INTRODUCTION TO
INTERNET
SECURITY

Other Prima Computer Books Available Now!

How to Order:

For information on quantity discounts contact the publisher: Prima Publishing, P.O. Box 1260BK, Rocklin, CA 95677-1260; (916) 632-4400. On your letterhead include information concerning the intended use of the books and the number of books you wish to purchase. For individual orders, turn to the back of this book for more information.

INTRODUCTION TO

INTERNET SECURITY

FROM BASICS
TO BEYOND

Garry S. Howard

PRIMA PUBLISHING

P™

is a trademark of Prima Publishing, a division of Prima Communications, Inc.
Prima Publishing™ is a trademark of Prima Communications, Inc.

Prima Online™ is a trademark of Prima Publishing.
Prima Computer Books is an imprint of Prima Publishing, Rocklin, California 95677.

Project Editor: Jeff Ennis

Prima Publishing and the author(s) have attempted throughout this book to distinguish proprietary trademarks from descriptive terms by following the capitalization style used by the manufacturer.

Information contained in this book has been obtained by Prima Publishing from sources believed to be reliable. However, because of the possibility of human or mechanical error by our sources, Prima Publishing, or others, the Publisher does not guarantee the accuracy, adequacy, or completeness of any information and is not responsible for any errors or omissions or the results obtained from use of such information.Opinions expressed in this book are of the author only and do not reflect the opinions of Prima Publishing.

ISBN: 1-55958-747-4
Library of Congress Catalog Card Number: 94-68676
Printed in the United States of America
96 97 98 AA 10 9 8 7 6 5 4 3 2

For Geneva M. Howard, Carla J. Howard, Jim Warren,
and Phil Zimmermann

CONTENTS

INTRODUCTION

In the hit 1995 movie, *The Net*, actress Sandra Bullock plays the part of a computer analyst who becomes swept up in a terrorist plot to take over the government using computers and the Internet. When Bullock's character discovers a disk with data belonging to the terrorists, they *delete* her identity. Actor Denzil Washington's character also faces danger in the Internet drama, *Virtuosity*. Although most Internet surfers probably won't experience anywhere near this level of intrigue, people are being damaged. Businesses are losing millions, children are being seduced and stalked, viruses are erasing years of work, reputations are being destroyed by technology and forces many victims don't even understand. Cyberspace is no place to play around unawares.

Other Hollywood depictions of hacking and surveillance are excellent: *the Conversation, Sneakers, Prime Risk, Wargames*, even the old *Mission Impossible* episodes. These works accurately illustrate how the right information in the right hands permit the good guys to win. They also show how the right information in the wrong hands destroys people, families, and law-abiding institutions. Hollywood has also illustrated what happens when the government turns into Big Brother. But somehow, people still don't see themselves getting *caught, bitten,* or *stung* by the *Net*. But as a thousand new Net-surfers sign up every day, it's happening to an increasing number of people.

Although these *hacker-movies* take some dramatic license, they educate people on how computers and networks control much of what happens in their personal lives, from their employability to their credit and to their health care insurance premiums—it's all determined by a few thousand bits of information somewhere in cyberspace.

But most Americans—inside and outside the information field—don't fully appreciate the extremely serious nature of online crime nor how a lack of privacy and security on the Internet can threaten and damage their businesses and personal lives and jeopardize their personal safety.

It is the purpose of this book to detail the wide range of threats to security and privacy while we are on or in the environs of the Internet. From protecting telephone systems, PCs, LANs, WANs—or the biggest WAN in the world— the Internet—*Internet Security: from Basics to Beyond* will discuss risks, past problems, and solutions.

The biggest threats in cyberspace come from telephone fraud, theft of laptops and other portable PCs, viruses, and vengeful employees, but another danger might very well pose an equal or greater threat.

Telecommunication writers and consultants, *cyber-activists*, and industry authorities see the federal government's Wiretap-Ready Law, the *1995 Anti-Terrorist Bill*, the Exon Amendment, and the Clipper Chip proposal as evidence that Uncle Sam is transforming itself into Big Brother. Many Net-surfers regard the latest proposals as no less than a direct threat to the Internet and the Constitution. Some civil libertarians claim that law enforcement's use the Information Superhighway is an illegal shortcut around Constitutional rights. But for most Americans, it's hard to distinguish Big Brother from *Uncle Sam* when he comes to you as a friend and protector.

Introduction to Internet Security: from Basics to Beyond will make readers more aware of the new wild conditions brought about by explosive growth of the Internet. Not since the California Gold Rush have we seen a massive rush towards one place *(in this case the place is cyberspace)*. Our leaders are passing laws that are not fully understood. Some laws are good, but others are questionable and represent major departures from the previous restrictions on law enforcement with respect to personal communications between private parties. The resulting confusion and uncertainty are already having a negative impact on both digital communication technology and the comfort level of people on the Net. In response to the new efforts by law enforcement to look deeper than ever into law abiding citizen's lives—many Net-surfers are rebelling. New technology is now being employed to sheath data messages with digital protection that even the government can't break.

One lone programmer, Phil Zimmermann, threw a monkey wrench into the government's program. By making *PGP-encryption* available free to all PC and Macintosh users, he has given them the ability to pass information that would take the government too long and cost too much to decode. But when somebody downloaded his PGP program from Europe, the FBI chose to use this as an opportunity to prosecute him under munitions law. One Zimmermann supporter considers the federal governments persecution of Phil Zimmermann by the federal government as similar to the People's Republic of China's arrest and imprisonment of human rights advocate Harry Wu (the U.S. citizen placed under house arrest after exposing human rights violations in China).

Although some people claim that Zimmermann's quest was based on a paranoiac perspective of government and the world—many share his fear of the government and Big Brother's efforts.

For years, I used E-mail to send network designs worth millions of dollars (to both my company and other companies). But until my e-mail (involving this book) was intercepted and contaminated with a virus, I never fully realized how vicious and destructive hackers and viruses could be. The FBI was very courteous when I reported the event, but they weren't knowledgeable enough nor motivated enough to solve the crime. I was told that unless I were a bank or had sustained a major loss, I was not a priority, no matter how potentially dangerous the Internet violation was. I realized that when it comes to protecting my data, e-mail, files, and images, I would have to take proactive countermeasures to prevent a repeat violation.

As the number of Internet users increases, I predict that Internet violations and virus attacks will increase. Now more than at any other time, people need to take steps to secure their private and business communications, their PCs, and other valuable information resources.

Zimmermann's act empowered not only improved security but also privacy and free speech in cyberspace, because one man recognized that the collective power of private encryption was greater than the power of Big Brother's supercomputers to break code (in most cases). Zimmermann strategically hurled *the small rock* of *encryption*—right between the eyes of Goliath. The only problem is, the *giant oaf* may not be dead. But at least— while allies of Zimmermann join forces to do war with what they regard as a frontal attack by Big Brother—citizens of *Cyberbia* can equip themselves with effective defenses, skills, and tools against violation. With the proper knowledge and predetermined procedures, Net-surfers can easily protect the their data from compromise and destruction.

Protect yourself and your data; for if they can read your e-mail, they can see inside your soul.

If you are looking for further information, Garry S. Howard is establishing a clearinghouse for information on all topics related to Internet and computer security, located at the following World Wide Web address (URL):

HTTP:\\www.wavenet.com\~Howard GRP.Intsec

Acknowledgements

Special thanks to John Lee Pryor of ASK Information Services in Los Angeles for his assistance with testing things within this book and providing information about e-mail bombs and dealing with online stalkers. E-mail him at tracy24@IX.netcom.

Thanks to Paul Smith of Oasis Interactive in Los Angeles for his assistance and use of his PC laboratory for testing the material within this book.

Also, special thanks to Bob Binkley.

chapter
01

WHO'S WATCHING FROM CYBERSPACE

Merging onto the Information Superhighway?

The Information Superhighway could be loosely defined as "a hardware and software infrastructure supporting the transmission of information in the form of voice communications, data, images, audio, and video." The Information Superhighway includes the telephone system (the present core of the Information Superhighway), but it also includes the Internet, television, radio, coax cable, copper wire, attached modems, LANs, networks, satellites, fiber, microwave links, and a whole host of related services. The Information Superhighway is in its infancy, and we are witnessing the convergence of formerly distinct technologies—computers, telephones, video, audio, telemetry, and other technologies. A world of information, education, entertainment, employment and enterprise will be available to everyone with properly equipped multimedia personal computers. Even now, this new

Introduction to Internet Security: From Basics to Beyond

convergence of technology allows a person to conduct a business video teleconference, or even to host a TV talk show from a laptop PC—on the beach! Simply plug a video camera into your computer's PCMCIA port and you can send live video and audio using a cellular modem link.

Nicholas Baran, in his *Inside the Information Superhighway,* describes the future as a world where all homes, neighborhood schools, colleges, and governments will be connected by fiber and coaxial cable attachments to high performance multimedia networks. In just a few years, when people turn on their TV, they will get choices like these from a user-friendly graphic screen interface, making menu selections with an infrared remote mouse:

Network TV
News
Movies
Interactive Entertainment (Games)
Shopping
Travel
Sports
Restaurants
Education
Community Services
Medical Hotline[1]

With the touch of the remote, the near-future *cybersurfer* will get a full-color screen from which to select and connect to one of these services, or get the groceries delivered in minutes, or call an ambulance for the old lady next door when she falls down. There will be movies to download in seconds on high-speed digital communication links, hundreds of times faster than the 2400, 14,400, or even 28,800 bit per second modems that are becoming obsolete as this book is printed. These services can be realized with very little investment and great economic, educational, ecological and civic benefit—but at what cost to our freedom of speech, security, and privacy?

Warnings from Ray Bradbury and George Orwell

In Ray Bradbury's *Fahrenheit 451*, the government could see and hear all citizens on television—whence all information came. The government burned all books and outlawed reading in an effort to stop all creative thought. Nonconformity was the enemy of the oppressive state.

In George Orwell's *1984*, a similarly grim picture of the future is painted—one of a futuristic dark age where "telescreens" are used by "Big Brother" to monitor and enslave citizens, controlling their every word, thought, and action. Posters remind the mind-raped subjects that "Big Brother Is Watching You." Orwell had witnessed what Hitler and Stalin had done to the world. Needless to say, the main character rebelled and was crushed by the oppressive government.

What is obvious from literature and studies about the loss of privacy? They all seem to confirm what is widely believed yet frequently forgotten—that a loss of privacy eventually means a comprehensive loss of freedom: freedom of speech, of the press, of religion, of thought, of choice, of movement, of belief—of all forms of expression. You don't need a deep background in history to understand the propensities of powerful governments to use technology to implement mass surveillance.

Introduction to Internet Security: From Basics to Beyond

In October 1994, the United States Congress passed the The FBI Wiretap Bill, which effectively gave law enforcement the power to eavesdrop on every telephone conversation in the country.

Another law is being proposed, and it has the support of a Clinton administration. The Clipper Chip proposal might outlaw all nongovernment unbustable commercial encryption products. FBI Director Freeh has said that if his agents can't decipher data that they eavesdrop on, he will recommend that the government outlaw private encryption—effectively ending all assurance of security and privacy for all transmissions on telephone, cable, fiber, and other media. If Congress hadn't tabled the preposterous proposal, there would be no guaranteed secrets while talking on the phone, sending e-mail, sending a fax, watching television, or transmitting sensitive data over a modem[2].

Introduction to Internet Security... will discuss these issues and more. Looking at PCs, WANs, LANs, telephone services, and the Internet, this book will provide practical, cost-effective solutions to problems of data security in down-to-earth language. There are lots of exciting horror stories about hackers, thieves, and government agents—but remember—they are only amusing when they happen to somebody else!

We'll deal with the critical issues of the cyber-revolution, such as anonymity, security, privacy, and trust, as well as their antagonists: hacking, stalking, pornography, and censorship. We'll treat the gadgets you can buy and the practical problems of encryption. We'll also show you where to get what you need—to keep someone from watching.

The Biggest Meeting Place in the World

Currently, the most popular stretch of the Information Superhighway is the Internet. Since Vice President Al Gore's public acknowledgment that he is an avid e-mail user, and that he wants to put America on the fast track to the "Information Superhighway," it's been the nation's hottest media topic. Gore's public endorsement of the new technology has had such a positive impact on the public's interest and participation in the Information Superhighway that it has grown obvious that such leadership is way overdue. Technology leaders, noting the extreme popularity of graphics and multimedia formats on personal computers, are saying that the World Wide Web will eventually replace a great deal of today's mass media—TV and radio.

Al Gore's quiet endorsement and image building, combined with recent increases in modem speeds, sales of multimedia computers, and popularity of high-speed CD-ROM drives, has created something more enduring than a fad in America. It has college students standing in line at university library PC rooms. It has executives staying late at the office chatting with others in online chat rooms with names like "Alone In the Office." The Internet, recognized as the most popular place in the Info-Superhighway, is more than hot—it's already the high-tech rage of the 90s! Unlike TV, radio, conventional cable, talk radio, 900 numbers, or even CB, the Internet allows users to convene by the thousands to participate in an online event, to talk to dozens of people at a time, to exchange ideas, words, unique experiences—without having to leave their homes or offices. New video-conferencing systems allow remote PC users to type, view documents and images, and hear the voices or see the faces of the other conferees if they so choose, using the new multimedia technology. The Internet lets people meet thousands of others with shared interests, communicating quickly and inexpensively.

The Internet currently consists of 30,000 interconnected networks and 4.8 million attached computers linking over 20 million users by copper wire, fiber optics, microwave, satellite, radio, and an amazing level of good will and trust[3]. Users trust not just that their data will be transmitted and stored properly—but that their communications will not be intercepted, rerouted, altered, modified, or read by the wrong set of eyes. The sheer open nature of cyberspace (that is, of the Internet), and the fact that it is connected to so many computers and people has made it a hacker's gold mine. It's also a favorite hangout for government spies.

Electronic mail (by far the most heavily used tool of the Internet) can be read by anyone and tracelessly forged, which means that no one receiving e-mail can be sure where it's coming from.

Record Growth in the Use of the Information Superhighway

Over three million new subscribers joined the commercial online services and the Internet between January and March 1995[4]—a record number of new subscribers in just three months. Twelve million new users are expected each coming year. Businesses are investing hundreds of millions to provide access, space, products, and services on and through the Internet—becoming in the process virtual gatekeepers and virtual businesses.

Chapter 01: Who's Watching from Cyberspace

The sharp increase in the Internet population is due to the recent strong sales of high-performance multimedia personal computers, equipped with high-speed modems (14.4 to 28.8 bits per second), and the recent addition of Internet access to CompuServe, America Online, and Prodigy commercial services. The use of the Information Superhighway is also increasing due to the recent convergence of personal computer technology with telephones, television, video and audio recorders, answering machines and voice mail, fax machines, copiers, printers, pagers, and even home security and control systems.

The capabilities of the new high-performance multimedia computers, modems, and networks have created unprecedented opportunities to increase every PC user's personal and business productivity. On the World Wide Web Windows and Macintosh users can point and click their way to full-color, high-fidelity pictures, sounds, and video—truly exciting new things to see, read, and hear. Businesses are now free to greatly reduce the amount of required office workspace or even to eliminate centralized workplaces altogether. Telecommuting, personal and business e-mail, video conferencing, online conferencing and chatting (text), advertiser-supported Internet magazines, entertainment, education, government archives, research, marketing, selling, product delivery, document tracking, finance, and press communications are all the rage in the American business world. America's traditional high-overhead office and storefront operations are disappearing, because so many wonderful things can now easily be done from one's home or even one's lap on the beach, using a notebook PC and a cellular modem.

An Investment and Technology Boom

The new technology offers access to a vast universe of information, education, entertainment, and communication—in just a few years, it will become the foundation for much of America's employment and commercial enterprise. Tens of millions of people already seem to e-mail and electronically chat with far more people (and organizations) than they would normally communicate with using "snail mail" or the telephone. Big players, such as Microsoft, Novell, IBM, and Apple, are ready. Movie, cable, and media giants have positioned themselves with acquisitions and new products. The products: movies, video shopping, online entertainment, education, adult photographs and video clips, programs and information. The rewards: hundreds of billions in profits.

Already, hundreds of millions of dollars are being made providing access and sending and receiving data, e-mail, video, images, and telemetry over the Information Superhighway. But very little consideration is being given to assure the integrity, the privacy, and the reliability of the Info-Superhighway. It's growing at a pace of thousands of new users every day, with no central traffic cop, formal rules or laws, no safeguards against one party getting too much power, and no court precedents to protect victims of abuse, vandalism, slander, theft, terrorism, or fraud.

From all appearances, there will be no letup to the phenomenal expansion of the Information Superhighway, but greater the explosion, the greater the opportunities for abuse, fraud, deceit, and so on. It's impossible to conceive that the Info-Superhighway can promise to be the future job site and commercial highway for America if it cannot assure its users complete privacy, reliability, and universal availability.

Missing from Most People's Computers and Networks—Security

I have consulted in computers and networks for over twenty years. After designing and implementing mainframe and PC networks in hundreds of large banks and retail, manufacturing, and aerospace firms, I am excited about the recent arrival of high-speed and high-performance computers and networks. The PCs are finally fast enough and disk and memory are affordable enough for the masses, and there are more than enough online resources to attract a lot of people. The Internet is truly hot. It's pretty much a foregone conclusion that access to PCs and the Internet an absolute necessity for life in the twentieth century. But I've always been amazed at the relative lack of concern with security on corporate mainframe, PCs, and LANs, despite the availability of very low-cost and even cost-free solutions to protect data files, disks, e-mail, confidential file transfers, and the accuracy and security of confidential and public records.

But businesses and private users are already losing billions every year by ignoring the threats of data theft and vandalism, wire fraud, telephone card and PBX fraud, wiretapping, corporate espionage, internal and external vandalism, and misuse. These private users, small businesses, and large companies have practically gotten away with murder, often leaving lines and systems open, sometimes with little or no password protection. The more open their data, voice, fax, conference, and other communications networks to the Internet—the more vulnerable they become to abuse, unauthorized penetration and use, vandalism, theft, and more.[5]

But most or all of the problems could be avoided if the proper procedures

Introduction to Internet Security: From Basics to Beyond

were practiced before failures and damage—from within and from outside. Solutions such as software virus scanners, hacker warning or trapping systems, disk backup procedures, double-password systems, software firewalls, callback systems, file encryption, data encryption, disaster recovery plans, and off-site backup have been around for over a decade, and even though data-processing operations are critical to the day-to-day operation of just about every small or large business—*very few businesses* (with the exception of some banks and insurance companies) take computer and network security very seriously. Because of the digital nature of most of the communications on the emerging Info-Superhighway, security breaches—legal or illegal—can be quite disruptive, often very destructive. It's no longer a joke or funny to have your business attacked by hackers. Extended disruption of computers or network resources can result in payrolls not being made, people losing jobs—these things could even put some companies out of business within just a few days. Whether the threat comes from thieves or hackers, the government, image forgers, plagiarizers, online con artists, invaders of your online privacy, eavesdroppers, malicious e-mail and chat stalkers, virus and Trojan horse terrorists, or other rogues—from within or from without—the Information Highway promises to be every bit as perilous as it will be exciting. When the majority of banking, commerce, employment activity, and communications are transferred from the highways of concrete and asphalt to the Info-Superhighway, *assuring the privacy and security* of your transmissions will most certainly be more important than the communication itself.

Phreaks and Hackers, or Big Brother?

From their very inception, telecommunications systems gained their security from secrecy and anonymity. They also relied too much on good will of users. People have long used telephones, for instance, as instruments to harass, track, stalk, and terrorize anonymously. In the same way, people are using the silence of computer files and the plain-text chat to secretly abuse, stalk, and harass others online. The anonymous nature of cyberspace (the electronic realm of telephones, computers, and the Internet) is an open invitation.

Since the very beginnings of the Info-Superhighway, security and privacy have been an afterthought. Whether the mischief took the form of a crank call or a computer virus attack, it is likely that you have already been a victim—"cyber-jacked" if you will—in cyberspace.

When dealing with computers and networks, you are identified by a fictitious user id, (usually a number or characters). A message appears on your computer screen, saying that you are being logged on and that a host computer is verifying your user id and password. But you don't really know who is on the other side or what they are doing.

After you download a few shareware programs from the Internet—cyber-violence! Your disk drive has been infected with a virus that has just erased your files, all of them.

Who are these invaders? Are they phreaks, hackers, Internet stalkers? Why are they waiting to strike your PC disk drive, your telephone, or your e-mail? How can they be caught? Just how easy is it for someone eavesdrop, listen, read, or watch?

The Telephone System

Initially, the nation's telephone system was quite insecure. Teenaged boys were the first telephone operators. Phones and swtiches were connected with wire cables, controled with analog signals and audible tones. Tones were used connecting major switches, so that a person using a plastic Captain Crunch whistle could make free long distance phone calls. Telephone switch maintenence ports were put on unprotected dial-up lines, soon seized by phone phreaks. Such access empowered the power hackers to forward unsuspecting telephone callers to new locations—without their knowledge. They could cut off telephone service to thwart investigations, shut down businesses they didn't like, harass other phone phreaks, or even probe for passwords and access codes. But, the U.S. telephone system has been modernized for the most part, with most long-distance services providing digital quality through fiber-optic links to all major cities in the nation. Digital technology made violation of telephone systems more difficult.

In the 1980s, none of the experts predicted how much Americans would soon increase their use of long-distance, cellular, fax, and networking services. Now that there are clearly defined standards and products (ISDN, FDDI, T-1, Frame-Relay, Sonet), companies are finally building corporate telecommunications infrastructures—commonly one of the largest overhead items in business. But there are some kinks in the telephone lane of the Information Superhighway.

There are three major long-distance companies, dozens of smaller well-equipped companies, and hundreds of resellers. There are hundreds of local telephone companies attached to most of these long-distance carriers.

Although digital systems are perhaps more tricky to violate, with the new features and capabilities bring with them the potential for more high-tech abuse, disruption, theft, and surveillance from people and computers on the Info-Superhighway. One a phone phreak finally violates a digital telephone control facility, the potential for damage and compromise is much greater, because of the increased capacity of modern digital hardware.

Changes from Deregulation

For over 20 years, AT&T had in place monitoring mechanisms to catch fraudulent toll charges. They were also able to catch many who dialed into local and long-distance telephone switching systems to reprogram the switching computers. But with the breakup of AT&T, many of the monitoring systems were dismantled along with the monopoly.

The deregulation of the telephone industry in 1985 brought with it lower rates, expanded services and features resulting from competition. But along with the degregulation, what security existed was somewhat diminished in the scramble. There are three major long-distance companies, dozens of smaller well-equipped companies, and hundreds of resellers. There are many hundreds of local telephone companies attached to most of these long-distance carriers.

Now, a phone call could connect you to a person serviced by a no-name telephone company you don't even know exits. Your name, address and phone are potentially entered into some unknown computer's database, which could be accessible by who-knows-what? You could say that it's written in a *black hole* in cyberspace. Who you talk to, who called you, when and how long you talk—all are written in cyberspace. It's all there waiting for a clever hacker and the unscrupulous bureaucrat.

The Legion of Doom

In 1988, a small group called the Legion of Doom raided companies for internal technical data and then posted them on computer bulletin boards. A special document containing information on the 911 emergency telephone system helped one hacker trigger the 1990 crash of AT&T's computer system. A culture grew in America—a culture of teens and young computer nerds (from decent homes) learning how to crack first telephone systems and then computer systems. This group at one point started a security agency. They were still hacking when they met up with another group of hackers—and got into a petty rivalry. Then they used the Internet and client companies as their battle ground—extracting vengeance for profit and destruction—at the expense of innocent businesses, parents, and phone companies.

Other individuals and groups have been hacking their way into banks, military and aerospace installations, radio call-in contests, universities, and corporate computer and telecommunications facilities—raking in billions, and causing billions more in damage.[6]

Telephone Hacking or Phreak Techniques

Telephone hackers are nicknamed "phone phreaks." These people don't just steal telephone credit-card numbers; they also penetrate central office computer systems and disrupt or steal services.

Among the techniques utilized by phone phreaks to invade public and private telephone facilities, *1800 toll fraud, fraudulent use of telephone credit cards, PBX toll fraud, c.o. and l.d.c. phreaking, cellular fraud, bugging and tapping, tracing, line blocking or seizing,* and other ways of violating your telephone system will be discussed in the chapter dealing with security in residential and business telephone system. Solutions will be discussed allowing weak points in residential and business telephone systems to be addressed, allowing individuals and businesses to develop security plans which protect their connection with the world—their telephone system.

Snoopy Employers

Over ten million American workers are being listened to over their telephones.[7] The airline, insurance, telemarketing, utility, and banking industries are the chief industries monitoring their employees. The exact number of companies who monitor employee phone calls is uncertain. Fifteen percent of American companies, however, are known to search their employees' voice mail.[8]

Telephones can be used to monitor employees' conduct with customers. Laws vary from state to state, but most require employers to inform their employees that their voice calls are monitored. Companies say that the monitoring is necessary for quality control. Perhaps. But you have to wonder.

Even foreign spies are snooping on American workers; in the late 80s, agents working for the French, German, Japanese, and Israeli governments have tried or actually succeeded in stealing American technology trade secrets.

The Government Is Listening: The FBI's Digital Telephony Plan

In 1991, the FBI attempted to get the telephone industry to voluntarily write digital wiretap trap doors into future specifications for all public central office switches. The bureau tried to convince the industry to cooperate voluntarily by indicating that the FBI wouldn't be able to protect national security without expanded wiretapping powers.

At the second Conference on Computers, Freedom, and Privacy in 1992, a photocopied document was the talk of the conference. It was a secret FBI proposal on "Digital Telephony."

The proposal called for both private and public telephone hardware to be equipped with "wiretap ready" software features. It would permit law enforcement to tap literally any phone line in the country, whether residential, business, or cellular, from a police station. Since the telephone authority was the only check citizens had assuring that court-ordered warrants were presented, the proposal was seen as a major assault on the Fourth Amendment to the Constitution.

What's more, the systems would permit the police to tap without the subject being able to detect them listening (as one can with most systems, which exhibit slight drops in signal level when taps are active). The bureau justified its proposal by saying that it was necessary for police to have such access, since it would be hard to get cooperation from the phone company if a crime boss such as John Gotti were to bribe phone company workers. Agents also told Congress that the new digital systems required special "wiretap-ready" features because they were harder to tap than previous technology. But the industry disagreed. The telephone equipment manufacturers rejected the government's proposals, and it was revealed the Feds had made previous efforts to gain "back doors" to telephone company facilities secretly without company officials' knowledge.

The FBI's PR campaign was relentless, using every fear-inducing tactic available, invoking "child pornographers," "kidnappers," "snuff movie makers," "terrorists"—nobody even asked how "wiretapping" was better than stings and other types of investigations that may be more effective. Agents lobbied the Bush administration and then the Clinton administration, which got completely behind the plan, along with Democratic Senator Christopher Dodd (Intelligence Committee). The measure passed in November 1994 and has been sending shock waves across the data processing and telecommunications industries, as well as disturbing civil libertarians and free-speech activists.

It was discovered that the FBI had mistakenly estimated the cost of implementing the plan at $300 million dollars. The bureau had completely overlooked the software maintenance costs of the plan and had not considered the impact on computer networks, cable TV operations, digital cellular systems, and many new time-sharing systems and PC networks. The FBI was looking only at telephone switches, but these alone would require four different versions of the program costing over a billion dollars in downloads per year. *CyberWire Dispatch* estimated that it would cost over a billion. The FBI plan calls for fining manufacturers $10,000 a day for noncompliance. The bill applies to "any person or entity engaged in the transmission or switching of wire or electronic communications for value for unaffiliated persons, but does not include persons or entities engaged in providing information services" or "telecommunications carriers."

The plan calls on the Attorney General to draw up a plan to provide easy wiretap access for all law enforcement agencies, to "accommodate all the communications interceptions, pen registers, and trap-and-trace devices" the Attorney General estimates the government will need—in other words, to put in enough "ease-dropping" ports per switch to allow the FBI and other agencies to monitor thousands of conversations simultaneously.[9]

Previous to this bill, it was less convenient for law enforcement agencies to tap anybody in a given area. They had access to local connections but would have to go through the telephone company in most (but not all) cases. But with "police station" access to every telephone in America, there are bound to be some serious problems with privacy ahead.

Given the government's immense computing power, government agencies have the ability to search for strategic keywords. First, they target certain sources—financially, socially, or intellectually active citizens. Because they don't need a search warrant, they have the ability to target people illegally without anybody knowing. If an inspector demanded to know if government

Local Government Is Just as Nosy: The LAPD Spy Unit (The OCID)

George Orwell would have loved the OCID. The Organized Crime Intelligence Division was a secretive unit within the LAPD that used an extensive high-tech spy network and illegal surveillance to spy on every one from Robert Redford and Jerry Brown to Connie Chung and Mohammed Ali. The original objective of OCID was to function somewhat like a mini-FBI, to monitor and bust organized crime operations without warrants. No criminals were arrested, not much management existed, and the officers were not responsible for any particular schedule, case, or organized crime entity. They wound up bugging and trailing movie stars and elected officials, trying to learn secrets about their sex lives.

Both Mike Rothmiller (former cop and author of LA Secret Police) and Luis Tackwood (former informant and author of Glass House Tapes) confirmed that the LAPD could tap any phone line in the entire city.

agents were not scanning national security targets but instead monitoring political figures, entertainers, or financial power players, he could be shown bogus computer records indicating random searches.

The word search list could be comprehensive enough to detect all communication dealing with specific subjects. I imagine such a list could consist of fewer than a thousand words. The government has given both law enforcement and military agencies permission to conduct such searches under the guise of national security, but as one might expect, their potential for abuse makes anything George Orwell thought of completely feasible—tragically and horribly—right now!

Computer Hacking

America's businesses rely heavily on computer resources to operate. Computers are used at every step in the delivery of retail goods, commercial services, manufacturing, and transportation. The personal computer is on millions of home and office desktops, expanding the trend towards distributed processing in American enterprise; with Local Area Networks and dial-up mode attaching PCs to Wide Area Networks located around the globe. More employees are telecommuting,

This capability permitted the OCID far more power than most people can imagine. The technique could be used to monitor and record just a select group of people every time they used their phones, or to scan a large group of numbers for key words, intensifying the scan on people who discussed certain topics. By tracing subjects' calls to and from their contacts, further surveillance could ultimately invade every private subject and relationship in a person's life. OCID violated the private lives of former Governor Jerry Brown, Attorney General John Vandicamp, Universal Picture's Lew Wasserman, the mayor, and many others. If agents wanted to get into a person's house, they could just break in, then claim that they got a burglary call at the residence.[10]

and more businesses are trading storefronts for home pages on the World Wide Web (the new multimedia segment of the Internet).

The computer is no longer an isolated entity but is permanently connected to the world of other networks and computers. Business will increasingly rely on computers, both for operations and to talk to customers and suppliers. Computers are still the primary target of forces in cyberspace, and distribution of information among many computers in many locations makes the information available to more users. It also makes them and the information they store and transmit more vulnerable to attacks from cyberspace.

Hacking Techniques

How do hackers get into your computer or anyone else's? Here are a few favorite techniques:

Scavenging, impersonation or piggybacking, wiretapping, data diddling, salami slicing, superzaps, asynch attacks, simulation and modeling, trojan horses, back doors, trap doors, logic bombs, password busting, dial-up line-blockers, and other computer hacking techniques will be discussed in Chapter 4, which deals with computer security. We'll also discuss serious security solutions for computer hardware, software, and environments.

In Chapter 5, on Local Area Network and Wide Area Network security, we will discuss popular LAN servers, security features of most popular systems, and security and privacy considerations in the various LAN topologies and media. We will then discuss the often difficult subject of securing Wide Area Networks (WANs), hardware and data communication facilities, suggested equipment to assure security, and procedures and practices to implement before major problems occur.

The King of the Hackers: Kevin Mitnik

Kevin Mitnik was a lifelong hacker, and now he's in jail. But Mitnik is, for the time being, the most well-known, ingenious, and infamous hacker. He started as a prankster, then went on to become a thief, and then a societal menace. His personal transformation almost coincides with the new trend leading from pranksters to malicious and vindictive destroyers of people and businesses. He made the transformation from dialing into computer installations to using the Internet to steal, abuse, and transport his electronic booty.

Mitnik gained national attention when he broke into the Defense Department computers, but his behavior degenerated, and he began altering credit reports of people who had offended him and disconnecting celebrities' telephones. He stole thousands of credit card numbers, ripped off critical information, stored it on stolen disk drive space, and tried to sell it to the highest bidders. With plenty of cash, he led the federal government on a long cyber-dragnet, which failed until agents got the assistance of a supercomputer programmer, a counter-hacker if you will, who helped to devise a strategy to eventually lure and capture Mitnik.

The Internet Worm

In 1988, Robert Morris, the son of the chief computer scientist at the National Security Agency (the agency responsible for protecting our nation's communication infrastructure) created a software worm (a close cousin to a virus) and injected it into the Internet. This network-equipment virus attacked the UNIX operating system controlling the victimized Internet node, which spread the worm to its attached neighbors, and so on, and so on. The worm had a time-delayed reproduction so that it was hard to track. Eventually it cloned itself in computer centers all over the nation, causing an estimated $90 million in damage.

Experts declared after Mitnik was busted in 1995 that if businesses employed just a few security measures, such as encrypting sensitive information, "hacker threats" would be significantly reduced. Even though Mitnik was highly knowledgeable, he was caught in just a few weeks when he met people who were his equals.[12]

"We are seeing a transformation in the type of hackers from the Mitnik type, young hackers motivated by a sense of anarchy, to those who commit computer crimes to make money or to get back at people. . . ."[13] So says

Mark Rasch, a Washington attorney who deals with cases of computer crimes, and who also prosecuted Robert Morris, the Cornell University student (son of a NSA official) whose Internet "worm" ate its way through the Internet and crashed hundreds of computers on the system.

Ironically, it often takes a hacker stunt to induce business to plug security holes. Since the Mitnik arrest in 1995, Netcom Communications—the large Internet access provider from which Mitnik allegedly stole 20,000 credit card numbers—no longer stores unencrypted card numbers on its servers. And imagine, he began his hacker career using computers and demon-dialers to gang-block radio-station switchboards, winning virtually every call-in contest. (He made a fortune before he grew obsessed and began to become reckless.)

The Inslaw Case

Another, more recent, case demonstrates a federal government that is exhibiting the type of behavior you would expect in some science horror fantasy, where it is attempting to assume the role of Big Brother.

The House Judiciary Committee described it as perpetrated by "high-level Justice officials and private individuals".

One journalist, Danny Casolaro, was found dead after meeting with a former government contact, and his boxes of documents relating to the case have been destroyed, stolen, or conveniently "lost" by the Department of Justice. *Wired* magazine launched its first issue with a comprehensive investigative report; their headline: "Software piracy, Conspiracy, Cover-Up, Stonewalling, Covert Action: Just Another Decade at the Department of Justice."[14]

So far, not a single person has been held accountable.

Chapter 01: Who's Watching from Cyberspace

It all started with a couple, Bill and Nancy Hamilton, who developed sophisticated CASE (Computer Aided Software Engineering, capable of permitting the users to develop specialized applications) software to assist law enforcement in tracking criminals through the legal system. The U.S. Justice Department originally purchased the software and then illegally sold it to 80 countries and used the money to finance the Iran-Contra operation. Former Attorney General Edwin Meece (the only Attorney General indicted three times) and his two successors allegedly benefited financially, but the couple's software company, Inslaw, went out of business—the feds didn't even pay their bill.

If successful, Inslaw Software would have installed their anticrime software, called PROMIS, in more than 74 federal prosecutors' offices around the U.S. The company went private, realizing that the market for automating the Federal court system was staggering: worth up to three billion dollars, according to developer and owner Bill Hamilton. But Hamilton would never see another cent from a federal government contract.

Designed as a case-management system for prosecutors, PROMIS has the ability to track people. "Every use of PROMIS in the court system is tracking people," said Inslaw President Hamilton. "You can rotate the file by case, defendant, arresting officer, judge, defense lawyer, and it's tracking all the names of all the people in all the cases."

Wired magazine spent two years searching for the mystery Inslaw poses: "Why would Justice steal PROMIS? Did it then cover up the theft? Did it let associates of government officials sell PROMIS to foreign governments, which then used the software to track political dissidents instead of legal cases? (Israel has reportedly used PROMIS to track troublesome Palestinians.)"

Inslaw insiders are insisting that the software, in its enhanced mode, would be easy to adapt to track political dissidents.

Wired says this case shows "how justice and public service gave way to profit and political expediency, how those within the administration's circle of privilege were allowed to violate private property and civil rights for their own profit... What the Inslaw case presents, in its broadest possible implications, is a painfully clear snapshot of how the Justice Department operated during the Reagan-Bush years."

It wasn't just the largest piracy case on record, and it wasn't simply that it was done within the law enforcement agency charged with enforcing antipiracy law—it was the type of software that they sold. Since the questions are as yet unanswered, and since nobody is taking responsibility for the biggest case of piracy in U.S. history right inside the Justice Department, we are now faced with basic questions about the legitimacy and propriety of those charged with computer law enforcement itself, with privacy and the protection thereof. It's likely that the worse fears of investigators may be true—that PROMIS software is being used as a type of Big Brother system for tracking all perceived enemies of the government—law abiding or not.[15]

Abuse of the Internet

Because the Internet has so many attached computers and millions of subscribers, the ability to attack from complete darkness may be only rivaled by the telephone system. Internet computers are often attached to unprotected corporate computers (not a good practice, by the way) that contain millions of dollars worth of data and proprietary software. Proprietary or confidential data are also stored in computer systems foolishly attached to the Internet and other publicly accessible networks, permitting penetration by unauthorized sources. But businesses don't seem to learn until they are burned.

The Internet has spawned a new bread of hackers, hackers who actually write down a shopping list of things they want and then proceed to find computer installations that may have those things. Most experienced Internet hackers are not vandals but thieves; they seek to operate in secret, often virtually lurking in the memory of UNIX servers—waiting for somebody important to type in their password or credit card number.

Internet Hacking Techniques

This book will describe problems of stolen access, stolen resources, worms or Internet viruses, e-mail counterfeiting, e-mail interception and corruption, vandalism, and other Internet woes, along with solutions to protect your online account, your online reputation, the security of your Internet business or enterprise, and the integrity of your data. We'll also discuss the controversial topic of Internet stalkers and show you how to stop the sick adults who use online chat and pornographic images to seduce minors on the Internet.

Mitnik Assaults the Internet

Remember Kevin Mitnik? He became rather wealthy, selling information collected on the Internet from various sources, stealing credit card numbers and living like a rich playboy—he lost sight of those who might be watching him.

He had been traveling all around the United States, using various user accounts and stolen computer systems to store his hot data and to program on. In 1994, he was lured onto one system called "The Well" by a San Diego[EnDash]based supercomputer specialist. The FBI helped in the operation, and when they figured out where Mitnik's cellular connection was, they busted him. Mitnik was given so much unchecked time and disk space, he never thought about the possibility that the FBI was watching him from cyberspace.

What Is Government's Real Fear?

Many *cyber-civil rights* advocates (sometimes called cyber-punks) claim that what our government really fears is *crypto-anarchy*—a *cyber-society* run by anonymous electronic commerce that could work to bankrupt and undermine government. But crypto-anarchy would certainly be destabilizing for any government, and most governments would probably seek to prevent this from happening. Since there would be no way of paying taxes on goods that were transferred completely in secret, many feel that the government wants to prevent this from happening, no matter what illegal and anticonstitutional measures must be taken. But if a government ever gains unrestricted free access to every citizen's phone, e-mail, and personal and business secrets, history indicates that abuse is likely, and that restoring privacy under such a regime would be extremely difficult if even possible.

A Final Assessment: No Inherent Security or Privacy in Cyberspace

You should expect someone to be watching in cyberspace because everything you do on the Info-Superhighway—from telephone calls and faxes to the Internet, from the movies you watch to electronic banking—is written in cyberspace. Somewhere a computer has recorded everything. The moment your modem is activated or you log onto the Internet, your electronic door is wide open, and you never know who or what is slipping by, unseen and untraceable.

Only one conclusion can be drawn: There is neither privacy nor security in the Info-Superhighway unless every individual user takes personal responsibility for his or her own defense.

That is what this book is about.

chapter 02

MAJOR LAWS IN CYBERSPACE

Privacy v. Freedom of Information

The U.S. Constitution First Amendment states the following: Congress shall make no law… abridging the freedom of speech, or of the press; or the right of the people peaceably to assemble, and to petition the Government for redress of grievances.[1]

This small sentence in the Constitution defines what may be the most powerful right we have as Americans. Since our country's earliest days the rights of free speech and the press have been guaranteed. But high technology seems to be at war with our freedom. It seems that ever since the American Revolution, the law and technology have been engaged in a combined effort to diminish our freedom of expression.

Early Americans appreciated the significance of freedom of speech and expression on individuals and society in general—they were denied that right in Europe, where speech and religion were severely restricted by monarchies and the church. They probably understood the potential positive influence of one person's words on the society around him. Americans in this century, however, need only look back fifty years to see the worst proponent of censorship—Hitler. The German dictator gained power by silencing dissenters and burning books. Since Hitler didn't use profane language or eat meat and considered himself a moral person, as one professor friend of mine said, Hitler would have probably would have supported total censorship of the Internet today.

An example of how one individual's words had a enormous positive effect on society—Dr. Martin Luther King Jr. He was able to change a nation with his speech. Another African-American by the name of Robert Smith was able to increase the number of Black college professors tenfold with an individual letter writing campaign to colleges in the Northeast over 60 years before Martin Luther King was born. Before Robert Smith came along, there were hardly any Black college professors in East Coast universities.[2]

The Information Superhighway presents a new challenge both to those who need to communicate freely on the Internet and those who do business supplying information to those who seek to pay for it.

But at some point, Americans must ask themselves, "Will we allow the government to assume complete intellectual control of our nation's telecommunications network, including telephone systems and the Internet?" Even though crime online constitutes an extreme small fraction of the overall crime in America, both the media and Congress focus an inordinate amount of negative coverage on the Internet. Materials derived from such sources as *Playboy Magazine*, which are available in many stores, seem to cause more offense in cyberspace. Why?

Other problems are more easy to understand; they deal with what information people want to access online. Some information is public and available in any government archive office. Other information is highly confidential and potentially damaging. Who keeps this information? Who has a right to access this information? What responsibilities do system operators have for accuracy? And what's to keep the wrong people from getting at this information?

Freedom of Speech

The explosion in global telecommunication networks has made the future of government regulation of media a major topic of industry discussion. The First Amendment assures Americans that there shall be "no law abridging freedom of speech or the press." But since the advent of electronic media, there have been many laws regulating speech when it is transmitted on government-regulated media—and the government regulates all media—telephone, television, cable, radio, even power transmission! The FCC has the right to revoke any licensed broadcaster who violates local standards of *decency* and *obscenity*. So, since most people get most of their information over electronic media—we have grown accustomed to censorship. But as the world moves into interactive communication, more online users complain of unprecedented levels of restrictions on speech and expression. Many cyberspace explorers are being turned off, or in some cases, kicked off the Internet. Many citizens and civil rights groups are asking, "What is happening to our freedom?"

One strand of fiber-optic cable (or coax) can convey the content of virtually every newspaper and current publication in seconds. It can deliver electronic mail, TV broadcasting, online shopping, video rentals, cable television, and a host of other information services. The data pass at incredible speeds and are often never preserved at the other end. How can anybody be certain about what's actually going on over the Internet? Some First Amendment scholars assert that in the very near future the government will no longer be able to license or regulate the media.

Because modern telecommunications technology has enabled the high-speed transmission of voice, image, and data—no laws, no state or national borders can absolutely limit transmissions. Radio, microwave, satellite, even light beam communications don't require cable installations—nobody necessarily knows where certain facilities are, let alone that a violation of some law took place.

Cyberspace is in many ways its own separate jurisdiction.

Freedom Is Threatened by Complacency

With the introduction of digital and high-technology electronics, and advances in efficiency and speed of communication—one major issue has been almost completely ignored—the right to privacy: the right against invasion of a person's home, one's telephone, one's confidentiality.

The founding fathers didn't trust government authority; they *expected* authority to abuse its power and placed sanctions in the Constitution to punish overreaching. Today, fewer Americans seem to question authority or recognize the historical pattern of government privacy violation.

How Ethical Are Large Companies?

No organization or system can be tested sufficiently under normal network conditions. The best way to determine the integrity of a party is to test it under stress. (Over 1000 GTE employees improperly looked at Nicole Simpson's telephone records on the last day she was alive—in June 1994. This was a serious breach of privacy and public confidence, yet only two employees were fired.)

Because of the incredible demand for certain types of information, thousands of government, utility, personal, and medical workers are illegally invading the privacy of other Americans, stealing confidential secrets (never secret again), often resulting in great damage to the victims' lives or jobs. The federal government has joined in the violation; instead of extending greater safeguards, it has proposed legislation to permit law enforcement to tap, track, record, and search databases on private citizens.

The futuristic movie *Fahrenheit 451* depicts a world in which the government controls speech, thought, activity. No books exist, nor anything that would inspire creative or analytical thought. George Orwell's *1984* paints a similar picture. But both works also illustrate how few people may even realize what has happened to them and their rights.

While researching a book dealing with a corrupt government agency, I was told several times that noises were heard on my phone line. I used different phones but was again warned about probable eavesdropping, later confirmed by testing. During the rest of the project, I was so paranoid, I pulled out my phone and used pay phones for research. I realized that the person who was bugging me could be working for the government.

Freedom of Information: Online Access to Public Records

Like so many other things, freedom has two sides—it's wonderful when you need the information to be able to access it quickly on an online service. Birth records, licenses, certificates, legislation, 800 phone numbers, census records, emergency information, court records, records on where toxic waste was dumped, USGS maps, NASA space photographs, and other tremendously important items of information are now being made available online.

But when others go after information about you, whether it's public or confidential—it doesn't feel so good. And illegal invasion of public records by advertisers and government agencies can be quite damaging. Even if the information is inaccurate, it can even cause permanent loss of reputation.

A battle is being fought, not just over censorship and antipornography laws on the Internet, but also over the availability of public records on the Internet. Many municipalities are making public records available on local Internet nodes with public access—called *freenets*. These Internet servers (in many major cities) are setting up menu systems so that citizens can access records previously available only through city and county clerks. The Federal government has made the Library of Congress and all congressional legislation available on the Internet, and many state governments are allowing Internet access to their records. It saves cities enormous time and space, but because many cities and counties make lots of money selling hardcopy photocopies of public records to citizens, some are trying to profit off pubic records by selling the databases to third parties, who in turn will charge the public to access what belongs to them anyway.

Jim Warren, a writer for *MicroTimes* magazine, has been leading the effort to make public records (among other things) available free to all Americans. He has posted information on freenets throughout the country instructing citizens on how they can lobby and make their elected officials work to establish public record databases in their towns, cities, and states.[3]

What Secrets Can Employers Access?

If you've recently been turned down for a job and you knew you were the most qualified applicant, don't assume it's because somebody unqualified slept with the boss or benefited from affirmative action. You may have been denied a job because of what some former employer said about you, something that may have been completely untrue. But you weren't able to tell. If you have made a workman's compensation claim in the last ten years, don't be surprised if computer records "snitched" on you.

Any employer can call 1-800-55-VERIFY to find out everything about your credit, employment, workman's compensation, medical, insurance, legal, and criminal background, and even your immigration status. Much of the information is unverified, inaccurate, even damaging.

This service charges under $200 for a basic check on a prospective employee. Certainly employers must verify the honesty of job applicants, but there certainly aren't many restrictions or protections for consumers and citizens who may be discriminated against illegally by what employers dig up on them legally. It's their lives which have been affected and their privacy violated—often without their knowledge.

The service, offered by the parent company, Information Resources, can find out a person's: 1) credit record, 2) criminal record, 3) employment record, 4) social security record, 5) driving records, 6) education, and 7) past worker's compensation claims for under $200, 8) court records (civil laswsuits). If you are applying for a job, none of these pieces of information need your authorization or approval, except for credit and worker's compensation. Nonetheless, with companies being destroyed (unfairly and often without even a statistical foundation) by massive increases in their workman's compensation premiums from chronically ill and patients who have been sick in the past.

The IRS Invasion of Private Databases

Several years ago, the IRS purchased commercial mailing lists of high-income recipients of junk mail and asked state licensing agencies to report all the people who take out occupational licenses or register expensive cars. The IRS was attempting to use its tax collecting authority to justify unlimited instant access to these records, computerized records of several major credit bureaus, and more. The same rationalizations could probably have permitted their access to everything from grade school records to visits to the psychiatrist, or even the confidential notes of your church minister.

The IRS *Big Brother* plan ran into big-time resistance.[4] Many Americans recall Senator Joe McCarthy's attack on free speech in the forties and fifties, when he called everyone west of the Mississippi a Communist, and many remember the government's lies during the Vietnam era. The general idea that government should not have unrestricted access to law-abiding citizens' private lives has been accepted as the *only* rational alternative to tyranny. It has been quite evident to all who have observed American culture and politics that the mere collection of personal information has the effect of inhibiting free speech, especially dissenting speech and views.

Underground Databases

Now that we've talked about the official sources of public and private information, let's talk about the unofficial, often illegal sources. Let's call them *unofficial databases.* There are people within and outside of governmental organizations who are stealing massive amounts of confidential data about Americans' credit, medical, dental, employment, legal, and financial backgrounds. These people establish databases on their own or stolen computer systems and then contact companies who can use this information to generate huge sales—albeit using illegally obtained information that the person whose privacy was violated may never know was exposed.

For example, what if you take an AIDS test and it comes up negative, meaning that you are free of AIDS. Let's say that you are fired the next day at work. Let's then say that you find out from your friend in Personnel that some "secret AIDS test database" was established at the large laboratory-clinic your test was performed at, and that the company sent your employer the following letter:

We have been informed that one of your employees has taken an AIDS test. Whether or not his test is POSITIVE or negative, your employee has felt the need to take the test. This may indicate something about the employee that you would find useful in assessing the risk of AIDS contamination, exposure, and communication at your office, customer environment, or elsewhere.

If you desire to know the name of the employee who visited: AIDS TESTING SERVICE, please reply with check for $5,000 to:

T.J.Snitch Inc.
222 E. Violator Lane
Dirtville GA 90722

How many employers would turn down an opportunity to reduce their employee health care insurance premiums by finding out who in their company had AIDS? I expect that more would respond to such an offer than would be willing to admit it publicly. This type of privacy violation is taking place all over the country—with AIDS victims having their medical records routinely disclosed—resulting in job termination using such excuses as "unproductive" or "downturn in performance."[5]

Computer Blacklisting Is Big Business

One inexpensive way of determining if you have been "Computer Blacklisted" is to simply check yourself. Call the 800 number and pay to have yourself checked out. This is your right, and they must do it. The Fair Credit Reporting Act covers all records related to a person's credit, employment, legal, criminal, and driving records. Any flaws must be corrected in 30 days. It's your right to demand of companies like Equifax, TRW, TRans Union, and others (Appendix) that they correct any incorrect charges, delinquencies, defaults, judgments, or inquiries. They must remove false or misleading information regarding your employment history, your criminal or court records, and your driving records. The penalty for not updating your records after they have been informed is quite hefty, so they are encouraged to make the changes, even if they don't have time to research them.

Who Is a Hacker or a Snoop?

There's something of the voyeur inside all of us, particularly when we know that nobody knows we're watching. Imagine being a government satellite observer, working in a high-tech video surveillance and reconnaissance center. You are capable of seeing humans, cars, and houses from outer space. You can see your spouse pull out of the driveway and determine if anyone else is at your house at the same time he or she was there. If you suspect your other half is cheating on you, you will be able to tell if a lover comes to your house when you aren't there. How many men or women would be able to resist checking up on their spouses? This spy capability has existed for years, and although the government has never admitted this type of capability, it does exist. Satellites are so good, there's really no more need for spy planes (people speculate that's why they took the SR-71 Blackbird out of service). Satellites are equipped with everything including infrared technology (so they can see in the dark), subterranean visibility, and even special telescopic features allowing them actually to see detail in a person's face, read license plates, or determine how many people are inside of a building (by heat).

The fact of the matter is, considering how many people cheat on their mates, it probable that this type of thing has taken place. Let's just hope our fictitious government person—getting his heart broken watching the satellite monitor—doesn't have a little *red button* within reach!

But the problem is, the same agents probably abuse their ability to "see" just about everything. They are capable of seeing the young woman sunbathing naked in—what she thinks is—the privacy of her own home.

Constraints on Speech over Online Services

Online service providers can make their own rules about the types of speech permitted on their services. America Online is regarded as the most stringent enforcer of online speech restrictions. The restrictions don't just apply to chatroom conduct and language. On America Online and possibly a few other services, e-mail content is also subject to review and evaluation by an unseen,

Introduction to Internet Security: From Basics to Beyond

unheard from group of people called Terms of Service Staff. If subscribers break the rather vague Terms of Services provisions, their service can be cut off immediately, with no prior warning or even the ability to have mail forwarded to a new address. The Terms of Service Staff doesn't typically respond to e-mail from those who have been kicked off line, they don't take phone calls, and they don't respond to faxes unless they choose to. In short, America Online (like possibly other services) does not provide an environment conducive to free speech.

Note, for instance, these points from AOL's general rules:

- AOL provides "parental control" features that can prohibit minors from accessing various areas of the service.
- AOL makes information on members available to third parties such as advertisers, unless members know how to prevent this.
- Members are not allowed to use "screen names" that are vulgar or offensive or that serve to impersonate living persons.
- Members are encouraged to report any violations to the Terms of Service Staff by various means.
- Chain letters and pyramid schemes are prohibited.
- "Vulgar, abusive[,] or hateful language" is forbidden and may lead to an "on-screen-warning" [sic] or immediate termination.
- "Unsolicited advertising, promotional material, or other forms of solicitation to other Members" are prohibited in most areas.
- "Room disruption," which is defined as "purposefully interfering with the normal flow of dialogue in a chat room" by, for instance, "repeatedly interrupting conversation between Members, or by acting in such a way as to antagonize, harass[,] or create hostility in a chat room" is forbidden.

- "Scrolling," or causing other members' screens to scroll faster than the can type by, for instance, holding down a Return key is forbidden.
- Harassing another member by targeting that person for "distress, embarrassment, unwanted attention, or other discomfort" or by attacking that person's "race, national origin, ethnicity, religion, gender, sexual orientation or other such affiliation" is forbidden.[6]

I recently spoke with an AOL official, who explained he could sympathize with the frustrations some users are feeling with strict and sometimes rather drastic terminations on user accounts. He told me that although he could sympathize with their complaints, that there was quite a bit of fear that too little self-policing by online services might bring about public support for— draconian laws like the Exon Amendment and possibly even more radical governmental control.

Prodigy considers itself to be Disneyland of the Internet. The service isn't quite as restrictive as America Online, but it does have a policy explicitly forbidding profanity. CompuServe is far less restrictive in its online censorship.[7]

Contracts and Commercial Arrangements Online

Businesses can negotiate and close contracts online. Using images, faxes, and electronic transactions, parties can build relationships, assume legal contractual roles, and exchange money and property without even meeting in person. How do you put together an online contract? Just like a regular contract, it starts with the offer. When two or more parties have negotiated all the details, the terms and conditions should be written down. Provisions for completion, contingencies, bad faith, missed deadlines, and other eventualities should be clearly written into the text of the contract. Signed contracts can be scanned and sent over the Internet just like faxes; fax/modem users can even send fax image files.

Because of the popularity of the Internet, many commercial enterprises are establishing reciprocal arrangements with television networks, movie studios, magazines, and newspaper publishers.

Online services shouldn't take the place of lawyers; you still should have good legal advice, and you can use the Internet to find lots of attorneys and legal services through lawyer-finder message boards. Many attorneys accept e-mail so that you don't even have to talk to them—how nice![8]

Copyright Law Online

Can copyright law as we know it be enforced on computer networks? Should international boundaries be placed on the Internet so that material cannot be sent out of the jurisdiction in which it's copyright protected? Should individuals refrain from sending all copyrighted material as e-mail?

If I have pirated software on my PC, can it be confiscated? Can I be sent to jail? These are some of the questions that surfers on the Internet may not think about much since people do these things all over the Net. But the fact is, copyright laws protect all original copyrighted work whether in printed or electronic form. There are, however, some exceptions to the copyright protection on the Internet.

Copyright protection is defined by a legal concept called the *idea-expression distinction.* This means that it is the expression of the idea, not the idea itself, that is protected. No one can copyright a pure idea itself, but authors can protect the unique way an idea is expressed within their writing.

One of the major exceptions in copyright law is the fair use principle, which permits quotation from copyrighted material when certain conditions are met.

If one were not permitted to quote others, the First Amendment would be compromised beyond repair. But fair use implies that people must avoid abusing this right by:

- Minimizing the amount of quoted text
- Making it a small percentage of one's overall work
- Ensuring that it does not compete with the sales of the original work
- Not depending on the quoted material as a way to sell one's work
- Making sure that the material is quoted for reasons of educational or societal benefit.

Examples of the fair use law are TV stations airing short film clips of new movies that have not been released, short excerpts from books in news, and limited photocopying for one-time educational use. All of these forms are extensible to online systems.

In December 1994, a U.S. District Court judge in Boston dismissed wire fraud charges against an MIT student whose bulletin board system allowed users to download unauthorized copies of more than $1 million worth of software. It was not something he physically did—those who downloaded the software technically created and obtained the copy. The kind-hearted student placed the software on his PC, turned it on and plugged it in, and loaded a legal bulletin board system on it. The United States faced a monumental task

Know your CyberRights

The only firmly understood part of copyright laws deal with the originality and style of the material, part of the original copyright law. There is a natural law that says that if you are providing information or a product that the public wants, your creativity will serve to increase your celebrity, popularity, and integrity. But since information files on the Internet are routinely transferred, edited, plagiarized, and embedded and redistributed in a different form, copyright laws crafted in 1787 will be difficult to implement. Barlow says an approach of collecting tolls on an information highway is wrong: "The Internet is nothing like a superhighway. It's an organism."

trying to prove that the accused student violated the law, when all of his actions were legal—it was others who created the illegal copies.[9]

The judge acknowledged the problem, calling the student's actions "heedlessly irresponsible,"[10] but confessed that convicting the student would make even legitimate copying, such as software backups, illegal.

Intellectual property expert Ann Branscomb agrees: "You cannot take an old law intended for telegraphy and telephony and turn it into a mechanism for criminalizing behavior that Congress has not addressed directly," she says.[11]

E-mail

E-mail and the law have had a little bit of exposure in the courts, but the decisions came out against privacy, and for property and propriety of the owners of the e-mail facility. E-mail is private if it is sent from one individual to another person or organization. If the e-mail is sent at work, through an employer's computer, it is not private and is in fact the property of the employer (employers aren't even liable if they lie and say that they are not monitoring when they are).

One factor that will impact both e-mail privacy and security and perhaps mitigate many of the problems resulting from unethical employers, is *encryption* (see Chapter 7). If employers continue to allow employees to believe e-mail is not monitored and yet monitor it, employees will begin to encrypt e-mail. Even if their employer is the federal government, their e-mail will be secure. If employers protest or try to forbid the use of encryption, they will be forced to answer the question—how did you know the e-mail was encrypted?[12]

Data Files

Online systems have store computer files in mass quantities. The basic rules of online ownership of data files are simple—the creator of the file is the owner of the file under copyright law. For a file to warrant this kind of protection, the work it contains must contain original, new, copyrightable material such as text, photographs, drawings, music pieces, or video material.[13]

Downloading Commercial Programs

Since programs are copyrightable, all provisions of copyright law are enforceable against those who copy programs. Various portions or segments of a program can be copyrighted. The downloading rules apply to e-mail, ftp, and all other types of network downloads.

If a person sends a commercial program to his friend, it's a copyright violation, unless they get special permission. But they probably won't get prosecuted (who would know?).

If a person posts a copy of a commercial program on a message board, it is also illegal—and may get the person in trouble.

If a software program contains a process or formula that is patented, such a program is also protected under federal patent law. Patents cannot protect numbers, but where formulas protect unique processes specifically related to the area of application of the program—those patents can be protected so that those who use the formulas must pay license fees to the owners of the patent. This is the case with a company called RSA, which purchased many of the patents that provide for private- and public-key encryption. Every software product sold in the U.S. that uses RSA-owned patents must pay RSA patent fees.[14]

Shareware

Many people confuse shareware with freeware. It is not. Shareware is regular software, and it is commercial. The term "share" is misleading because it's actually not shared (like multiuser software), it's just distributed freely. Shareware is passed from one user to the other on floppy disks or posted on BBSes, online services, and the Internet. There are hundreds of thousands of shareware programs, and everyone is free to load them onto their systems.[15] The authors simply ask that if you use the software, you pay their asking price, usually printed when you initialize the program. Nobody will ever break down your door to confiscate your computer with shareware. But every time you boot and see that message, it works on your consciousness, and you eventually pay, just to get rid of that message, "You aren't registered yet; would you like to register now?"

Vendor or Developer Time Bombs

A software developer has the right to be paid. If buyers have made payment or credit arrangements and miss paying the developer, there are cases in which the vendors or developers have written routines that automatically erase the unpaid-for software. Even if this was something the customer was aware of and had agreed to in writing (which would not be advisable), surprising customers with past-due time bombs is not legal. If damage results from the removal or as a result of the customer not knowing about the lack of software (hardware damage or detrimental reliance)—the customer could seek civil damages that could probably pay for the software many times over.

Nor is it legal to send an employee to a customer site to destroy data—even if the customer is late on his software bill. Recently, a software vendor used a repair visit as a pretense to delete software from one of his customer's computers, both the vendor and the employee, sent out to repair the equipment, were prosecuted and imprisoned for felonious trespass.

Freeware and Public Domain Software

This software is completely and totally free of charge, with no restrictions on the transfer and use of these programs. Some people actually sell this software. Although this practice is not exactly ethical—there is no law against this, anymore than there is one against selling Bach recordings.[16]

Images

Images online are fully copyrightable upon their creation by the photographer or artist. If images are copied and used in another image, it is a copyright infringement. Unfortunately, with electronic photo-retouching, it's possible to modify, cut, paste, morph, distort, and combine images with other images—often making identification of the original image difficult or impossible. The general rule says that if the original image is recognizable, the act of copying is possibly an infringement. In FPG v. *Newsday*, the computer-art images were cut from FPG's photograph and placed on the cover of the magazine—the images were altered quite a bit, but still recognizable enough for a $1.4 million judgment against *Newsday*.

Similarly, the widespread practice (even today) of scanning *Playboy* pictures and distributing them all over the Internet was declared completely illegal by a judge in Florida, who held the bulletin board owner liable for infringement damages. In the case of *Playboy* v. Frena, the court ruled that those who uploaded the nude photos were giving the BBS an implied license to distribute, and the downloaders an implied license to download the image.

Since picture files are some of the largest files in the PC world, downloading graphic files takes more time and makes more money for the online services. They are one of the most popular items people seek online, and we're probably in for quite a few legal challenges in this area, because pictures from cyberspace are now easier and faster to get and cheaper than photographic stock.[17]

Music

Sounds are also protected under copyright laws, as rapper Biz Markie found out when he failed to get permission to digitally sample copyrighted music for his rap arrangements. But musicians (ASCAP, BMI, SESAC) are also attempting to extract both copyright and performance fees for copying music from the Internet (copy of music, plus performance on TV-like media: multimedia computers). Experts predict such fees will be claimed only for live Internet performances.[18]

How to Name an Online Business: Trademarks

The name and logo you choose for your business or products constitute one of the most important—and possibly valuable—assets in your business. The trademark inherits the benefits and liabilities of the company's reputation. It can take the form of a graphic logo, the name of a product, online screens, or computer art.

Competitors know how effective trademarks are and will try to capitalize on your good name, so it's important to protect your business against impersonators who violate trademark law. When choosing a trademark, you must avoid selecting a trademark that is already taken.[19]

Online Criminal and Civil Law

Generally, in order to be guilty of a civil infraction, for which a damaged person can sue you for conduct or acts online, you must do something either wrongful and deliberate or reckless and negligent. Defamation and online invasions of privacy can also be treated as civil infringements, as can the deliberate dissemination of misinformation or copyrighted material.

Choosing a Trademark

The best way to go about selecting a trademark is to get a book on the subject and fully educate yourself on the ins and outs of trademark law. You will be in a good position to choose a trademark if you know how to:

Find out if someone is using the name you choose

Protect your trademark by registering it with the U.S. Patent and Trademark Office

Keep the registration current

Look up trademark laws

Settle trademark disputes out of court

Locate a reputable trademark attorney if there are legal issues needing resolution[20]

The separation between civil and criminal violations is not precise; a person guilty of a criminal act may also be found financially responsible for damages including punitive damages by a civil jury. Much of the civil claim may hinge on the degree of the wrongful commission or omission (failure to act), the degree of recklessness involved, how "reasonable" the alleged violator's acts were, and other factors.

Commonly alleged breaches of civil law include conduct by online system operators that violates the First Amendment guarantee of free speech, operator neglect for permitting offensive or illegal information to be made available online, fraud or online rip-offs, and more.[21]

Defamation

The definition of defamation is a case in which a person makes a false public statement that injures another's reputation (online or otherwise). The injured person can sue both the people responsible for originating the false information (not true information) and the system operator if there was definite knowledge and negligence involved in their failure to stop the action. The system operator, however, can't always be held responsible.

Fearing a flood of online defamation cases, some legal scholars suggest that the courts should not involve themselves, since damaged parties online can post rebuttals—on the same forums or areas they were damaged in—making repair of reputation much more obtainable than on traditional commercial media. Others say that the law should require the violators to post retractions as punishment. But more realistic debaters on the issue note that negative impressions take much longer to overcome—even when retractions are made.[22]

Privacy Rights

People don't lose their legal right of privacy in cyberspace. A woman who had her naked picture published in an advertisement without her knowledge (photo take secretly) was able to sue and win in a New York court. A celebrity may be able to sue an online service or business if it uses the name or image of the celebrity to make a profit without asking permission. Even if a business uses movie-star look-alikes, if it is using their likeness to sell products and services, the act may be interpreted as stealing the real celebrities' "right of publicity."[23]

Misinformation

If an online service misprints critical information from another publication (as by misprinting the *Wall Street Journal*), it's been ruled a civil violation. If a cookbook prints a recipe that is poisonous, the publishers may be sued and held liable for injury or wrongful death. If a textbook mistakenly says that a nonlethal product IS poisonous, the courts have ruled the publishers liable. One bank was forced to pay huge damages to absorb a $28,000 note by an Arkansas Supreme Court because of a computer error in software which calculated payments; as a result, they charged an illegally high rate of interest, but the courts penalized them severely.[24]

Computer Crime Law

In 1928, the Supreme Court ruled in Olmstead v. United States that the prohibition against unreasonable searches and seizures covered only material items. Conversations on the telephone, the court said, weren't material goods. Thus, the use of recorded conversations taken from phones that had been tapped wasn't covered by the part of the Constitution that requires a search warrant.[25]

In 1934, Congress passed the Federal Communications Act, which specifically forbade the interception of wire or radio communications. Finally, the Supreme Court ruled that information obtained by a tap and not backed up by a court-ordered warrant could not be used as evidence in court.[26]

During the Second World War, Congress again authorized wiretaps of spies. Then the court modified its position on wiretapping, permitting conversations obtained through "other" means admissible without a warrant. In the case of Irvine v. California, a spiked mike allowed agents to hear the conversation from a room next door without their actually trespassing into the suspect's office, but the court ruled that the Fourth Amendment's prohibition on unlawful search had not been breached. In a 1954 case, the court extended this ruling to include microphones hidden in the walls of a suspect.[27]

But in 1961, the court reversed its position, asserting that information gathered from a spiked microphone was inadmissible. In 1967, the court ruled in Katz v. United States that public phone booths could not be tapped without a warrant—although in a public place, they carry with them a reasonable expectation of privacy.[28]

This case led to the rewriting of the federal wiretap laws in the 1968 Omnibus Crime Control Act, which passed when people feared a rise in organized crime. Wiretaps were promoted as the only way to catch and convict organized criminals. The use of wiretaps increased significantly, and with society's growing familiarity with electronic equipment, the threat wasn't perceived as being as serious as it is now.[29]

The Electronic Communication Privacy Act of 1988

The Electronic Communication Privacy Act is sometimes called the anti—wire tapping act because it was passed after the Watergate scandal in the 1960s. Thousands of law-abiding Americans' telephone and facsimile transmissions were monitored to serve the political objectives of president and bureaucrat. The late 80s Congress expanded the coverage of the anti—wire tapping laws to protect electronic communication so that it covered not only voice communication but also digital communication, including text and images. The law also prohibited eavesdropping of all persons and businesses, not just the ones the ECPA prohibited—both the interception of messages and unauthorized access to messages after they had been stored on a computer.

The problem with the ECPA is that it is so complicated and filled with exceptions that it is difficult either to enforce or to interpret. Messages that are moving are treated differently from messages that are idle, but overall, the ECPA protects voice messages; it does not give online system users the same rights of privacy it assures users on public telephone systems (even though the vast majority of online users use the public telephone system). There are criminal penalties for violating the ECPA, but their use depends on how badly the government wants to make a statement.

Another weakness in the ECPA is that online services have the right to ask their subscribers to permit them to disclose information without being held civilly liable.[30]

The Credit Card Abuse Act: 1991

The credit card abuse law deals with the use of counterfeit or stolen access devices. It is a crime under 18 USCS 1029 (1991) knowingly to defraud with the manufacture, use, sale, or distribution of unauthorized access devices, with the intent to defraud or illegally sell equipment or the use of the equipment, with the use stolen credit card numbers in the commission of the fraud. The law was designed to stop the use of communication devices that make phony credit card purchases.[31]

The Computer Fraud and Abuse Act: 1991

This act makes it a crime to use a computer without authorization to access national security data. It makes it a crime to misuse a federal government computer (or one accessing such a computer) for misdeeds, fraud, damage, harm, or interference with an official transmission.[32]

The New York Computer Crime Statute: 1992

New York State took leadership in its computer crime law, defining such terms as "computer program" and "computer data." It makes crimes of committing computer trespass, tampering (first, second, and third degree), unlawful duplication of computer material, and unauthorized criminal possession of computer material. Defenses under the law include operator belief that there was authorization, the right to alter or delete the data in question, or the right to copy the material.[33]

The Child Porn Statue: 1991

This law makes it a crime to knowingly transport, receive, or distribute any visual depiction of a minor engaging in sexually explicit conduct. It covers distribution by mail or over an interstate network (crossing state lines).

Punishment includes ten years in federal prison, heavy fines, and seizure and forfeiture of all equipment and software used in the violation. The law permits the seizure of equipment belonging to parties who engage in "third party transfers" of the child-porno images.[34]

State Computer Crime Laws

All 50 states have enacted computer and network criminal statutes. These laws change frequently and often exact stiffer penalties for crimes involving computer fraud, misuse, hacking, child pornography, and the like. Because they deal with non-Interstate computer crime, the federal government would not be involved.[35]

The FBI's Digital Telephony Plan

As mentioned previously, the FBI attempted to get the telephone industry to voluntarily write digital wiretap trapdoors into future specifications for central office switches in 1991. The bureau tried to convince the industry to cooperate voluntarily by indicating that the FBI wouldn't be able to protect national security without expanded wiretapping powers. (The story of the FBI's campaign was recounted in Chapter 1.)

The FBI conducted a full-force campaign and the Congress passed the wiretap-ready bill. With HR 3422, including the "wiretap ready" provision for all equipment installed in the future, the FBI has gained access to virtually everyone's home phones, cable connections, cell phones, and even faxes.

This capability would remove the separation between the FBI and the phone company when they want to tap your phone. Without needing a search warrant, they could tap not just one person's phone, but the phones of an entire city, with just one attendant.[36]

The 1995 Antiterrorism Law

Taking advantage of the panic and anger after the Oklahoma Federal Building bombing, the FBI recommended even further expansion of its powers to eavesdrop, wiretap, and snoop on suspected citizens and groups who fit the profile of a "violent group." The antiterrorist legislation was passed; greatly expanded powers by the FBI to use wiretaps against "suspected" subversives, violent organizations, and terrorists. Many of the provisions have been under attack, critics citing the ability to deport suspects without allowing them access to classified information against them. One thousand new law enforcement personnel would work on "terrorism" cases at a proposed new "antiterrorist" center to be run by the FBI.[37]

The Exon Amendment: Death to the Internet?

Mike Goodwin of the Electronic Frontier Foundation states that that Exon Amendment (to the current telecommunications legislation in the Congress) would threaten the Internet by placing enormous penalties on online providers if they were to make obscene material "available to children." Goodwin fears that because children find ways around age restrictions, online providers would fear being fooled and prosecuted (for five years in prison with fines of up to $100,000). His fears are being echoed by an overwhelming majority of industry professionals, and according to a *Time*/CNN poll, a majority of Americans are against Exon-type censorship (approximately 48 percent compared to 42 percent supporting it).[38]

Goodwin and others site the availability of software that gives parents the right to restrict their children's access to adult areas of the Internet from the desktop (with *Surf Watch*—type software products). He says that the Exon Amendment would transform the Internet into the equivalent of an international children's library, since there is still no real definition of "obscene" or "filthy"—so online providers would be forced not even to allow posting of controversial literature such as *The Satanic Verses (which provoked the spiritual leader of Iran to issue a death sentence on its author, Salman Rushdie)* because it might be deemed "obscene" or offensive to Muslims, for example. He says that the Exon bill would be extremely hard to enforce and would put in power a group of unelected bureaucrats under the president to be a "Big Brother" committee to tell Americans what speech, text, and images they would be allowed on the Internet, and to recommend who should be jailed for violations. The sidebar on the next page includes an analysis of the latest version of the Exon Amendment by another civil libertarian:[39]

Crimes against Online Systems and Operators

Users who upload viruses or dangerous code, trespass into private network or computer facilities, hack into systems or steal copyrighted, secret, or proprietary material from a system may be in violation of both state and federal computer laws.[40]

Can the Police Take My Computer?

Yes. If your computer has been used in the commission of a crime by yourself or a subscriber to a BBS, newsgroup, or online service, it could be confiscated by state or federal law enforcement with a search warrant. With no search warrant, there is no requirement that you allow them into your home or office, but sometimes they get a little pushy and don't give you much chance to get out of the way of their gang tackles.

   If you are the subject of a civil suit and information on your computer is evidence, your computer could be seized, but since civil actions are friendlier,

An Analysis of the Exon Amendment

Legislative analysts have raised some legitimate concerns about the Exon Amendment's potentially chiling effect on the information provider industry, particularly online providers and bulletin board systems where providers could never monitor everything which goes on (no more than a phone company). The legislation also expands the prohibition on knowing use of telephone facilities to knowing use of telecommunications facilities.

The carrier could all potentially be held liable, and subject to up to $100,000 in fines or up to two years in prison if something took place which someone didn't like.

The Exon bill would amend current law from dial-a-porn to include the Internet; current law prohibits use of the telephone to make obscene communications for commercial purposes, whether or not the maker of such communications placed the call (i.e., regardless of consent). The Exon amendment might make the provider responsible if the offended party meerly stumbled onto an offensive message, photograph or soundfile.

and because arrests aren't made, you have a better opportunity to discuss providing an "original backup" with the peace office executing the subpoena.

The government really doesn't understand computers or telecommunications. Government agents tend to grab everything that looks high-tech. The rules are more strict, but judges let law enforcement get away with a lot of overreaching. The government can take the BBS, Web server, or other device belonging to the owner, involved subscribers, uninvolved subscribers, witnesses, victims, e-mail contacts of victims or others, suspects, press, and other knowledgeable third parties in contact with the principles. And they can keep the equipment—for a long time—unless you do something to prevent them from destroying your business machine.[41]

Do Police Warn You Before a Computer Raid? NO!

Because police argue that there is the possibility that you will destroy the evidence, you will never be warned. You must always be prepared for the worse if you are the target of an investigation.[42]

Can Police Confiscate My Disk Drive?

Yes! But if you can persuade law enforcement to allow you to back up the drive (if they won't take the backup themselves), do it.[43]

After the Search or Seizure

The police burst in on Tony Davis, owner of a BBS system in Oklahoma City, confiscating his computer and 57 of his CD-ROMS. TV reporters zoomed in on the computer, with the screen names of those who had downloaded "dirty" pictures online. The *Your Busted* TV show raided a perfectly legal store and wound up hurting a law-abiding business, it did get high ratings.[44]

What Can You Do to Recover Your Property?

There's no way around it—individuals and businesses must cooperate fully with law enforcement. But too often, police have left businesses destroyed, equipment confiscated, innocent third parties destroyed. If you don't want that to happen to your business and won't stand for being a victim of the system, then you are going to have to use the law and your rights to defeat the ignorance and overreaching of sloppy law enforcement. Since the federal government typically doesn't sanction agents for collecting too much evidence, and because judges seem to be almost blindly pro-law enforcement and anti-Internet, the only way to protect your rights and property is for you to protect them yourself! If you are an innocent party—don't lie down for a bulldozer just because Uncle Sam's in the driver's seat?

Attack the validity and execution of the search warrant; you as the operator can move for return of seized computer under Rule 41(e) of the Federal Rules of Criminal Procedure due to violation of warrant requirements. You can move for suppression of any evidence that was seized if you aren't able to get the computer back. Some of the following arguments can be made:

- There was no probable cause for the search.
- The warrant was defective because it wasn't specific in its description of items to be searched.
- Agents applied for and obtained the wrong kind of warrant.
- The search was unnecessary; for example, if the data were available on a public BBS and were not illegal.
- The actual search as executed was overly broad in scope; for example, where it described a specific disk, the policy took the computer, the desk, the backup tapes, and the wife's lingerie in the closet.[45]

Back up with a tape drive before police remove data, and inform them of law that says copies can be used as original evidence. Most federal agents are trained to take "original" evidence, but they don't appreciate that copies of digital mass storage media have identical data.

Most law enforcement officials in most jurisdictions are not familiar with computer law or with online crime and technology. Chances are they will err in obtaining or executing the warrant. If you can prevail at this early stage, you have the best change of getting your material back. If you have to wait until the case is closed or has gone to trial, it's a good reason for off-site backup. Here are some further tips for minimizing your losses from searches and seizures:

● Try to communicate to agents, judges, and all law enforcement the urgency of returning the material, which could decide your future livelihood.

● Tell them that if you could make copies, it would mitigate major losses in money and eliminate risk of civil damages if the warrant is challenged as invalid and losses result.

● Consider getting a publicist to expose law enforcement improprieties. District Attorneys must be elected, and bullying law abiding citizens is something that destroys their public image fast!

● If materials were not seized as tools of crime or a weapon but used by subscribers instead, the judge should be informed that this is important, since your intent is an important issue.

● If other subscribers were damaged or had their systems confiscated, joining forces with them can help to turn the tide against the federal government around.

● Challenge the claim that authorities need the original data files as evidence for trial, the computer owner can respond that under Federal Rules of Evidence, Rule 1001, agencies can use copies of disk files as original evidence for trial. This prevents companies from going out of business in the time it takes to get some federal trials completed.[46]

Introduction to Internet Security: From Basics to Beyond

Avoiding the Risks of Legal Action

Here are some tips for keeping out of the civil and criminal liability zones, so that operators and systems can be equipped with the structures and procedures needed to stay out of court disputes.

- Establish clearly separate "red-light districts" for adult areas online, where there are stringent restrictions on age, and where consumers of the service agree to conditions by which little or no policing by the online operator takes place.
- Require strict proof of age, and make sure that the proof is verified before granting access to a subscriber. The FCC recommendations (for assuring adult status are excellent: 1) require credit card payment or 2) obtain a written application in which the prospective customer declares his or her adult status and provide a special revocable access code that must be used to go online.
- Scramble or encrypt all indecent materials and provide a de-scrambler only to adult users who can prove their age.
- Act immediately on all suspicious users and potentially illegal materials or activities.[47]

chapter **03**

TELEPHONE
SECURITY

Operating a
Secure Line
Of Defense

This chapter will discuss problems with the telephone system, and how to implement security for business and residential telephone systems. The chapter will deal with systems ranging from the one- or two-line home-office environment to business PBX systems, voice mail, and voice response systems, and it will show you how they can be protected from tapping, PBX-toll fraud, voice mail abuse, and even telco improprieties. It even describes what you as a businessperson can do if you are overbilled by your telephone company or stuck with an unauthorized 900-number telephone calls on your bill.

The Telephone System

Our national telephone system has been revolutionized, physically, organizationally, and technologically—with most of the telephone systems providing advanced digital features such as call waiting, call forwarding, three-way calling, callback, call blocking, and caller id (offered in limited areas).

The phone company is no longer one monolithic monopoly or one long distance carrier and a few small Baby Bell companies (RBOCs or Regional Bell Operating Companies like NYNX, Pacific Telesis, Ameritec and Bell South). It's now a telecommunications supermarket for the residential and business consumer, sometimes more resembling a jungle, but an environment with perhaps more options for public and private networking of voice, data, audio, and video than there are varieties of game in Africa, and with over a thousand long distance companies and probably just as many local carriers coming to compete against the local carriers.

Digital telecommunications technology can convert audio, data, and image signals from their analog forms into digital streams of zeros and ones—binary data. Cell phone service has exploded into a multibillion-dollar industry in its own right; with prices going down and phones getting smaller, and over 28,000 cell phones being sold per day, it's expected that in a few years, over 50 million cell phones will be in use.

New technology and deregulation will allow present local and long distance companies, online services, and even cable TV operators to offer both long distance and local service. Many long distance carriers are already offering local service across the United States (AT&T, MCI, Sprint, and more). The demand for telephone numbers has increased dramatically in the last decade, causing many area code splits due to the boom in fax, data, and voice telephone use in American businesses and residences. The use of 800 numbers connects customers to the trillion-dollar direct-mail industry (from *Home Shoppers Network* to infomercials), and 900 numbers (although tainted with a bit of scum) generate billions in revenue from callers seeking entertainment, information, and help.

ISDN, FDDI, T-1, satellite, microwave, and other digital services allow companies to pass images, audio, video and data at very high speeds—connecting people in aerospace, design, broadcasting, and entertainment. But with more phone lines, products, cable plant, and advanced equipment, more people have access to your lines, upon which ride your voice, data, and images. More people can listen in on your conversations and access your customer records. And even though fraud and abuse are increasing, telephone companies have not done much to improve their ability to detect or cut down the chances of human or equipment problems that compromise privacy and security.

The telephone layer in the Information Superhighway has been and will most likely continue to be the main source for all the services that connect us to cyberspace. But the security considerations are critical, since valuable information—the substance of all business—is traveling over two pairs of copper wires, to the local exchange carrier, to the long distance carrier, to the destination LEC, and finally to the other party.

Along with the deregulation have come some growing pains, particularly with respect to privacy and security. Actually, they are more than growing pains; they are critical problems with the potential for extreme consequence. Properly treated, the telephone facilities in every home and business can be protected from most threats to privacy and security. That is what we'll be discussing in this chapter.

Telephone Hacking or Phreak Techniques

Telephone hackers are nicknamed *phone phreaks.* These people don't just steal telephone credit card numbers, they also penetrate central office computer systems and disrupt or steal services.

Here are a few techniques used by phone phreaks to invade public and private telephone systems:

- **Toll Fraud**—The easiest way to cheat is simply to dial a company's 800 number and then use touch-tone codes (through trial and error) to break into private PBX remote-access units (subsystems that permit company employees to call their home office, obtain a dial tone, and then call the world.). These units feature security codes for outgoing calls, but often company VIPs don't want to remember passwords, so hackers can go crazy once they find an unprotected PBX. Estimates range from a few hundred million to a billion break-ins per year. Relentless trial-and-error dialing—often using automatic computer-based speed dialers (demon dialers) are the next easiest way to break into private PBX systems.

- **Telephone Credit Cards**—When phone cards first came out, they were mostly numbers made up of the area code, the number, and an office code, followed by a "check digit" that was derived from the other digits. Operators performed a simple calculation to determine whether a particular credit card number was valid. But phone phreaks quickly found out the simple formula used to calculate the check digit, allowing them to generate a phone credit card number for any telephone number. Now, numbers are more difficult to calculate, so most are stolen by eavesdropping, "shoulder surfing," finding discarded bills, or stealing the card itself.

- **PBX Toll Fraud**—This is done by gaining access to a company's private PBX, figuring out the codes to gain a dial tone out, and then using this company's telephone service to make long distance phone calls. Recently, MCI Telecommunications refunded about $50 million to customers who were victimized by toll fraud.

- **C.O. Phreaking**—The most dangerous and perhaps neurotic "phreaks" are those who actually invade telephone company facilities, access maintenance ports, or break into operator consoles on switches and test equipment. CO Phreaks often reconfigure lines, modify and execute software functions, or even disable service entirely. They invade both local and long distance carrier facilities.

- **Cellular Fraud**—Every cellular telephone call starts with a broadcast of the unique serial number and billing number. Cellular switch customers check both numbers (unencrypted) against the active customer file and place the call. A thief can impersonate a legitimate caller by using a special "listening device" to "steal numbers from the air" near a highway—or anywhere near cellular activity. In a busy downtown area, a thief can sit in an expensive restaurant eating and drinking. With a pen and paper in his hand, he can copy enough numbers to pay for the check, an expensive hotel room, plus a high-roller's life to boot.

- **Bugging or Tapping**—Bugging or tapping is where someone has attached listening equipment to residential or business telephone lines and is listening to the voice, fax, and data transmissions. Without special equipment, it's more difficult to bug or tap digital communications lines (for example, ISDN, DDS, FDDI).

- **Tracing**—Tracing used to require a person to go to the central office and note the number of clicks in the switch-relays to determine the calling party. Now tracing a call can be accomplished by looking in an area of computer memory holding the switches' records. It is illegal to trace numbers without legal authority. If a phreak is tapping the line, he can monitor the DTMF pushbutton (touch tones) and, with a decoder, learn who you are calling.

- **Line Blocking or Seizing**—Kevin Mitnik used this technique as a teen to use several personal computers and autodialers to "seize" all the lines at radio stations, until he was recognized as "caller 10" by the unwitting contest organizers. This technique effectively "blocks" other callers and assures the "gang-bangers" domination over any small corporate switchboard. This method is also used to disrupt a business, particularly an 800 number, which the person doing the harassing may be calling from out of state, generating expenses while disrupting the victim's incoming calls.

Basic Two-Wire and Four-Wire Connections

Even though all the top long distance companies' transmission systems and switches are entirely digital and fiber, and even though local carriers have digital facilities, most residential and small business telephone connections are still two-wire copper. Voice-grade lines are either switched (dial-up connections for voice, modem, fax, and the like) or leased-line connections; these make up the bulk of all customer connections for both residential and business sites. Voice-grade lines operate at frequencies between 300 Hz and 3,300 Hz. Tapping two-wire voice-grade circuit is simple; so you can put a pair of alligator clips on and actually listen or see data. And so can a hacker.

Tapping an office's telephone lines or a PBX (or small telephone system) is the most effective way to monitor all types of data coming to and from a particular computer/telecommunication facility.

Direct Access

Larger customers have recently migrated to the new cost-effective T1 access (also T3, ISDN, FDDI, frame-relay) to provide for multiple inbound and outbound voice and data (integrated voice/data) facilities. New digital services provide high-performance digital features. Digital transmissions are more difficult for low-budget wiretapping, and digital services are now becoming affordable for even the home office; sometimes access costs less than for some analog products (such as the new lower cost digital switched ISDN and fractional T-1 circuits). If a phone phreak gains access to such a system, he potentially has access to voice, data, conferencing, and other services. Some consultants recommend against such shared access because of the potential security concerns, but the functionality and cost effectiveness often allow many customers bandwidth they could not justify without direct access.

 Securing the Business Premises

It doesn't really do much good to secure hardware and software against attacks from cyberspace if an intruder can walk right into your office area, turn on your PC, and copy all the data to a floppy disk during off hours. Securing the physical location is the very first step in securing a site's gateways into cyberspace. The following list details some considerations and suggestions for securing the office and plant premises:

- *Conduct a proper and thorough review of each new and existing employee.*
- *Conduct independent audits of computer operation.*
- *Minimize traffic and access to the computer and network equipment area, logging all people coming in and out.*
- *Erase all blank tapes and shred all hardcopy confidential reports.*
- *Inspect all items coming into and going out of the computer facility.*
- *Do not label tapes—use serial numbers*
- *Ensure that hardware and software vendors have integrity.*

Introduction to Internet Security: From Basics to Beyond

Weak Points in the Telephone System

Because DISA (direct inward system access, sometimes also called T1 access) provides cost savings, it has become a very popular access method for businesses. But hackers are also able to exploit more access to *all* your communications if they break the security. There are four highly vulnerable areas in a modern phone system:

1. Unsecured PBX systems, and other telephone hardware
2. Unsecured voice mail systems (which often allow access into phone lines)
3. Inside information known by employees without management's awareness
4. Direct inward system access

Tapping can take place at the individual telephone line, at the wall jack, and at the computer. It can be at or leading from the PBX machine. It can take place down the hall, in the customer's wiring closet at the outside terminal box (which connects telco wiring to the building). It can take place at the telco box outside the building (or at the B-box which connects several hundred phones in an area.), where a man in a truck, armed with two alligator clips and a telephone set, can hear a private conversation. If a hacker is equipped with an identical modem, he can attach it to the line (with certain signal level adjustments) and view and save the data, even passwords. If someone has access to a telephone company cable servicing many customers, he can wiretap everything in a whole area. Fax, mail, programs, financial reports, and other data can be wiretapped if someone has access to your telephone line coming into your office or home. The telephone system is the entry point and the transport mechanism in the Info-Superhighway, and perhaps its most vulnerable component.

One of the most frequent methods used to gain access to a dial tone from a private company's PBX is to call a voice mail box, press "0," and then input the trunk access code to get access to an outside line. From there, the caller can make any long distance call permitted. Recommendations to prevent access to the PBX and voice equipment violations include these:

- Change passwords regularly and immediately, if victimized by fraud.
- Disable outward calls from voice mailboxes.
- If outside calls are permitted, program the PBX to connect only to area codes you do business in (except management stations).
- Never use the voice mailbox number as the password, not even when it's an unused voice mailbox, nor assign actual numbers or extensions to the unused mail boxes.
- Monitor incoming calls that are rejected by the system (after failed passwords); attempt to identify the caller (using caller id) or keep him on the line until the calling number can be traced by the phone company (this takes only seconds now).

Physical Access to Telephone Lines: Danger!

Figure 3-1 shows the route and facilities providing end-to-end telephone service along its route over the public-switched telephone network (DDD network). Telephone facilities on customer premises, including telephones or phone sets, wiring, PBX, punch-down blocks, and distribution frames, are vulnerable to violation unless preventive measures are in place. From the customer premise to the wiring center, there is vulnerability. *B-boxes* (area serving green-boxes that connect customer lines to the local central office) and manholes don't provide much security, and considering that the information passed on business lines

Introduction to Internet Security: From Basics to Beyond

may be worth millions, it's amazing how easy they are to break into. One day as I left my apartment in Mar Vista (near Beverly Hills), I saw a man in a truck with two alligator clips connected to one of my neighbor's telephone lines. He was in a T-shirt and didn't seem at all concerned that I saw him tapping into the phone line. Since that time, I've been particularly conscious of who is working on my neighborhood's public telephone company B-Box.

The Cable Plant and the Telephone Closet

Cables and wires must be sheathed. Tie-wrap should be employed wherever wires and cables are not completely enclosed in conduit. This will allow data security professionals (your staff or a consultant) to check your facility for intrusion—not from a burglar—but for wires and cables that shouldn't be there. This could be a sign of corporate espionage, where other parties, interests, companies are interested in your company's secrets. Cables and

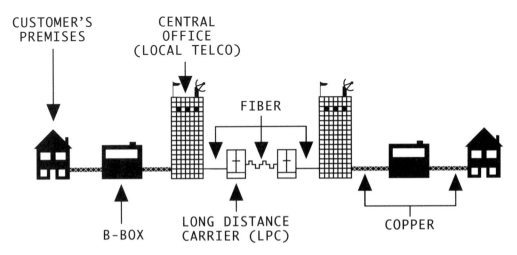

Figure 3-1. Possible routings for your telephone calls.

wires carry with them all the information transmitted internally and externally about your company.

Access to the telephone wire closet should be restricted to authorized technicians. The wire closet may be the most important space to protect in your business. One thing to remember about stealing data—you don't necessarily ever find out how it happens, only that data are lost or damaged. If you don't protect your cables and wire closet, you are permitting easy access to virtually all the networks using the wire cable plant.

Phone Company Connections

Unless service is digital, two-wire circuits are typically copper wire to the local telco's central office, and so connections from the telephone set to the area wire-center are vulnerable to tapping. Most telco wire and connector boxes are unlocked and easy to acces. B-boxes and manholes aren't difficult to violate, and most bystanders wouldn't necessarily notice the violators— even in broad daylight—if they looked remotely like phone company employees (all it takes is a hard hat) and drove an unmarked van.

Long distance phone company connections are typically fiber and microwave, which are relatively hard to tap, since tapping these media cuts off communication and alerts the operations support staff (although someone claims to have found a way to tap fiber without breaking it). But despite secure facilities, some telephone companies don't have the best records for customer service, billing integrity, responsiveness, and repect for customer privacy.

Employee Working Conditions

Here is the best way to stop providing the fertile soil to sprout new hackers in cyberspace. Try not to abuse, exploit, or take advantage of your employees. It would also help to remove conditions that may lead to injuries to employees at work on the company computer system, where their wrists, fingers, eyes, and backs can sustain serious injuries if proper ergonomic and safety considerations aren't taken. Also, employers who treat their employees like numbers or who violate private aspects of their lives are more likely to face retaliation by an employee hacker. Bad working conditions and unaccessible unresponsive management can breed vindictive hackers, thieves, phreaks, and corporate espionage agents from *cyber-hell*. It's no joke. Hackers have the potential to put companies, their employees, and even their customers in the unemployment line, or even federal bankruptcy court.

Because increasing numbers of companies are beginning to adopt *bottom-line finance-type ethics* , we'll probably see more horror stories of companies creating environments which increase hostility, and the employee victims retaliating — in this case — using cyberviolence rather than physical violence. Because the motive is often vengeance, not profit, it's often more difficult to anticipate or even understand the threat of a vindictive hacker. But employees do far more damage—billions more—than the more glamorous hackers and phreaks.

The Battle of the Phone Phreaks

Recall when the Legion of Doom met with another hacker group, called the Masters of Deception and caused mass havoc in the business and telephone industry during the late 80s. They also had fun with chosen targets, such as corporate voice mail—busting the passwords (with DTMF touch-tones) and leaving obscene messages and connecting callers to adult 900 services when they called the home office. Soon, these *super-phreaks* were charging customers for security consulting services and began to develop a bitter rivalry. Customer equipment got caught in the middle of a *phone phreak–war* of sorts, where the members and families of each group engaged in technical attacks against each other.[1]

For years, telephone hackers or phone phreaks would boldly post stolen telephone credit card numbers on BBS systems and "borrowed" boards. They also posted pirated software and confidential documents. Phreaks would hold message board discussions on how to break into just about every telephone system—and some could back up their boasts. Telcos and banks, not to mention law enforcement agencies, were no longer amused with these teenagers and young adults. On May 7,8, and 9, 1990, the FBI, Secret Service, and other federal agencies launched a major Hacker-crackdown in Los Angeles, Cincinnati, Detroit, Miami, Newark, San Diego, San Jose, San Francisco, Richmond, and Phoenix. It was called Operation Sundevil by the Feds, and it was designed to stop the PBX, wire fraud, and credit card fraud, and most importantly, to seize hardware used by the scores of phone phreaks to break into the phone system and disseminate their technical hacker-bases on BBSes and the Internet. One hundred and fifty Secret Service agents seized about 42 computer systems and 23,000 floppy disks. But after they were done, there were few arrests, fewer indictments, and over 2975 "outlaw" BBS groups still actively displaying phone phreak technobabble all over cyberspace.[22]

The Breakup of AT&T Also Dismantled Security

After the Bell breakup in 1984, AT&T was no longer the only long distance carrier. MCI, U.S. Sprint, and other carriers began carrying greater and greater volumes of long distance and leased-line service. Thousands of companies with their own PBXs (private branch exchanges) took advantage of their own private internal telephone networks to offer sometimes millions of dollars in savings by utilizing existing private links (leased line IMTs) between their major locations. Calls from within and outside a company's facilities could be routed over these leased lines, avoiding all long distance charges. Hackers soon found their way into private corporate telephone networks, permitting them to reek havoc anew. And more long distance carriers dramatically increased the quantity of telco to telco connection points, making more connections vulnerable to phreaks—who often took advantage with skill.

Basic PBX Toll Fraud

Recently, MCI Telecommunications refunded about $50 million to customers who were victimized by toll fraud (described under "Telephone Hacking or Phreak Techniques" earlier in this chapter). AT&T was initially reluctant, but changed their tune when MCI and Sprint used this policy to steal AT&T customers. Phone operators need to be cautioned about providing dial tones manually to strangers on the phone.

As with other "black holes" in the Info-Superhighway, no one knows the full cost of this fraud. Often the companies hide the expenses in their telecommunications expense reports, so even stockholders are always kept in the dark. Loss Estimates range from a few hundred million to a billion dollars per year. Relentless trial-and-error dialing—often using automatic computer-based speed dialers (demon dialers) are the next easiest way to break into private PBX systems.

Individual hackers can make tens of thousands of dollars in calls before being detected—but they are seldom caught. Many, as mentioned before, sell long distance service out of storefronts in impoverished immigrant neighborhoods of big cities. The customer comes in, and then the crooks will step across the street, dial the number free, and allow the customer to talk as long as he wants to Puerto Rico, El Salvador, the Dominican Republic, Cuba, and elsewhere. Some shops actually set up extensions or pay phones in the storefront and run an operation until the telephone police close down the operations. Unfortunately, the employees are often hired by the crooks and are usually not the brains—who are free to set up another operation down the street. (Telephone police are made up of phone company personnel, the FBI, and other federal authorities. Often, they are unable to follow up on local areas to catch the real thieves, who steal and exploit unauthorized PBX access and phony calling card numbers).

If businesses cannot block calls to nonbusiness locations (if employees must have access to all area codes), checking the PBX call record by employees and then billing employees for personal calls can reduce unauthorized outbound activity and charges. Authorities lament that most company managers don't understand how toll fraud works or even what it is. It's doubtful that they are anxious to report the problems to internal management or authorities when it makes them look neglectful and ignorant. Authorities assert that ignorance and passivity in corporate telecommunications staff is the biggest problem. Many sites are unmanned at night, when hackers attack the most.

Voice Mail Invasion

Just like PBX fraud, access to voice mail equipment can be secured simply by making sure passwords have been applied. The phone phreaks use poorly managed voice mail systems for their own messages, stealing the service by configuring their own voice-mail box for whatever features they want (including paging, call forwarding, and more). These phreaks' pranks eventually come to the light when victimized businesses receive their phone bill. The phreaks use cellular phones so they can retrieve their messages without fear of being traced.

Toll Fraud, Shoulder Bandits, and the Black Boxes

For over 20 years, AT&T had put in place monitoring mechanisms to catch fraudulent toll charges. They were also able to catch many who dialed into local and long distance telephone switching systems to program the switching computers (these folks actually implemented a sort of "black market" phone company within the phone company) Such access empowered the power-hackers to forward unsuspecting people's telephone calls to new locations— without their knowledge (since you don't hear your phone ring when calls have been forwarded). They could also direct the specific routes of calls around the world (like a skilled operator or computer routing program). They could even cut off telephone service to thwart investigations, shut down businesses they didn't like, harass other phone phreaks, or trigger service activity—permitting them to tap unwitting technicians' passwords, access codes, and procedural practices (as failed lines were being serviced). Sometimes, aggressive phone phreaks would actually draw service activity in order to steal equipment from trucks and even hold up telephone service personnel.

Cellular Fraud

The cellular companies efforts to cure "phone phraude" have been mostly limited to monitoring calling patterns. But industry engineers have hardware solutions that they claim may block the overwhelming bulk of fraudulent cellular calls. In late 1993 TRW publicized a new technique for analyzing the analog transmission "signature" of each individual cellular telephone, storing it with the PROM-burned serial number and cellular telephone number. This would give every cell phone in the world an individual digital profile. A phony unit's serial number and telephone number would be rejected before the call was placed, since the supervisory computer would see that the unit did not match the signature. But this system could be defeated if details of the "signatures" don't remain secure. If industry historical patterns hold true, within a few months, the hacker-geniuses will already have devised countermeasures. Remember the first coded cable boxes with scrambling for HBO and other movie channels? They were supposed to be secure and unbreakable. But just like the telephone black boxes, fraudulent cable boxes still provide millions of citizens with free cable service on premium channels.

The measures proposed by TRW and others are only stopgaps. Most of the large cell carriers are replacing analog cellular-phone systems with a digital ones.

Digital Cell Phones Are More Secure

Digital-cellular standards are more secure, requiring the calling cell phone to answer a mathematical challenge based on serial number and telephone number, as opposed to just sending the actual numbers. Some units actually encrypt conversations to prevent cellular eavesdropping; ironically, law-enforcement agencies outside the United States are opposing such security.

Some carriers are able to encrypt your account number as it's transmitted to the nearby cell; this prevents hackers from using special scanners designed to pick up and display customer account codes, which are then burned into the chips of nondigital cellular "hot" or "cloned" cellular phones. It isn't unusual for victims of cloning to receive a cellular bill for $20,000 or more; and even though telcos give full credit for fraudulent calls, digital phones with secured transmission are worth the extra money (Motorola and Nokia both make cell phones with this capability).

900 Fraud

The system of 900 numbers provides many useful services, including sports and weather information, financial information, sports handicapping, technical support services, research, entertainment, and of course adult chat lines. Because updated 900 services allow providers to supply the most current information to their databases, it may prove worthwhile to permit limited access of 900 numbers from phones in a restricted area. These 900 services *(although some feel the Internet will eventually replace them)* provide information critical to your interests.

But some who have checked their 900 calls on their bills may find that even the most reputable services (such as the now defunct *L.A. Times* research 900 number) are subject to serious overbilling. These overcharges are all refundable, and customers should deduct the amount from the very first bill and *not* pay the overage. By federal law, customers can't be disconnected for failure to pay for 900 charges (even when they are valid).

But unless you protect yourself from invasion of phone phreaks, your residential or business telephone may be used to make such calls without your authorization and not even from your usual billing location. A group of phreaks seized a dial tone from a business PBX and then made thousands of dollars in 900 calls. You can bet that business blocked its 900 services after discovering the little surprise.

Originally, it wasn't unusual to hear stories of night watchmen generating $10,000 900-number phone bills until the business world protested and telephone companies encouraged businesses to block 900 numbers. But there's still millions of dollars in 900 abuse and fraud reported, and still more millions lost by those too ashamed or embarrassed to report it. Although there is much fraud on both sides of the 900 number game, it's important for all consumers of 900 services to know how their privacy may be compromised by calling a 900 number, how you are within your rights not to pay for services that are not completely satisfactory, and what the 900 company can and cannot do if you refuse to pay. You cannot use a calling card to place a 900 phone call. Your phone records could be subpoenaed in a court of law, so as in Murphy's Law of anti-Murphy's Law preparedness (Everything which can go wrong will go wrong at the worse possible time — be prepared for the worst consequences), forewarned is forearmed. It is also a reality that many phone abusers make 900 phone calls in homes without the owners' permission

Important 900-Number Facts

- It's best to block 900 numbers at the office.
- It's best to block 900 numbers at home if you have children.
- When such calls are necessary at the office, attempt to make 900 numbers available to only one phone (like the president's or the director's) so that there is some control and ability to manage calls.
- No residential or business customer has to pay 900 bills if service is not what was advertised or is unsatisfactory.
- Don't answer personal questions; 900 providers can use it in court to confirm your identity, since they can't see your face.
- Check to make sure the 900 company credited your account—examine their next bill carefully and write the FCC if they continue to add this amount to your bill.
- Your phone and long distance service can never be disconnected for failure to pay for 900 bills.
- If you demand a refund but the 900 provider wants to challenge you in court, they may just do so and try to convince a judge or jury that you should pay your bill.

(although not nearly as many burglars as customers tell the phone company). Here are important facts (hard to find) on consumer rights with respect to 900 phone service:

Carrier Integrity

In 1991, AT&T's network experienced a major failure in its Manhattan switch, which brought down communication to millions of customers and also shut down air traffic control. A previous AT&T failure brought almost the entire nation's phone service down when the company attempted to test new software. The Manhattan switch failure was prolonged because the technicians didn't switch over to backup power (required at all major long distance points of presence). The software failure was avoidable, and customers weren't impressed at all with AT&T's excuses and attitude about reliability. Many companies lost significant revenue; some decided to give some of their business to MCI or Sprint so that future AT&T crashes wouldn't disrupt their businesses again. Other phone companies have been luckier technically but have exhibited almost bankrupted ethics.

Bell South, for instance, became tremendously profitable after the breakup of AT&T. Bell South was also busted by authorities for overcharging millions of cutomers for years; it was cited by the FCC and forced to refund millions to its millions of customers.

Many consulting firms make millions every year helping customers identify overbilling and collect what is owed them. Since customers can often obtain phone bills on floppy disk or tape, and because all rates are published, customers can develop software to expose all instances of overcharging. All overcharges are 100 percent credited to customers by law.

GTE and Private Records

When the news media announced that Nicole Simpson placed a call to her mother just before she was killed, the question of the day became "When was the call made?"

Confidential, private information was almost instantaneously ravaged by over 1000 GTE employees all over the country. Just about every telephone company employee had authority to view customer records, and of course, there was no precise way of determining exactly who accessed Nicole Simpson's phone records. Two employees were fired, and they indicated that they were simply trying to prove OJ's innocence.

MCI Slams Its Way into Market Share

MCI started it all—the decade-long battle that started with MCI's challenge to AT&T's monopoly of the long distance phone network eventually led to Judge Green's comprehensive breakup of the nation's public telephone system. MCI fought hard for just a small market share, although they offered what seemed to be discounts *(although longer call completion time and quality were problems at first)* and solutions. AT&T often didn't service their business customers satisfactorily, and often their lack of flexibility created a major exodus from AT&T to MCI and Sprint.

Then MCI attracted more customers with their "Friends and Family" calling circle discount plans, where individual residential customers could get discounts for calling other MCI customers.

But the marketing at MCI became extremely aggressive, with telemarketing centers set up in several parts of the nation, and telemarketers paid by commission. Many helped augment their salaries with an old sales technique—*lying!* The actual term is "slamming," but rather than just lie about the product, these telemarketers were allegedly telling people things like, "Ma'am, you must change long distance companies because AT&T is going out of business." AT&T responded with their own telemarketing campaigns, and they also took liberties until the FCC stepped in and warned them.

In 1994, an MCI employee was charged with stealing many thousands of telephone calling card numbers, which were eventually used to make over 50,000 fraudulent calls. (Wall Street Journal Report, NBC August 20, 1995).

Friends and Family and George Orwell

Can the government subpoena persons listed on a list of an MCI or other carrier's calling circle friends? Yes. Both state and federal (and maritime) authorities have access to all telephone company records, including calling circles. If you don't want your calling circle friends to wind up being subpoenaed as possible witnesses to some event, crime or action, you might want to check out the law in your state before *ratting-out on your friends"*(as the AT&T adds playfully euphemize their competitors product).

Security for Residential Phones: Caller ID Is Coming Nationwide

Caller id service will go nationwide (except in California) in December 1995, and it will be available in California in the first quarter of 1996, according to FCC and regional telephone companies (RBOCs). Simply put, this service allows you to see the caller's area code and phone number on a numeric display on your phone.

Many areas in the country already have caller id and advanced caller id (in which both name and number are displayed). Ameritech makes an enormous amount on caller id; in fact, the biggest portion of the company's $60 billion in revenue is from this feature, bringing home the reality that customers want security.

Why, Why, Oh MCI?

I was working as a network designer in the San Francisco complex bid office for MCI. I had been transferred from my office in Los Angeles to San Francisco. I went home to Los Angeles on the weekends but gave my boss all the phone numbers I could be reached at. When an emergency came up when I was in L.A., some of my friends and relatives told me that my boss had called and left a message. He identified himself by name but left no phone number, only a message to call as soon as possible. The only problem with this situation was that I had never given him the phone numbers he was calling.

I realized that my boss had no respect for my privacy. He could have called the numbers I had supplied, but instead he called people whom I had called, not knowing if they were friend, business contact, plumber, or even court adversary. He probably had lost my emergency numbers and took a shortcut, but didn't realize that by breaching what was thought to be a private and confidential phone

Caller ID Block

The phone company offers a service, something like an unlisted phone number, that blocks a caller's number and name from being displayed on a caller id phone (at the other end). This function can be turned on and off, just like call waiting.

Blocking All Caller ID-Blocked Callers

Finally, the phone company, for an additional charge, will block a call from going through if the person calling you has invoked their caller id block. Until they disabled the caller id, they would receive a recorded message that tells the caller the person will not accept your call as long as it is blocked. :) And so it begins. . . .

Residential Privacy: Multiple Numbers, One Line

Distinctive ringing service from the phone company only costs about three dollars per month, and the phone company will give you an additional phone number that just rings differently on the same single telephone line.

number, he destroyed any trust I might have had in him (no, I didn't have any trust in him before that).
He had apparently taken numbers off the PBX call records and called the numbers assuming they would all be my friends. Some were not, and when I confronted my boss about the situation, he didn't deny calling. When I filed an official complaint, nothing was done. I resigned a few weeks later over another issue, but it was a relief knowing that certain people couldn't eavesdrop on me.

When this number is called, you hear the differently patterned ring, and you know which number the caller has dialed.

Ring n' Route is a product that allows you to dedicate this distinctive ring number to your fax so that if you have a separate fax machine and PC, you don't have to leave your PC on 24 hours a day, which may permit hackers to access your computer. Instead you can give your fax number out freely on your business card and keep your PC modem number secret.

Ring n' Route can also be used to dedicate the two numbers (with different rings) to separate answering machines. Some phone companies offer three and four separate ring patterns, and this product works with both, offering privacy for people, security and protection for your computer. At only $45, this new product saves the cost of another line. (Fax switches often do not work; CNG tones often do not accompany the fax handshake.) Because you can audibly tell which number is ringing, it can be used to prioritize calls, and filter — business calls on one line, personal on the other can prevent disruption in one area from NOT taking calls in the other.

CALL BACK OR CALL RETURN — For areas which don't have caller id yet, you can get a feature which allows you to returned the last call in which you missed. When you call the number back, it appears later on your bill, so you have a record of the harassing call in your calling area (but not long distance). You can get a phone which displays digits of the number, so you don't have to wait for a bill.

CALL FORWARD — Besides being a nice way to link your home with your business, call forward is a neat way to deter crank or harassing callers. You can forward your number to a number which has been disconnected, and leave it that way for a number of hours or days — telling your clients before hand that your service will be out of order for maintenance. You can also forward calls to your local police department, with their permission. The call will be automatically recorded, and often traced by many police agencies. Selective call forwarding (used as call return or call trace) allows you to "peel off" crank calls, directing them to a disconnected number or the authorities (with permission).

CALL TRACE — This is a new feature, which allows a person to document harassing incoming calls. After receiving a harassing phone call; the operator comes on the line and the call is documented.

People who act aggressively against phone abusers, cranks, phreaks tend to feel liberated from the feeling of victimization. Once I had a good time busting a particularly malicious crank caller for a family member. I forwarding his call to the front desk sergeant of a local police department. Don't ever allow yourself to be intimidated; take control and use technology to bust those who would disrupt business or your home.

Special Screening Answering Machines

There are many machines that use caller id to screen calls, provide personalized greetings to those assigned personal voice mail-boxes, and provide call waiting with no bothersome "click." There are non-answering machines that also screen all preprogrammed numbers out—you don't even hear the phone ring.

Years ago, I ran across a product that worked on a non–caller id number, that allowed complete call filtering of all unwanted calls (no ring), using a secret ring, and offering a ring-again procedure (within a time window).

Cordless Phones—Insecure!!!

Most inexpensive cordless phones, like cellular phones, can be easily tapped using a inexpensive police scanner. Because the frequencies used by cordless phones and baby monitors are easy to listen to, it's recommended that they simply not be used for any confidential or personal communications. People could be recording your friends', business associates', and others personal information, not to mention your own. More expensive cordless phones (Sony) have encryption so that they can't be tapped. Because the frequencies used by cordless phones and baby monitors are easy to listen to, it's recommended that they simply not be used for any confidential or personal communications.

People could be recording your business and personal (sometimes very personal) information, not to mention your own. More expensive cordless phones (Sony) have encryption so that they can't be tapped.

Three Types of Stalkers

There are basically three types of persons who engage in harassing calls, which often escalate into stalking in person.

They are the rejected lover, the spurned admirer, and the linkage stalker. Celebrity stalkers, like John Bardo, who stalked and killed actress Susan Schaffer, look up computer records (motor vehicle records are available on CD-ROM) and attack. It's important that citizens realize that instead of letting stalkers use their phones as intelligence devices, they should turn technology on the stalker.

Stalkers also conduct repeated telephone calls and hangups, repeat calls, lewd and threatening messages—all of which should be dealt with aggressively and with sound use of technology.

Many small business phone users also get harassed. Here are a few tips to help both homes and businesses avoid being victims:

- Don't leave a number on an answering machine, only say, "Leave your number at the beep."
- Don't leave your name on an answering machine, why give out information?
- The callback feature allows you to call the harasser back and register his number on your bill (if local).

- Call block permits you to block the harassing call immediately after the harrassing call is made.
- Caller id allows you to see the caller when he's ringing and filer it out.
- Put a fax on line (hurts ears).
- Get the harassing call on your answering machine, but don't tape without knowledge.
- Report the call to authorities if it's a repeat caller, or if threats are made.

Video Phones

Video conferences can contain extremely sensitive and important information, which could be very damaging in your competitor's hands. Video conferencing taps allow your competitors to attack your venture or business with incredible effectiveness—they know what you're going to do. MCI recently announced a new product called network MCI, which combines video conferencing, e-mail, and faxing in one product. There's no mention of encryption in its product description, so customers desiring security may want to check and see if that is now available.

Introduction to Internet Security: From Basics to Beyond

Counter-Measure Equipment

There are antitap products that can detect phone taps, hidden microphones, video equipment (micro-miniature), hidden tape recorders. A company in New York called the Spy Shop bills itself as the authority on spy gadgets and has a whole range of products and prices for the person who wants to have more assurance of security. Digital taps by law enforcement may not be detectable, and with the implementation of the "wire tap ready" law, it will be impossible to tell when law enforcement is listening. There is also more expensive testing equipment available designed to detect line impairments, line breaks, and signal level problems.

COMPUTER
SECURITY

Programming
Protection into
your System

I t isn't the purpose of this text to cover the subject of medium and large computer system operation procedures; there are enough comprehensive reference texts covering installation, organization, scheduling, backup, fault tolerance, software and hardware change control procedures, disaster contingency and recovery, and the rest. But it needs to be said that without proper management, allocation, and protection of its computer resources, an enterprise is much more vulnerable to destruction when it does eventually become the target of hackers, viruses, Trojan horses, and PBX-phreaks.

It really isn't a question of *if*, but *when* a computer facility will fall prey to cyber-terror, which when it strikes can rip the heart out of your computer system and destroy a company very quickly. When will they attack? When Murphy's law says—when you least expect it, and when you need your system the most (this book was almost destroyed at deadline time by a hard-drive crash, two virus attacks, and intercepted e-mail—my backup spared me a fool's fate). If the computer installation is prepared, you can minimize disruption of its operation; otherwise, an attack could create enough confusion to permanently damage your enterprise. The key to a secure computer environment: reliability, integrity and availability.

Reliability and availability may mean having these elements in operation:
- A UPS or uninterruptible power supply
- Power Surge Protection
- A secure and padlocked CPU enclosure (housing or cover)—prevents tampering
- Keeping the environment dust-free
- A backup CPU, tape storage, a disaster recovery planbackup site

The Weakest Point In the System— Incompetent Management

If MIS or CIO managers have practices of implementing untested software, installing unproven hardware, or simply implementing changes on your computer system without gradual phased implementation—chances are your business will suffer greatly from its own devices. I remember taking a part-time job working for a large telemarketing company. They had implemented the newest version of a leading NOS (Network Operating Security). It was extremely unstable and caused their automatic calling system and database to freeze continually. Telemarketers had to be sent home constantly, and the company lost millions. They claimed that they had to "upgrade" their system because of capacity, but they suffered so many down-hours with the new software, it would have been less costly to their revenue and reputation to have purchased another building and constructed a second network. The moral of the story? Don't change anything unless you have to, and when you do, implement network, computer, and application changes in a gradual way, always allowing your business to "fall back" on the previous configuration of software or hardware if things don't work out.

Seeing multimillion dollar computer installations become crippled by incompetence and lack of preparation is not unusual. Unfortunately, poor management will often withdraw in the face of crisis, further jeopardizing the health of an organization. In the midst of a crisis, management of this type is often paralyzed and unable to make sound judgments. Even when computer systems have been crippled by circumstances they created, they often repeat the same mistakes over and over. In some cases, even if a company is losing millions from interruption and disruption due to poor planning or implementation, stubborn MIS managers and CIOs often don't seek help from consultants when they really need it; they fear being exposed for what they are. And what else would you expect from a MIS manager who runs a disorderly shop—they are of course, more focused on job security than the health of their business.

Business consultant and author Stanley Foster Reed identifies the symptoms of poor management—recklessness, laziness, egotism, dogmaticness, and destructiveness—in his book *The Toxic Executive: A Step-by-Step Guide for Turning Your Boss or Yourself from Noxious to Nurturing.*[1] Any management that ignores standard operating procedures of data processing and telecommunications is taking risks with a company's future. The necessity of hardware and software change control; contingency planning during project implementation; and planning on device, software, and power failures (as well as earthquake, fire, and security threats) demands competence. With poor management over a good company, even the most valued and productive employees wind up in the unemployment line (in a company bankrupted by MIS-buffoonery). With "let the chips fall where they may" management in place, many things besides "chips" tend to "fall," and the highest degree of computer security will not necessarily help.

Computer Security

Although the Internet is the primary thoroughfare on the Info-Superhighway, the desktop computer is the primary target of those who seek the booty—information. A recent study recently found that there were 40 million PCs in the U.S.A. (6 million sold in 1994), and that there are many households with two PCs—usually the kids get the one with the CD-ROM reader and the multimedia games. The PC industry generates about nine billion dollars per year in hardware and software sales alone. But the hardware and software that Americans are investing in is not the most valuable asset placed on personal computers. The data that people create, save, and transmit from the personal computer are the most valuable—both in the collective monetary value of the information stored on tens of millions of spinning disk drives and in the intangible but immeasurable value of these data to the owners. The data on personal computers are confidential, private, personal, creative, often irreplaceable. You don't appreciate the meaning of the term "priceless" until you have lost computer data that are irreplaceable.

Personal computers are now the core data processing machines in the modern business, industry, and home. The PC is quickly becoming the preferred video game platform (with CD-ROMS, Pentiums, and Power-PC speed), and it will soon be the tool that will change retail business—with *virtual shopping malls* and ordering goods and services. It has long ago revolutionized mechanical engineering, word processing, accounting, publishing, art, aerospace design, prototype fabrication, all types of modeling and simulation, statistics, chemical and biological sciences, and many other industries. Roughly 90 percent of personal computers are IBM compatible, with about 10 percent being Macintoshes. Amiga, Commodore, and other personal computers are a distant third and fourth and don't have much presence outside of music, graphic, and game applications.[2]

Performance Improvements

With speeds of PCs approaching 100 Megahertz, and processing approaching the MIPS ratings of mainframes just a few years ago, it's not hard to understand why personal computers are now doing the bulk of scientific number crunching, financial bean counting, administrative text processing, and electronic messaging. A 100-MHz Pentium processor is capable of performing as fast as expensive minicomputers and mainframes were just a decade ago—many of these old computer systems cost millions, and millions more to maintain and operate!

Although Macintosh Power PCs can run IBM-compatible software, Intel Pentium processors equipped with high-speed CD-ROM drives offer noticeable improvements in multimedia performance, and IBM has announced a Power-PC product that will allow PCs to run Macintosh software. Sales of computers continue to rise, and manufacturers are offering better price-performance ratios in products costing less than their predecessors.

Statistically Speaking

Who Threatens Computer Data?[3]

Employees:	*81.60%*
Outsiders:	*17.30%*
Others:	*1.00%*

Major Causes of Loss To Business[4]

1) Accidents

2) Dishonest employees

3) Computer failure (software or hardware)

4) Network failure

5) Disasters

Minor Causes of Loss[5]

1) Viruses

2) Hackers (inside and outside)

Business PCs Infected by Viruses[6]

None	*42%*
Less than 25%	*45%*
26% to 50%	*5%*
51% to 75%	*4%*
More than 75%	*1%*

Just When We Were Starting to Have Fun

Even though consumers are taking advantage of the cost-effective processing and power capabilities of modern PCs, there is little or no appreciation for the importance of privacy and security. The indifference starts in the design of PCs—typically few have security for hardware or software resources. Hardware and applications are frightfully vulnerable to tampering and hacking, and operating systems are only recently being shipped with antivirus software. The security gap continues at the retailer, where the PC salespersons typically don't sell customers security products, conditioned power, or repair service contracts. Why is this? Because even computer professionals aren't very familiar with security software or hardware issues, and they are encouraged to sell exciting CD-ROM programs or business applications.

They don't emphasize security issues, not even how to prevent viruses from damaging disk drives. Too many people still consider the PC as a toy, used for games and *sometimes* business. Customers actually expect the PC will last forever, so most home and office PC users fail to get the proper preventative maintenance until something is broken. Since *all* personal computers break at some point, just about every PC is subject to major security and reliability problems.

Both physical space and cyberspace can conceal threats to computer security. A poorly managed, unsecured computer can actually be used as a burglar device in your own home or office. Whether it's an unfriendly software *agent* residing in a hidden directory or a bundle of floppy disk sitting in an unlocked cabinet—both could provide an internal "window" for your CPU to be "stolen," damaged, or secretly altered. Let's look at the real threats to computers and get some perspective:

Virus Vigilance

A computer virus can damage a single PC or wipeout an entire network system by inserting copies of itself into computer files and other executable programs. As the infected file is loaded into memory the virus can attack other files, giving it the opportunity to cripple or destroy the infected computer or find its way to other computers through a company's computer network system.

Minimum Security Procedures

- System disks should not be used to copy or install application programs.
- Do not borrow or exchange system disks with other users.
- Don't exchange or share **any** floppy disks with other users if you can avoid it.
- When a computer is just set up, and after each new program install, print all directories with dates and file sizes and also save the output on disk for reference.
- Do not run programs from unknown sources.
- Scan all floppy disks when they are first inserted into a drive (using a virus scan program).
- Run antiviral software on all disk drives daily or at the very least, weekly.

Maximum Security Procedures

- Don't attach any user stations to the Internet, only to one or more Internet PC.
- The Internet PC saves files only to floppy disk.
- The Internet PC saves files to one hard drive only.
- Turn the PC off after saving to one drive, flushing memory in case a virus is memory resident.
- Large LANs (Local Area Networks) and computer businesses need to establish a comprehensive Internet connection strategy, incorporating packet filters, firewalls, and further measures to restrict outside access.

Virus Contamination Route

- The virus contamination route begins with the contaminated medium: a floppy disk or Internet file download to a hard drive or another floppy (minimize the risk of spread by copying to a second floppy if possible).
- The next step the virus takes is to spread. The virus will try to spread to another file on that volume, to another disk volume, or, most dangerously, to main memory. This happens very fast if the program containing the virus is run or executed by the unwitting user.
- If the virus remains on the disk (in the system, the startup area, or another program) or in main memory, it can then infect and/or damage every file written to disk and every uploaded file or backed-up file. In a matter of days, the virus can modify every batch file or script file, in fact, every program executed on your system.

Isolating Viruses

To reduce the possibility of viruses spreading, use a completely separate Internet PC, one not attached to other company computers, to test all new programs. If this isn't possible, then here are a few steps that can isolate viruses before they spread throughout your system and your business:

Virus Mitigation Procedures
- Write-protect all system files and use a "test volume" (dedicated to testing new disks, programs obtained from the Internet, and even data files).
- Use a floppy disk if possible.

- After a transfer from the Net or a floppy disk, power the PC off to flush main memory of potential viruses.
- Run a virus scan on a downloaded file as soon as you power-up the PC.
- Perform a check of main memory (using DOS CHKDSK or the Mac's "Get Info and Memory" icon in the Control Panel) before and after you test-run the program or use the data file—is all normal afterward? Are the normal memory usage and disk state subsequently altered?
- Run a virus inoculation program at the outset of any suspicious symptoms.

Of all the human threats, it seems that the vengeful employee is the most dangerous threat to the corporate computer system. Employees have the advantage of site familiarity, physical and system access, and knowledge of the computer system's vulnerabilities and most valuable data. But beyond revenge and retribution, other motives include money, fear, politics, industrial spying, power, and ego. The people who seek to disrupt our info-nirvana have an advantage—plundering data is a relatively low-risk undertaking, vastly more profitable than robbing banks. History tells us that with each phase of new technology comes a new type of crime.

As previously discussed, information is by far the most expensive business commodity, and our business and personal computers are the vaults in cyberspace; they contain infinitely valuable personal information, documents, and images. The information on computers contains the equivalent of *money*: quantifiable, time-critical, or irreplaceable information—which businesses almost universally fail to appreciate fully until after it's compromised or stolen. The resulting lax culture in the computer and telecommunications industry has caused lazy MIS managers, CIOs, telecommunications managers, and system administrators to seriously under-protect data in their charge. This situation is slowly changing in most of America's Fortune 500, but not fast enough to prevent some inevitable tragedies—inevitable because of the degree of threat in relation to the lack of protection.

Employment and Commerce

The computer is already both the *virtual automobile* and *office*—the future is now. New multimedia PCs and Macintosh personal computers have built-in telephones, headsets, voice mail, modems, video cameras, microphones, and scanners. The new convergence of computers, telephones, and video transports American workers, via a modem, to whatever or wherever they want, allowing them to communicate with others and to access and forward vast libraries of information via e-mail, file transfer, fax, and voice. One online service actually offers high-fidelity real-time voice communications through the Internet. Businesses are being born every day at home using personal computers.

A Sales Call from the Near Future

Its 1:30pm when a multimedia PC equipped salesperson makes a phone call to a customer, he double-clicks a Windows phonebook icon and chooses the client to call. Instantly, the client is auto-dialed, and after a two-second pause, his picture appears on the computer, and they see the salesperson's picture on theirs. The client picks what items he wants to order by double-clicking on pictures of those items, and an order form is instantly presented, which the client then signs with a digital signature. The customer's credit card is instantly billed for the order total plus tax. Two minutes later the shipping department receives a printed shipping request; in fifteen minutes, the clerk sends an e-mail message to the customer reading, "ORDER #3445 SHIPPED 4/20/96 at 2:05:02 PM"

Computer Hacking Techniques

How do hackers get into your computer or anyone else's? Here are a few favorite techniques:

- **Scavenging**—The simple act of looking for valuable data, whether the information is online, stored in tapes or disks offline, or on printouts in the dumpster.

- **Impersonation or Piggybackers**—Individuals "slip" though security doors by pretending to have their hands full, or they introduce themselves as "reporters" to get full tours of computer facilities. Or an impersonator can use an phony terminal (programmed with the address of the real one), wait for the real user to sign off, and then use the unattended terminal to gain access.

- **Wiretapping**—This involves tapping of telephone lines, computer ports, modem ports, or other hardware, but it's also possible to "eavesdrop" or "tap" someone's communication I/O buffers or memory areas so that whatever is being send or received can also be recorded by unknown parties.

- **Data Diddling**—This technique uses the complex codes in the computer to direct funds or other valuable resources to an unauthorized account. The numeric codes often conceal where the funds are taken from, so "diddling" is often hard to find if applications don't permit easy auditing of funds distribution.

- **Salami Slicing**—This technique is used to "skim" funds secretly from one account to another, so that one person or organization receives the funds in their account. The same thing could be done with other valuable nonmonetary assets. The salami-thief may be able to make repeated small electronic transfers of small change from thousands of accounts, as did one resourceful hacker did at a Hughes division. The law at that time didn't allow prosecuting the wire thief for more than a misdemeanor (on thousands of counts) because he "sliced" only a few pennies per employee check. Ledgers and checking accounts aren't balanced to the penny, so "slicers" can drain accounts over many weeks or even months and never be detected—never! Is your payroll department slicing your check? Since this can also happen to a banking account, one wonders how many hundreds of thousands of accounts are being sliced—with nobody even aware.

- **Superzaps**—When a systems programmer loads a special operating system and then uses expanded system privileges to access privileged files and transfer money from one account to another—it's called a "superzap."

- **Asynch Attacks**—When programs pause in main memory, hackers can sometimes access their data and use them to penetrate the system.

- **Simulation and Modeling**—Some hackers actually use a company's own computer to model or simulate the necessary adjustments necessary to hide their theft.

- **Trojan Horses**—Trojan horses are viruses hidden inside of software. They may damage or erase data files and programs, but they may also display messages or images and even steal money from computer accounts and anonymously send e-mail to the hacker who introduced the virus. "Worms" are similar but designed to spread through a network, consuming memory or disk space in a node until it fails. A new virus type, called a cruise virus, attacks a specific target on a network or computer.

- **Back Doors**—Systems programmers of network and computer systems often have secret passwords to gain operational control of a computer or piece of network equipment. These passwords are normally easy to break, allowing hackers to do incredible damage and theft.

- **Trap Doors**—Often, programmers will build "hacker routines" into their programs, taking advantage of the program's access to critical areas of memory, CPU registers, and disk space to perform functions not available to interactive users.

- **Logic Bombs**—At a system time or date, or after a certain event on the system (after the execution of a certain program, after a certain user logs on, after disk space consumption reaches a specific level, or after any other event trackable through the system) a destructive act is done. It could be erasure of disks, system shutdown, or viral incubation and proliferation.

- **Password Busting**—This is a technique to find secret passwords. Some hackers use random number generators, special password analysis software, or other techniques, combined with repeated calling of the same dial-up computer to gain unauthorized access to a host.

- **Dial-Up Line-Blockers**—These are used by constantly dialing an access number, particularly an 800 number and then hanging up. This costs the company money for the 800 number and ties up a communication line or a computer port for a time. These attacks are hard to defend, because even if they are temporary, they permit one person with an auto-dialer to seriously disrupt business.

Viruses

Viruses are programs that have the ability to destroy computer data files, program files, entire disk surfaces, and sometimes even computer hardware. Viruses need access to the processor in order to execute their program functions—the same specific input, processing, and output commands used to normally process data are used by viruses to destroy. Viruses are serious business and can be murder to companies, careers, and computers. Even though most businesses have yet to experience serious shutdowns, I anticipate that viruses will become increasingly destructive—especially to small, home-based computer businesses.

The rather perverse science of virus programming started in 1986, when Baset and Amjad substituted the executable normally found on the boot sector of a floppy disk with their own code. From there viruses began to show up in universities and military computer facilities, mostly infecting .COM files on IBM PCs and eventually finding their way into .EXE files. Viruses attacked the file allocation tables, system files, even data files, and there weren't any antivirus programs until S&S software created the first antivirus software (the Anti-Virus Toolkit).[7]

Viruses can be introduced onto a system from a floppy disk, network downloads, and of course, direct input at the computer keyboard. Viruses are typically written for a specific platform or computer type, such as the IBM compatible or Macintosh. Although they are mostly disk resident, they also can also "hide" in memory (be memory resident) and have delayed execution (based on date). They can alter the content of a data file just slightly so that a decimal point is moved one position.

Scientists have proven that it is impossible to scan a file and determine it's

How Viruses Are Introduced Into a System

- *Floppy disks*
- *Bulletin board systems*
- *Connection with another computer*
- *The Internet*

Signs and Symptoms to Watch For
- *Disk read and write activity occurs when users or programs are idle.*
- *File sizes of system and other program files are larger than normal—a very good sign of trouble.*
- *System and other program files have been updated—not normal on a PC since most programs are off the shelf and never altered for the life of the PC—this might mean something that is quite unusual.*

Defenses	*Used by How Many Businesses*[8]
Anti-virus software	*86%*
Training	*65%*
New policies	*29%*
Other	*34%*

a virus 100 percent of the time, and sick virus writers are creating new-generation viruses that are encrypted, so that they can't be examined easily without complex algorithms (which are beyond the budget and capabilities of many of the software companies producing antivirus software). The result is today's state of affairs—someone must be bitten before antivirus inoculations can be developed.[9]

The most destructive viruses are *invisible*, erasing disk contents. Some viruses can make disk drives clatter until they break, monitors go up in smoke, or computer chips overheat and fail. Some chips actually contain viruses, and in addition to performing standard processor functions, they spy on the computer owner and report back to the hacker on the contents of the target disk. New-generation viruses are performing hacking tasks in secret, making computers send mail with secret passwords of the owners.

Billions of dollars have been lost each year in damage from viruses, and after large companies like Novell and IBM began to infect their customers inadvertently when distributing software, antiviral software has become a staple in computer software distribution on floppy disk and online.

Viruses have many forms, for instance: 1) simple viruses, 2) Trojan horses—which act like good programs while actually doing something else, 3) logic bombs, which are triggered when an event occurs, such as a date or the entry of certain information, 4) worms or agents, and 5) cruise viruses, which target specific programs (often antivirus programs).

Because most new viruses must be detected before there can be an defense against them, it is almost impossible for heavy PC users who download regularly from the Internet and bulletin boards not to be infected. Viruses that operate in secret or are time delayed during a long contamination cycle are very hard to defend against because you often don't know they are present until they have replicated themselves through an entire office (if office workers exchange disks—a practice that is not recommended).

One virus scare surrounded a software strain called "Michelangelo," which was supposed to go off in 100,000 computers at once, coinciding with the birthday of the artist. It affected only about 30,000 people but caused quite a bit of disruption and stress. There have also been phony virus rumors.

At the time this book was written, there was a version of PKZIP which people were downloading off the Internet, which, when executed, would erase a person's hard drive. WATCH OUT!

Viruses usually exist inside of programs, but it's easy to disguise a program as a data file. Some particularly dangerous viruses actually lodge themselves invisibly inside of data files and then crawl out of their cyber-cloaks into system and application program files—wreaking havoc and terror in those individuals and organizations whose computers are affected. Some programs are hidden, so that the files they are based in are invisible to users and absent from the system directory.

Three thousand viruses were documented in 1993, with 100,000 expected by the new decade, and the billion-dollar losses are adding up every year.

The Life Cycle of a Virus

A typical virus's life consists of: first, entry into a host system (computer or network equipment); next, replication within the system; and finally, activation to perform its destructive work on a program or data file (Figure 4-1). Sometimes this last stage occurs immediately—resulting in an erased disk or altered programs. At other times, viruses can be set with time-delayed action, blowing up at a critical time in a business, such as during Christmas season (when many businesses make the most profit).

Defenses to Viruses

Surprisingly, the best defense to virus attacks is to expect them—to actually anticipate virus attacks on every front and implement procedures and practices that will not only reduce the chances they will infect one computer but also lessen the chances that viruses will spread to other computers in a particular organization.

Virus Vigilance: Minimum Security Procedures

- System disks should not be used to copy or install applications.
- Do not borrow or exchange system disks with other users.
- Don't exchange or share *any* floppy disks with other users if it can be avoided.
- When a computer has just been set up, and after each new program install, print all directories with dates and file sizes; also save the output on disk for reference.
- Do not run programs from unknown sources.
- Scan all floppy disks when they are first inserted into a drive (using a virus scan program).
- Run antiviral software on all disk drives daily or at the very least weekly.

Antivirus Software

There are hundreds of antivirus software products for IBM and Macintosh computers, and any good product will check your data files, program files, and system environment for known viruses, Trojan horses, and other cyber-strains. When new viruses are discovered and can't be removed with current software, new routine are added to regular software releases to deal with the new viruses.

The three basic types of antivirus programs include: virus scanners, which constantly search for virus activity and signatures, rule-based TSR (Terminate and Stay Resident) programs (which in many cases constantly ask PC users if they are experiencing "virus" symptoms and can be quite distracting to users trying to be productive), and antivirus utilities that run on demand when users execute them. The problem with the last type is that, by the time you run your "on-demand" antiviral program, the diseased files may include that program itself. Many viruses go after antivirals. This is not to say that they aren't capable and known for attacking the scanners and rule-based TSR programs also. The Macintosh is also a frequent victim of viruses, and many scanners and other programs are available to keep its disks *disease-free*.

The programs all basically work the same way: Identify the virus, determine where its code exists, and remove it from the disk drive. Most antivirus programs can't search and identify new viruses unless they are similar to previous ones.

Without an aggressive, proactive antivirus program, your computer operation is probably doomed. I have found that Murphy's law is incredible for timing viral attacks at the most critical times in your personal and business life. Employees should receive constant memos on virus alerts and be encouraged to report all known symptoms of viruses. Viruses often are assigned numbers but more typically given thematic names consistent with how they affect their targets or with their intended dates of detonation. The accompanying sidebar shows a partial listing from a virus information BBS:

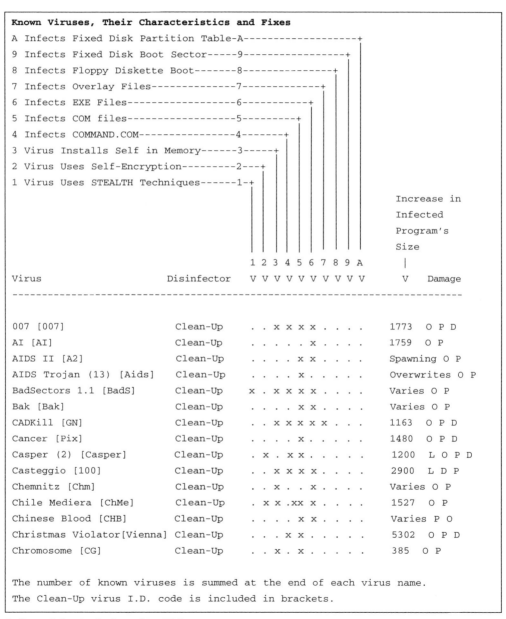

```
Known Viruses, Their Characteristics and Fixes
A Infects Fixed Disk Partition Table-A-------------------+
9 Infects Fixed Disk Boot Sector-----9-----------------+
8 Infects Floppy Diskette Boot-------8---------------+
7 Infects Overlay Files------------7-------------+
6 Infects EXE Files----------------6-----------+
5 Infects COM files----------------5---------+
4 Infects COMMAND.COM--------------4-------+
3 Virus Installs Self in Memory------3-----+
2 Virus Uses Self-Encryption---------2---+
1 Virus Uses STEALTH Techniques------1-+
                                              Increase in
                                              Infected
                                              Program's
                                              Size

                           1 2 3 4 5 6 7 8 9 A    |
Virus            Disinfector  V V V V V V V V V V    V   Damage
-----------------------------------------------------------------

007 [007]            Clean-Up   . . x x x . . . . .  1773  O P D
AI [AI]              Clean-Up   . . . . . x . . . .  1759  O P
AIDS II [A2]         Clean-Up   . . . . x x . . . .  Spawning O P
AIDS Trojan (13) [Aids] Clean-Up . . . . x . . . . . Overwrites O P
BadSectors 1.1 [BadS] Clean-Up  x . x x x x . . . .  Varies O P
Bak [Bak]            Clean-Up   . . . . x x . . . .  Varies O P
CADKill [GN]         Clean-Up   . . x x x x x . . .  1163  O P D
Cancer [Pix]         Clean-Up   . . . . x . . . . .  1480  O P D
Casper (2) [Casper]  Clean-Up   . x . x x . . . . .  1200  L O P D
Casteggio [100]      Clean-Up   . . x x x x . . . .  2900  L D P
Chemnitz [Chm]       Clean-Up   . . x . . x . . . .  Varies O P
Chile Mediera [ChMe] Clean-Up   . x x .xx x . . .    1527  O P
Chinese Blood [CHB]  Clean-Up   . . . . x x . . . .  Varies P O
Christmas Violator[Vienna] Clean-Up . . . x x . . . . . 5302 O P D
Chromosome [CG]      Clean-Up   . . x . x . . . . .  385   O P

The number of known viruses is summed at the end of each virus name.
The Clean-Up virus I.D. code is included in brackets.
```

* from Cybertech Security BBS

Hackers

After famous hacker Kevin Mitnik was busted in 1995, experts declared that if businesses employed just a few such security measures as encrypting sensitive information, "hacker threats" would be significantly reduced. Even though Mitnik was highly knowledgeable, he was caught in just a few weeks once he met with people who were his equals.

Ironically, it often takes a hacker stunt to induce business to plug security holes. Since the Mitnik arrest, Netcom Communications—the large Internet access provider from which Mitnik allegedly stole 20,000 credit card numbers—no longer stores unencrypted card numbers on its servers. And imagine, he began his hacker career using computers and demon-dialers to gang-block radio-station switchboards, winning virtually every call-in contest (he made a fortune before he became obsessed and began to become reckless).

The Home-Office PC Environment

The only way to run a computer business from your home is to do so as discretely as possible. Don't let everybody know that you have your PC in your home, or you've immediately compromised your security. Businesses never advertise the location of their computer facilities; that's like putting a sign in front of their company reading:

"This Is Where My Computer Is, Come and Get It."

The easiest way to secure a computer facility at home is to put it in a large walk-in closet or enclosed area not frequented by either occupants or visitors. You can even shield the room with wire mesh to cut down on the typical interference computers give off that ruins TV and radio reception.

Office Security

Office environments are blessed to have the benefits and productivity of computers and networks. Unfortunately, they are cursed with the inferior security of the cubicle-office. Not only do cubicles and open workspaces deny the modern office professional the wonderful privacy of the private office, they also deny the computer desktop protection from office visitors who will take over your desk the first day you are on vacation. And of course, if you tell your cubicle neighbor your password, he may tell the visitor—just so he can use the PC for a few minutes.

Burglars also like open-style offices, and thousands of PCs are stolen each year, often by thieves posing as repair men. It's important that all PCs in open environments be secured to the desktop. Implement password protection on the PC and encrypt important files, or save all data to floppy disks (which in turn should be stored in a strong locked drawer or—better yet—in another part of the office).

Businesses Should Implement the Following Security Measures

- Follow the steps mentioned in the text, and also cover exposed CPU ports and lock or tie-wrap all cable connections.
- Put cables and wires in conduits so that access to cables, wire, and even fiber is made more difficult.
- Implement security systems, such as modem callback, multilevel password protection, and built-in bait-and-trap systems (keeping hackers on the line until they can be traced, luring them into taking bigger chances).
- Put cameras and security around communication centers: Protect the modem racks, multiplexers, front ends, computers, and wire facilities. Not only are these systems links to the Information Superhighway for every business, they *are* the business, because more business operations cease when they have had anything in their computer/network operation stop than for any other reason.
- Back up disk drives daily; implement off-site storage and redundant disks.
- Arrange redundant locations or reciprocal-cooperative arrangement with another firm.
- Implement firewalls (secured access to the Internet and other networks through systems such as Pilot); maintain separation from corporate network and computer facilities.

Passwords

To Improve Home-Office PC Security

Passwords are the universal security tool for computers, networks, software, and related systems. They are used on many devices, are created in a variety of ways, and come in several forms. Passwords and password files are the most sought-after plunder in cyberspace—at least for computer hackers. Special programs called

- *Use internal modems and a hidden or locked CPU unit (so that no one can open or move the PC easily).*
- *External modems should be hidden out of sight: under the desk, behind the desk, in a drawer.*
- *Wires and cables should not be visible.*

password busters are employed to input and test tens of thousands of combinations repeatedly, as shown in Figure 4-2. To be effective—must be selected from among words or phrases that the password buster won't try automatically.

But passwords can't be of excessive length or formed of an item you won't remember if it isn't used often. With so many passwords, PIN numbers, and other identification numbers and codes—if you forget the right password on the wrong day—it could have major consequences. That is why when individuals are responsible for systems, software, and the administration of other users—it is mandatory that more than one individual have access to critical passwords. The more often passwords are changed, the more secure is the account or accessed entity. When passwords are written down, they must not be located near where they are used. Thieves will stop at nothing if they need data, including looking under a desk or breaking into a file cabinet or floppy disk holder to search for a piece of paper with a password (sometimes taped underneath something). System administrators should limit login attempts to no more than three tries.

Figure 4-2. How a password buster works

Passwords, when properly generated and administered, work quite well at protecting their hosts. When they are used in combination with other passwords, the hacker must invest significantly more time in his busting attempts. If passwords are required at more than one location in the same host, the resources will be all the more protected.

Don'ts in Selection of Passwords

- Never use your initials, wife's birthday, or address! Forget important names, dates, and numbers.
- Never use anything that is close to you: persons, numbers, things on your desk.
- Never use a phone number, driver's license, license plate number, or social security number.
- Avoid regular words; put numbers at the end of a word, or use mixed-case words.
- Never use passwords shorter than six characters; they makes password busting easier.
- Never use anything popular, exciting, or obvious.
- If you have the ability to use a pass phrase, make it an entire sentence like: "Dick and Sally play and run."
- Never use less than six characters. It's best to use two words and a numeral, such as "BearGrizzly18."
- Don't use same password you use for other logons; this is quite a common practice, and it permits hackers to completely destroy a person's access throughout the Internet.
- Never use a color; there are too few, and too many hackers will try all of them.
- Don't use the make or model of your first car—DMV records may give you away.

Suggested Passwords

If you are selecting a password yourself, it's best to use nouns—persons, places, or things. They tend to be easier to remember since you can visualize them. The more characters, the better, but the password must follow the grammatical guidelines of the operating system running on the computer. The password should be based on something significant in your past, something that you will never forget. Something like the color of your first bicycle or your first dog's name. If you use something more recent, such as your wife's name, a hacker will bust your password much more quickly, since that will be one of the first things they will try to use. In general, if you select a password from a real-life experience that few people know about, it creates a more difficult challenge to the password busting programs, which repeatedly try passwords based on individuals' names and other *known* information about them. The second sidebar offers some good suggestions.

Password Generation Techniques

- Host vs. user generated
- Static passwords
- Random change passwords (user must supply personal data on which to base password)
- Pass phrases generation (algorithmic)
- Personal or *diary-type* passwords
- Group password (must be changed when any one member leaves)
- Backdoor passwords for maintenance entry into computers and network equipment

User-Generated Passwords

- Mixture of letters, numbers, and punctuation marks
- Name of first dog combined with first cat and a number
- Favorite vacation site combined with six digits
- Name of bird combined with a number and punctuation marks
- Name of teacher with six digits
- Name of first summer camp plus girlfriend's name reversed
- Combine two words from a list of words
- Passwords of whatever kind should be changed frequently.

The two best ways to administer passwords are to do so at the computer, where either the user assigns his own password or phrase or the computer chooses it. No printing of the password to a printer; that could allow operational staff to see it. There is no stuffing of the "secret" password document into an envelope, where an administrative assistant can get it. Nor is a person asked to give the password to you in the envelope—which by the way, the administrative assistant forgot to seal.

Different Types of Passwords

Power-up passwords, E-PROM based, start up program input

Menu system passwords for access to directories, programs, and files

Application program passwords

Encryption program passwords

LAN interface passwords

Network application passwords

FTP or remote-site passwords (sometimes)

Chat-room passwords (room names)

Pass phrases (like passwords but longer. Often used to access digital signatures for e-mail)

Always let a second person know your password or store it for you. Don't put your name on the paper.
Do not use power-up passwords on critical applications, such as a network server PC.

After the password is printed on the screen, the user should write it down but keep it totally confidential, never telling anyone the password, not even the administrator. Employees who use the computer system should be trained never to give their passwords to anyone.

Password Processing

Most computers and other systems requiring a password automatically disconnect a user after two or three failed attempts. Each instance of failed password entry should be registered in systems designed to monitor possible hacker intrusion. Repeated failed password attempts are a good indication of hacker password-busting activity, and procedures should be set up beforehand to deal with these possible violations. The best action to take against the hacker is to set up a plan that could lead to apprehension.

Power-Up Passwords

Power-up or boot passwords are stored in the PC's battery-backup CMOS (E-PROM) memory, together with the setup information on the disk, in memory, and so forth. The PC normally requires a password to get the user past the password prompt, but if the memory is intentionally damaged, corrupted, or lost when the battery fails, the system doesn't retain the password, or the password protection of the disk. Laptops and notebook PCs all seem to have this feature, but they are still very vulnerable to breakins, since a hacker need only let the battery drain to disable the password mode and erase the password. It's better than no password, but sensitive data should be kept off of the hard drive. Floppy disks are best, with encryption of *all* data files as the next best option.

Catching the Computer Password Buster

1. For dial-up host access:
    - Obtain the telephone number of the possible hacker using caller id from the telephone company(if possible).
    - Work with the local telephone company and request that a trace be placed on the line
    - Use the telephone feature callback several hours later, and if the hacker answers , tell them that you dialed the wrong number. *(The hacker's number will appear on the phone bill when it is within same calling area.)*
    - If the hacker hangs up too fast to trace the call, find out what he's after, and offer phony data files that look like ones he may try to download. Any time you prolong the session of a hacker is time that can be used to trace his calling location.

2. For leased-line or locally attached computers:
    - Monitor the LAN or WAN data as the hacker attempts to break the password.
    - Determine which PC station or terminal and/or controller is under attack, and note its location. (Work with your LAN administrator or network manager, who will have a listing of the "network configuration.")
    - Give the hacker access to a harmless area to keep him online.

● Identify the actual person who is attempting to break the system while he is online, even if it must be done later on; the hacker is probably gaining access to the company's private facilities, so he is more easily located than dial-in users.

Smart Cards

A *smart card* is a floppy disk with an encrypted key or else another type of intelligent hardware unit that carriers secret information. It usually contains a user id and a password, and it is inserted into a reader (which can be in a time clock or a PC), after which the user keys in the same information and then is either rejected or accepted by the reader host computer, which verifies that the correct password has been entered. The smart card works like a PIN number, because somehow people seem to act more responsibly when they can touch something (for example, service station owners put bathroom keys on huge rings to induce their return).

The smart card–type disk can be easily written by a programmer, so that an encrypted digital signature can be read off a disk file and compared to the user's key-in. This is probably one of the most cost-effective ways to physically verify a person's presence. Problems with these smart card–type disks include the fact that, if users lose them, they must be replaced immediately (if used in logon or clocking employees or jobs). Other problems are associated with their physical nature—they can be lost (which compromises security to some extent), and if parties ever write their smart card password onto their personal disk, they essentially have handed over access to whoever holds their card and has access to the proper system. Newer smart cards, soon to be announced, will make these cards an even more usefool tool with computer security.

Other techniques for verifying physical presence are biometric identifiers: voice, palm, hand, signature, retina-pattern readers. These methods are accurate within a certain margin of error but become less accurate when the number of people needing identification forces the administrator to provide wide tolerances for identification patterns. These systems are rather expensive, but the technology is improving, and they have the advantage of allowing employees and workers to avoid unnecessary and unwanted paperwork. As these devices become less expensive, they will assist companies who hire telecommuters to gain visibility, control, and identification of their employees without requiring physical presence of the workers.

Tempest Standard

The EMR (electromagnetic radiation) emissions from devices such as keyboards and video monitors can be picked up by well-equipped vans parked near a facility with special instrumentation to pick up all keystrokes from keyboards and characters from video screens (which exist in video memory and in the monitor). This technique is much less expensive than using supercomputers and wiretaps to record and bust computer messages. The eavesdropper actually sees the plain-text characters as they are typed or displayed—giving him access to what is input from keyboard or displayed from keyboard, disk, tape, or other media.

For this reason, the U.S. government has established a shielding technology standard known as "Tempest" to protect government agencies' and defense contractors' data. Special Tempest cabinets are used to enclose computers, data communication equipment, and connectors. Special shielded conduit and cabling are also required by the standard.

Mainframe and Minicomputer Security

All major mainframe and minicomputer companies have equipped their hardware and software products with proprietary security features and/or products. Most are sufficient, but customers should consider supplementing their environment with third-party products to add further security. Most medium and large businesses have millions invested in their data and telecommunications equipment, and where security problems and omissions exist, they are usually treated as serious emergencies and addressed quickly. As mentioned previously, most mainframe and minicomputer systems are capable of running UNIX, the operating system that supports TCP/IP and Internet services such as e-mail, telnet, and ftp. Depending on the implementation of UNIX, these systems would inherit the same security features offered by the version. Proprietary operating systems often run UNIX and/or TCP/IP as subsystems (operating systems running under larger operating systems). These UNIX subsystems would inherit the security features in the particular version of UNIX running as a subsystem.

IBM Mainframe Security

The Resource Access Control Facility (RACF, which is pronounced "rack-eff") is an IBM program product that limits access to data sets (files) residing on direct-access volumes. IBM's RACF product was one of the first computer security products, and it set the standard for current products. Without password and RACF-protection, data sets are available to anybody who has access to the system. RACF and other programs provide group, password, and user security parameters, and users code these parameters into their job statements before executing a program or utility. Attacks on the system are reported and logged to system operators. Many fine security products are available to IBM mainframes and mainframes from Amdahl, Hitachi, and Fujitsu, as are programs that monitor system activity. Minicomputer manufacturers have also made security a top priority in their hardware and software features, yet there have been some oversights.

Large CPU and Network Monitoring

Omegamon, by Candle Corporation, allows IBM mainframes to be monitored comprehensively, with graphic and quantitative utilization levels reported throughout memory, mass storage, processors, and other systems. Resource management allows computer professionals not only to determine what's happening to the system at a particular time but also to adjust resource configurations to improve performance. Computer resource monitors exist for virtually all computers, minis and PCs.

Put simply, resource monitoring allows an environment to continually inspect the victim of hacking—the computer. Typically, even destructive hacking takes time. To erase a large drive might take several minutes. If a monitor program were set to note certain suspicious conditions, an operator could be alerted to something quickly enough to do something about it. Otherwise, the operator might not spot a problem on a trouble log.

Console Logs

Not having console logs has been known to kill a computer system. Like passwords, console logs are almost a universal feature on all computers and network equipment. Virtually every mainframe, mini, and PC computer system permits the continual logging of all events. Log files can be printed, saved to disk, displayed on a console screen, or any or all of the above. These logs allow data processing and network staff to determine what was going on and who was using the system when certain events occur. For example, if a hacker broke a password and erased fourteen disk drives, a manager would be able to go to the log listing of the disk drive erasure and see who was signed on at the time. With comprehensive audits of every keystroke, virtually every act and event on the system can be linked to the individual who caused or triggered the event. Organizations who do not fully audit important inquiries and updates to private, confidential records are being irresponsible, yet this is a common practice in American business—both small and the multibillion-dollar variety.

Console reports document when user ids have logged on and off, what applications they were using, what they did. These logs, combined with other corresponding tangible evidence, can be converted into a comprehensive audit trail for each employee. Such auditing may be essential in financial, government, engineering, utility, aerospace, or professions where personal accountability is critical for the protection of assets.

A trouble reporting function is a necessary element in computer (and network) security. One central office and staff should be trained and set up as the sole first contact for all they are designated to service. The users, like log reports, can be of critical importance in preventing hackers and viruses from taking out entire computer systems every minute of the day. Users are in a position to contact the system operators when there is a compromise of the system—sometimes fast enough to mitigate the threat to the system.

DOS Security

Microsoft's MS-DOS is the most popular operating system for the IBM PC and compatibles, comprising about ninety percent of the PC market. Unfortunately (perhaps fortunately), there is no built-in password protection in MS-DOS, but certain files and programs can affect data integrity and system performance. Some areas are more vulnerable and need constant attention. Let's examine the security issues and problems in MS-DOS and other ver-

A Sun Micro- systems Mishap

Initially Sun Microsystems shipped a multimedia-equipped workstation with its microphone enabled (by default). The feature was designed to allow the manufacturer to talk to the customer operator when troubleshooting the system. This microphone was set up to allow the vendor to call and listen to anybody standing near the system—without their knowledge. Nobody knows if this actually happened, but when the oversight was discovered, it was corrected. The moral of the story is, you can't assume that computer security exists no matter how expensive the hardware is; in fact, it's safest to assume no security exists.[11]

sions of DOS. One benefit of the current MS-DOS VERSIONS 6.*X* and Novell DOS 7.*X*—they are both equipped with antivirus software. (Novell 7.*X*, in fact, has advanced security, as described later in this section.)

MS-DOS 6.0 has a problem of corrupting files when operating the Windows disk caching feature (and other TSRs). There were also other problems with the integrity of the data and legal disputes. These complications led many users to simply install MS-DOS 6.02 (available free on CompuServe), which has no disk compression. Or they are upgrading to MS-DOS 6.21 for a small change (about $10). Version 6.22 fixes the DoubleSpace-TSR data integrity problem with new compression code and memory management. Customers can switch to another vendor's DOS, such as Novell DOS 7.0 or PC-DOS 6.3 or even load another operating system—such as UNIX.

Novell DOS 7.0 has the most advanced security features among DOS operating systems. It features master key password protection and floppy boot prevention for the hard drive, screen saver with lock for keyboard (TSR program) with password required for reentry. It also allows users to disable security, recover deleted and damaged files (and track them), make full backups of all systems, and use antivirus TSR and scan software.

With the directory arrangement shown in Figure 4-3, and if the graphics directory in the far right were hidden, it would be harder to see all the subdirectories under it, and the hacker might just assume that all the programs were in the phony program directory, and that all your data was in the phony data directory for Microsoft Word and Lotus 123 *(it's legal to have a backup copy of a program on the same PC)*.

TYPICAL DOS DIRECTORY STRUCTURE:

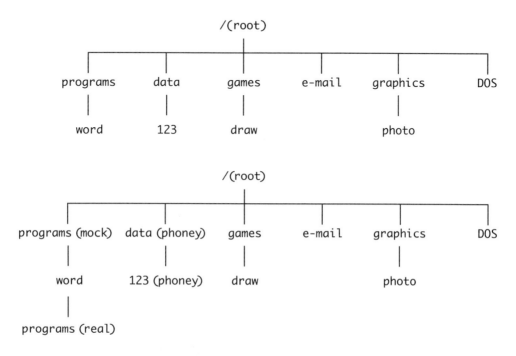

Figure 4-3. A misleading DOS directory structure can disguise hackers

If you want additional security, you can put programs in the data directory and data in the program directory, also putting spreadsheets in the word processing subdirectory and vice versa. An experienced hacker might see right through this, especially if he's invaded your system this far—especially if he knows what he's looking for. But a novice is likely to give up and go on to another computer.

DOS Commands Affecting Security

You can use these DOS commands to gain some extra control over security on your system.

- **ATTRIB**—The DOS ATTRIB command gives you an extra level of protection for data files. You can specify a file as read-only, so that it can't be altered or deleted. (ATTRIB =R,-R,+A)

- **BACKUP**—The BACKUP command archives one or more files from one disk to another. (BACKUP *filespec* C:*filespec*)

- **CHKDSK**—The CHKDSK command displays the status of the disk drive, fixing any errors found in the directory or file allocation table, reports all fragmented files, and sends a status report to the file called DSKSTAT. It also provides memory information; used and unused. This command can aid in determining if changes exist in your environment from one day to the next. If you run a regular report using CHKDSK, you can determine if significant portions of your memory are being suspiciously used, or if programs suddenly are taking more memory. This program is like a magnifying glass into your computer's internals.

- **FC**—The FC command compares files on your disk. This is handy when you want to determine if files have been altered, modified, or infected with viruses.

- **FDISK**—This command creates a partition on the disk, changes partitions, deletes partitions on a DOS disk. Since this command simply segments one disk into two logical ones, it can confuse some users, but it is required when PCs can only configure disk drives up to 33MB each (the old limitation under pre-4.0 DOS).

- **FORMAT**—This command formats the disk in the specified drive, writing zeros and ones to the surface of the drive. If data existed before the format command, they no longer exist.

- **DELETE**—This command removes the file marker from the area used to store your data. The data are still intact if the disk has not experienced any writes since the delete, or if you are lucky. With Norton 8.0 for PC or Norton Utilities Version 3 for Macintosh, you can "undelete" files (with the Macintosh, you must load a utility program first).

- **ERASE**—This is the most dangerous DOS command, in that it replaces the data with zeros and completely removes the possibility of recovery. If you have accidentally deleted your file and you aren't backed up, be prepared to accidentally type your resume.

- **REDIRECT OUTPUT**—Because this command can direct print from the parallel port to the serial port, or vice versa, it has a lot of potential to cause problems if it's altered. It could send data designed to go to a disk to a printer instead—perhaps it was a confidential financial report.

- **RENAME**—The RENAME command will change the name of any file to the new filename. A common prank involves the doctoring of COMMAND.COM or renaming of other .COM or .EXE files, so that, for example, the COPY command calls one of the destructive commands— such as DELETE or ERASE. This prank would cause the user to actually destroy his own files. This is why it's important to back up all disk files, save file directories, and password protect all desktops.

- **COPY**—When the destination file exists, the COPY command overwrites the data, making it unrecoverable. This command is dangerous when a person doesn't know what he's doing, but it can also make an innocent-looking batch file destroy an entire disk.

- **XCOPY**—The XCOPY command can cause an entire disk's content to be reproduced on a target disk. If the target is unformatted, this command will format the disk. The contents of the target disk is completely overwritten, including the volume name. There is no way to recover existing data.
- The following files are used by DOS and Windows to load and boot your operating system. They allocate memory; load files, buffers, and drivers; and set up your configuration. If they are tampered with, serious problems can result, sometimes permanent.
- .BAT
- CONFIG.SYS
- AUTOEXEC.BAT
- Windows files
- ANSI.SYS
- Other SYS files
- DEVICE
- .COM files
- .EXE files

Windows 3.X

Since Windows 95 will probably never be a standard for all IBM PCs, it might be safe to assume that half the current Windows 3.X users will stay put. The newer version of Windows, however, features password protection and file attribute protection. If you forget your password in a Windows-supplied screen saver, open the Control.INI file (using Notepad, not edit), look for lines that read "PWProtected=1" and change the "1" to "0." This disables the password without removing the currently assigned password. To remove the currently assigned password, find the line that says "Password=" and remove everything on the right of the equal sign.

Third-party software exists to provide access and virus protection, protect of boot sectors, and prevent unauthorized copying or installation of any software. But it must be remembered that, if a user gains access to DOS or the Windows File Manager, he can typically get around application programs that attempt to restrict file input or output. (Disk Tracy and other copy prevention can easily be bypassed with the File Manager.)

Write-Protection

Files and directories to write protect or restrict (hide):
DOS COMMAND.COM
Other .COM files
System files
Windows files and directories
AUTOEXEC.BAT
CONFIG.SYS
.EXE
.BAT
.DEV
Other required files

Windows 95

You would have thought it might have come in the later 80s, when everyone conceded that the Macintosh graphic user interface was by far easier than DOS and Windows 3.X. But it has finally happened with Windows 95: With folders instead of directories or group windows, the new user interface for the PC platform is the most powerful and aesthetically pleasing (with 32-bit video) operating system for the PC platform. Windows 95 will feature stronger password management in the Security Control Panel, which allows centralized control over passwords. The Security Control Panel will allow all application passwords to be unified around one, something that is more convenient, but potentially dangerous. Once access is gained to a breached password, an unauthorized user has access to all systems. High-security PCs should refrain from centralized passwords. Because of Windows 95 advanced multimedia features, it will probably become a huge hit and a standard for all PC platforms; many prerelease users of Windows 95 say that they like it better than the Macintosh interface.

Macintosh Security

With the new Macintosh System 7.1 operating system, the Apple Menu (which already has folders and advanced GUI) now features hierarchical submenus so you can quickly access your Control Panel items and your most recently used applications, documents, and servers.

Security features include *DigSign Digital Signatures*, built-in digital signature software, which allows users to send mail with the same legal validity as a real signature.

PowerTalk Key Chain Security saves time when accessing your password-protected resources such as servers, online services, and e-mail. A single password does it all. Like the Windows 95 unified password feature, this can be dangerous.

System 7.5 has a built-in Telephone Manager; this architecture incorporates telephone technologies into applications programs so users can take advantage of new features as they're released.

Scriptable Finder allows users to automate routine and repetitive system tasks with scripts. The Desktop Hiding feature is designed to keep novice users from becoming confused when they click outside an application and find themselves on the desktop.

There are several security-oriented menu systems for the Macintosh, like *At Ease*, which provides password protection for folders, files, or the entire disk. It supports multiple passwords and can assign passwords freely to any disk file.

Here are the critical folder and files to lock and/or password protect in the Macintosh environment: system, finder, password, programs, and utilities.[12]

Personal Computer CPU Unit Security: CPU Enclosures

Many companies enclose CPU units in metal boxes, attached underneath or on the sides of the desk. The wire connections, cables, and CPU box itself are protected against theft and intrusion. Locks and other enclosure protection are available to prevent access to the internal hardware, which if modified could be converted into a device that could be used against you. Homebrewed hacker processors can actually contain built-in code to e-mail information to your competitors. Even if a thief doesn't remove the CPU, it's important to remember—if he can remove your disk drive, he has information that may be worth vastly more than all the hardware in your office environment.

Desktop Security
Security cable locks are available for desktop PCs and laptops; they are hardware mountings to secure PCs to the desk or desktop of the owner, making it more difficult to remove the PC. *Port-Lok* protects the boards from being stolen from the IBM platform.

Unalterable Clocks for Reliable Time/Date Stamp
A PC product that allows the personal computer be have just as much reliability as a notary public.

Floppy Disk Drive Security

A special device called the Floppy Disk *Drive Loc* neatly covers disk drive doors for several models of PCs, preventing the insertion of disks and also preventing pirating off the hard drive. This small feature can save businesses thousands in copyright infringement settlements, not to mention secret virus contamination.

Hard Drive Security

There is no more valuable piece of property in any business than the hard disk drive. If the drives fails, business stops—it doesn't matter whether it is the drive in a computer-based phone answering system, voice mail, automated receptionist, fax send and receive, or the office PC. As a consultant, I've seen hundreds of computer installations, and it's amazing how even though the personal computers perform most of the processing in business—people do not back up their disk drives. In order to save a few hundred dollars on tape backup (which is now extremely inexpensive), companies put their entire operation, reputation, and future on the line.

Data Compression

Before discussing how data must be backed up regularly, let's talk about compression and encryption—technology that can save drive space and money and provide for cost-effective security for data resources.

For years, data files have been compressed to reduce their size. This not only saves a tremendous amount of disk space but also greatly reduces the amount of time it takes to transmit that file. Compressing a file 50 percent reduces its download time by 50 percent. DOS and Windows users typically use PKZIP, which can create both standalone compressed archives and self-extracting archives (so the receiver need only double-click, or execute the archive file before it decompresses itself). Macintosh uses Stuffit and Stuffit Lite to accomplish compression on Macintosh files. These programs are both available all over the Internet and are necessary to decompress files that are not self-extracting.

Compression and Data Integrity and Recovery

Because compression removes repetitive characters and alters the format of the original data—it is more difficult to recover, rebuild, or restore that data if damaged (since the loss of one repetitive character means the loss of many other identical characters in the file).

Encryption

Encryption decodes data using sophisticated formulas that are extremely difficult to "bust" as hackers break passwords. Encryption is the most secure way of hiding the contents of electronic data. Government standards like DES are set up by the NSA to establish levels of security of data using these encryption techniques. Many commercial and shareware encryption programs are available, and many on the Internet are free (like PGP). As will be explained in the last chapter (which deals with encryption), encryption is considered the best way to protect your disk files and transmitted data, be they voice, data, sound, or image. To bust one well-encrypted message may take as much as a year using the fastest computers on earth—and that's if there's only one algorithm used.

Back up or Else

Backup Strategy

- *Back up daily, no excuse. Mirror if possible, dual disks prevent shutdown.*

- *Understand that change-control, OS, and NOS failures are more common than hackers.*

- *Find Partner Companies for remote storage.*

Failing to back up is worse than a thief robbing you in the night, but so is an earthquake, fire, flood, or other disaster. Off-site storage of backup resources adds security in case of a disaster. Tapes, removable drives, or even DAT and VCR recorders can be used to back up data.

Off-site backup is possible now without even transporting floppies, tapes, or disk cartridges. With multisite LANs and WANs, remote backup is inexpensive to implement (on PC and minicomputer file server networks, a company's computer facilities can be located in ten different cities, serving ten separate departments, but all providing universal mail delivery and receipt.). If dual backup sites are configured at implementation time, and auto-backup tape drives archive all vital disk drives every day, companies can often protect themselves from millions in losses without adding much work to their already busy operations.

Personal neglect of backup, compression, and maintenance causes more disk drive problems than all the hackers in the world combined. Hundreds of millions of dollars worth of data are destroyed each year because of individual reliance on something that is not reliable. No matter how many years your disk drive works—just like an automobile engine—it's going to break at some point in time. Because Murphy's Law rules the computer and network world, your computer disk drive will fail at the worse possible time.

Disk and File Maintenance and Repair

Norton Utilities 8.0 (for PCs) has many extremely valuable utilities to repair, defragment, optimize, and undelete files and disk drives (including floppy disks). Norton for Macintosh Version 3 (from *Symantec*) is also an effective tool for repairing and recovering data from damaged disk drives. Norton for Macintosh (which has an undelete feature that aids recovery when you have thrown things away accidentally) was responsible for helping to repair a drive that stored the manuscript of this book, not to mention several design, word processing, and database files damaged in the not-too-distant past.

Both the PC and Mac products feature emergency boot disks in case your situation left your computer unable to boot. Most of the disk management programs (Norton, Disk Tools, and more) are amazingly effective.

The success rate for Norton is probably over 95 percent of the data. So, when you have a drive failure—and you will definitely have one—don't worry until you've tried to repair your damaged drive. Even if you aren't successful, there are many drive recovery services that can do more than you and can probably recover as much information as exists on the drive's surface. These services are somewhat expensive, but they are worth it if your data are valuable. It's amazing, though, how people will gladly pay a recovery service $1000 to recover a $200 hard drive for which they refused to provide a $200 backup tape drive. Sounds penny wise and dollar foolish, doesn't it? But most standalone PCs today aren't equipped with backup tapes or drives.

Screen Protection

Most people think that there isn't much chance someone is going to steal your password—unless you type it right in front of their face. Not true. These days, you never know where a camera is, and you never know what prison the security guard just checked out of. So, you probably want to assume the worst about every environment, at least until you are familiar enough with it to trust the unknown. You could be displaying none of your keystrokes, but a camera from a hidden mirrored bubble is zooming in on your hands, picking up your password and your user id. The guard then sells it to your office competitor, who signs on using your name and sends death threats to the company VP. Certainly, this is a bit extreme, but if the company VP is like my old one, he would fire you first and then ask questions later. Then he would promote the guy who used you to get ahead.

Keyboard Protection

You may not realize it, but what if somebody were to attach a second cable to your keyboard, so that it sent its ASCII codes not only to your computer's CPU but also to somebody else's computer—so that he could see every keystroke you made? Keyboards can be locked.

What if somebody were to mount a camera near your desk? (See the section on premises security.) A keyboard is one of those things that—when one can see—one can gain much information—especially when played back on slow-motion video.

Modems and Modem Banks

The modem is the most critical element of any computer that wants access to the world. Without the modem you can't connect off-site, unless you go though a host or a server. Your modem is particularly vulnerable to tapping, and it's not even necessary actually to access it directly. Anybody who gets to your serial cable, your modem itself, or even the phone line afterwards, can capture every bit of data that is transmitted across it. Internal modems are more secure and less expensive but subject to obsolescence. Certain huge parties are now able to tap phone lines without even the telephone company's notice, without even altering the signal level. In other words, nobody could sense (even with equipment) that law enforcement was tapping their lines.

Mysterious Fax Phone Calls

Unless you are expecting a fax or modem transmission, *leave your modem power switch off!* You could be getting a call from a hacker who wants access to your system. Fax software permits him to do that. If a hacker finds away to bypass the fax receiving program that accepts his connection (as a fax transmission or data transfer), he may find a way to gain access to your data files, programs, and system—in order to steal, alter, or destroy your data!

CD-ROMs

Windows, Apple, and Novell are releasing their new operating systems on CD-ROM. The advantage of CD-ROMs, like all write-only or write-once media, is that they are bulletproof to viruses, and operating systems can't be corrupted anymore. They are extremely durable, and a person can save the contents of an entire disk on another computer. There are services that will save the entire contents of your hard drive on a CD-ROM for less than $200. CD-ROMs can store over 600MB of information.

Printer Security

Just like the monitor, the printer is not the most efficient place to steal your data, but it's an extremely easy way, since many offices have several employees share printers. If you have an enemy who shares a printer and decides to read your hardcopy, or to copy and replace it—there's no way you know it's been done, unless you stand next to the printer when your output is coming. What then do you do? Stand next to the printer when your output is coming. You don't have to do that if the document isn't confidential, but if your work is sufficiently sensitive (the personnel department should never share printers, faxes, and the like), you *need your own printer!*

Here's some information that may make you think twice about putting your printer in a hallway at night, rather than locking it up or securing it in a printer cabinet.

Printers have large buffers, sometimes 12MB or even 24MB of memory. If a hacker wanted to, he could sneak in your business, modify your printer, install static RAM memory chips to copy every page of information printed from your computer, and put an internally installed cellular phone on your cellular account. Of course, it would call his home computer at midnight every night, with his PC-modem equipped with a stolen cellular phone and stolen account (which changed every day). So, without even going back to your office a second time, he would be able to see virtually all the work you put into hardcopy. And as long as nobody took the printer apart (which isn't likely until it received major service), no one would ever even suspect it had been modified. Since the cellular phone could charge and run off the printer's AC input, your business would be stolen without even leaving the exit doors.

Run, Don't Walk!

Offices with shared printers and confidential data should advise employees to go directly to the printer so that others can't take or look at output (same rule with laser fax output).

Digital Cameras

Apple, Rico, Casino, Pentax, Kodak, Minolta, Fuji, and Cannon either already have or are going to offer high-resolution 35 mm digital cameras, which can take full-color photographs and save them digitally on data cards or disks.

Some digital cameras allow you to review the photos on small LCD screens and then delete them if you wish. Images can then be loaded on a personal computer, where they can be enlarged and saved on hard drive, even run through OCR software, converted to text, and then e-mailed to a publisher in a matter of seconds. But these devices could also be used against your privacy and security.

Digital cameras offer enormous advances in the field of imagery, information gathering, and documentation of phenomena. One data card in a Pentax digital camera can take over 350 photographs. Just imagine what one of these nice gadgets could do if mounted above a board room or conference table. Just imagine what could happen if such a camera, armed with secret designs worth millions, fell into the hands of competing designers.

TV and Video Security

Small cameras will soon be packaged in every multimedia PC configuration, allowing the new PC user to immediately teleconference with friends, customers, and employers. This will serve as the immediate de facto way to verify an employee's presence at home when he's supposed to be working at the computer. This presents some new problems for the employee in that portion of his home.

Other ways might be developed in the future permitting verification of the employee's presence without "taking" away any degree of privacy from his home environment.

Security in Popular PC Applications

In addition to making PC applications easier to use, menu systems offer great security benefits, providing numbered system schemes or point-and-click graphics selection screens so that the users can open directories, files, and applications. By custom designing menus, users and system administrators can limit access to disk drives to certain applications. Used in conjunction with other security features, menus can prevent employees from inserting disks and removing confidential files, or from running games or their own personal programs on employer-provided personal computers. Netware's menu limits users to those areas that they are permitted to visit only. This relieves the administrator from having to adjust menus for each user.

Lotus Notes

Lotus Corporation has a product called Notes that provides secure e-mail, documents, and even live communication sessions (brainstorming sessions). It has a unique preponderance of built-in security features and safeguards to protect all data from a violation.

Notes automatically backs up databases and e-mail and gives different data sets various private looks—depending on the user's assigned rights (by the creator or administrator). At the same databases it completely certifies the ID and authenticity of each user before granting access to a resource. It provides encryption of e-mail, whole documents, communication sessions, and even fields within docs. Lotus notes has password access control, tamper prevention, source verification, and public-key encryption to authenticate both users and servers. Lotus Notes and a full line of office software products from Lotus bring users the state of the art in groupware security.

Word Perfect 5.0

Word Perfect 5.0 has integrated security features, including password protection on all files over and above the security provided by network operating systems. If a user forgets his password, there is absolutely no way he can recover his file because the process used to encrypt it is a one-way or hash process. Use extreme caution or avoid this command.

The Role of Consultants: Technical and Political

Whether developing a security plan or reacting to a security incident, computer and telecommunication security consultants can be extremely helpful to small and large businesses. Consultants tend to be expensive, but when specific objectives and goals are put in the form of a consultant service request for proposals, skilled professional consultants can save companies much time and millions in damage. In addition to their role of providing technical, logistical, and strategic planning, consultants often see the problem more objectively than proprietors, managers, and staff, since they are not affected by decisions that would affect employees, and they see the problems and solutions from the perspective of the entire organization—without fear of internal politics. Internal politics become critically important in company politics, since upper-level management will usually insist that the parties involved in developing a perceived "failed" plan be held responsible.

Laptops

Since laptops have no real effective security (power-up passwords can be defeated), it's essential to encrypt data files and to store all data on floppy disks (kept away from the laptop). While transporting laptops and notebooks, users should consider not carrying laptops and notebook PCs in a case that looks like a briefcase, so that muggers won't be tempted with the obvious *three-grand grab* opportunity.

Computer Surveillance Equipment

1. Electromagnetic surveillance equipment

    There is a company in Texas that supplies extremely sophisticated equipment to the United States military and intelligence community, which don't even acknowledge the company's existence. The company manufactures the most sensitive eavesdropping equipment in the world, and among the equipment reportedly made are devices utilizing "Van Eck radiation" technology, which is able to pick up electromagnetic radiation from computers, keyboards, monitors, communication links, and more. In 1991, Geraldo Rivera demonstrated the first electromagnetic eavesdropping (Figure 4-4). Demonstrating the effect of Van Eck radiation can be easily accomplished; a normal TV set can pick up a computer screen simply by adding two signals to the source—vertical sync and vertical hold. The hardware to accomplish this costs roughly $5.00. This technology can be used to eavesdrop in situations where wires would be too obvious. The NSA and other intelligence organizations have gone to ridiculous lengths to maintain the secrecy surrounding Van Eck radiation, but the word is out; Watkins-Johnson of Gaithersber, Maryland and other companies working with the U.S. and other governments have devices that are capable of reconstructing video signals from computer monitors. Chase Manhattan Bank ran a test on its terminals and became extremely concerned after realizing that "screens [were] being read." Chemical Bank, in 1992, was targeted by an unknown hacker who directed an antenna towards the ATM machines. From appearances, it seems Chemical Bank became the first target of a such a "Tempest" attack.

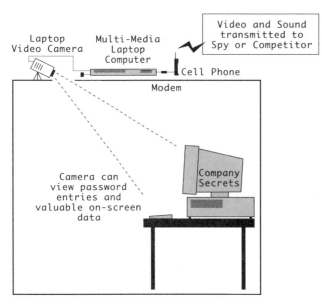

Figure 4-3. With today's technology, companies can keep tabs on competitors using a special video camera, laptop, modem and cellular telephone

2. A personal computer can be an automatic hacker.

    As mentioned previously, the computer itself can be used as an instrument of surveillance; computer chips planted inside a PC can in fact seek, gather, and transmit information to a spy. Or small cellular phones can be secretly installed, equipped with a miniature modem—anything transmitted over the computer's internal bus or I/O interfaces could be transmitted to the hacker—with no ability for users to trace the cellular call.

3. Chips that snitch, chips that fail.

    Foreign chip makers have been cloning U.S. chips; recently, they have begun placing built-in timers that make the chip fail on a certain date. More dangerous chips actually can be equipped with (when technology advances just a bit) an info-gathering program that could then utilize Van Eck technology to transmit the information without wires. EPROMs and EEPROMs are inexpensive memory chips that can be equipped with programs that survive without power. PALs are also inexpensive. Chipping is bound to become more of a problem as software viruses become less effective against antivirus programs. This method of spying could in fact be used to steal information for years without an organization even knowing.

4. Data scopes and protocol analyzers and data traps

Protocol analyzers or "data scopes" allow a person to see the physical, data-link, presentation, and application-level messages as they exit the computer (before the modem) information on a voice-grade or digital line. Depending on the interface, protocol analyzers can attach to any line, and because they utilize comprehensive software features, you can search for a specific address, user, and string and copy the information to a PC. Data scopes permit users to see protocols, user addresses, connections, and hardware and software negotiations online. These devices support most speeds, protocols, and interface types.

5. Rogue modems

The data are converted to analog or digital once they leave the modem or digital data set, and in order to convert the data into a code that can be understood, they must be demodulated or decoded by an identical or compatible modem, digital data set, limited-distance modem, line driver, or the like. If a hacker can tap the copper line and disable responses from the device (for invisibility), it can be used to see the data passing from two or more points (single- or multidropped).

6. Hidden microphones (passwords, applications, and so on)

Wireless microphones come in very small sizes, so small in fact that some can hardly be seen from a few feet back. These bug devices can be wired or wireless and range in price from $30 to over a thousand dollars.

7.   Miniature video cameras can pick up (passwords, all input and output, plus sound) Surveillance equipment companies have been around for years, supplying private investigators with micro-miniature cameras to snoop on couples and individuals. But these cameras, when directed at a computer, video monitor, or other exposed area, can reveal everything from passwords to information displayed on the screen or a printer. The best defense to this type of spying is to secure the facility at all times, so that planting such a device would be difficult. After they are in place, video scanning equipment must be used; even if a building is torn up, you still may not see a well-hidden and disguised video camera.

If such a video camera were connected to a portable notebook PC with multimedia microphone, video clips could be saved and then transmitted to the hacker remotely using a portable cellular phone. Such a notebook PC could broadcast almost real-time video to a information-hungry hacker.

8.   Baby monitors

As harmless as these devices seem, they utilize cordless telephone frequencies and are extremely effective at monitoring all sound and words in an entire small building. These monitors are proliferating throughout American neighborhoods, and one day I walked down the street with my Uniden Bearcat scanner, I was able to listen to sounds and words from about five homes per block—some people leave their monitors plugged in for years. They forget that while they leave such as device plugged in, the privacy and security of their home can be compromised with the flick of a scanner switch.

9. Digital cameras

    As mentioned previously, new digital cameras have the ability to save still 35 mm photographs onto disks *and* then dump them into computers. If such a camera were connected to a portable notebook PC with a multimedia microphone, it could be planted inside of a business or a residence. Equipped with a portable cellular phone, this notebook PC could essentially broadcast both sight and sound to a information-hungry hacker, or someone who just wanted to take embarrassing pictures or obtain damaging secrets in order to harm or blackmail you.

10. Phone (voice and data) taps

    Phone taps are designed to eavesdrop on either voice or data communications conducted on a phone line. Phone taps can be wired to the actual phone lines (2- or 4-wire), or phone taps can operate wireless. Taps on voice-grade lines can pick up voice conversations with ease. Digital taps can be implemented using data sets equivalent to those on the line.

11. Demon dialers

    The demon dialer is a program (or dialer plus software) that dials thousands of numbers, searching for a computer line. Once finished, it reports those numbers to the owner, so that he is able to start his hacking campaign effectively. There are standalone devices that are capable of as many as 60 dials per minute.

12. Password-busting programs

    These programs were discussed earlier; they work by calling numbers detected as computers (often using demon dialers) and then attempting to gain entry into the system using any known user ids and intelligently selected passwords. Most hosts will cut off a logon session or hang up after three failed attempts, but the busting programs call over and over, with new passwords. A site that doesn't log the failed attempts will permit these repeated calls to continue until the hacker breaks a password; from there they often go after the password file or other valuable files.

13. Encryption-busting programs

These programs are used to crack one message and then use the key and algorithm combination to crack other messages.

Baseline Security Procedures: the Best Defense Is a Good Offense

- System monitor programs and trained operators; a security manager; management, departmental, and individual accountability for protecting passwords; and independent auditing, and security consultants
- System procedures, encryption, password file encryption, system logging and trouble reporting, and logon, file, and resource access restrictions
- Directory hardcopy records, so that virus and hacker modifications and file erasures can be detected.
- Use of the CHKDSK command and others to check backup files' checksum values against the new files, so that a contaminated file can usually be detected

- Data integrity and virus check programs
  Programs that check data integrity (like Norton Utilities and Disk Tools) are extremely important for all computers—PCs and larger. The first sign of random corruption (virus- or hacker-generated) is a file reported as corrupt. Norton actually fixes corrupted files and disks.
- Virus programs at every PC, with virus reporting procedures in place
- System procedures: password accountability, encryption, password file encryption, system logging, and trouble reporting; program testing on separate system files; resource access restrictions; consultants
- User training: virus, backup, hacker detection, file management
- Backup, redundancy, disaster site and recovery, fault tolerance, conditioned power
- Site security: cables, access, badges, data cards, man traps
- Network access: separate from Internet, firewalls, dial-back, caller id and router filters to protect computers from outside damage

SECURITY ON THE INTERNET

Defensive Driving Along the Info-Superhighway

The Internet is sometimes referred to as the center of the Information Superhighway; actually it's only one part. But it's the part that everybody's talking about. Crimes in cyberspace are not as physically threatening as violent crime, but they are a valid concern, not just because of the media hype, but because cyber-crime is becoming a serious issue. Just when people were beginning to gain some ground on the Internet hackers, viruses, and thieves, a new threat has cyber-citizens more threatened than ever. Far-reaching and unprecedented proposals about the Internet are being made by little-known bureaucrats in Washington D.C. and being passed in the face of protests by science, industry, academia, and constitutionalists. The proposals concern your privacy.

Introduction to Internet Security: From Basics to Beyond

As American businesses have shifted from mainframe computers to networks, the number of access points for intrusions increased significantly. Because the Internet is the world's largest network, there are infinitely more access points for hacking than in any other place in cyberspace. New data bear this out.

The FBI reports that in 1994, there were 2,344 reported computer break-ins of American business (up 75 percent over the previous year). Eighty percent of all computer crimes are estimated to take place using the Internet.[1] There is an increase in the age of the average hacker, indicating a more intelligent foe. Also, the Computer Security Institute in San Francisco estimated a total of $66 million in losses from computer crime in 1994 (*Wall Street Journal* Report, NBC, August 20, 1995). With millions of new users expected to sign on the Internet in coming years, and with tens of billions of dollars to be generated, we can expect unprotected entities in cyberspace to come under incredible assault.

As thousands of *newbies* subscribe weekly to time-sharing services and Internet access services, the opportunities and opportunists flourish, as do all forms of electronic fraud.

Armed with custom programs or off the shelf auto-dialers, the hackers, whether they are private, corporate, or government employees—go to work. With speed dialers, multiple lines and multitasking, a single radio contest contestant has the power of 40 callers combined. But such hackers also bust into corporate and government files, compromising our national security and sometimes selling secrets to our enemies.

The network now referred to as the Internet used to be called ARPAnet. It was initially limited to use by military, researchers, and educators. But its growth since the 90s has been phenomenal.

Initially, lack of security on the ARPAnet permitted easy attacks. Robert T. Morris, Jr., a Cornell graduate student, release the now famous Internet worm His attack halted most Internet traffic for several days, and it actually was intended as a test, not as a malicious act. Since then, thousands have attacked the Internet's vulnerabilities or used it to access the some 20 million attached computers.

With the introduction of computer bulletin boards and online discussion groups and download facilities, online users sometimes feel overwhelmed and intimidated by the unknowns in cyberspace. But the benefits and fun of the Internet so outweigh the risks of the cyber-bogey man and his bag of space viruses, it's worth putting up with the present potholes in the Info-Superhighway.

The Scope of the Internet

The 30,000 interconnected networks and 4.8 million attached computers with over 30 million users are attached through copper, fiber, and an amazing level of good will and trust (Figure 5-1)—not just trust that information will be transmitted and stored properly, but trust that it will not be intercepted, rerouted, altered, modified, and read by the wrong eyes. The sheer openness of the Internet, and the fact that it is connected to so many computers, has made it a hacker's heaven and a favorite hangout for government spies. And neither side has conducted itself in a friendly way.[2]

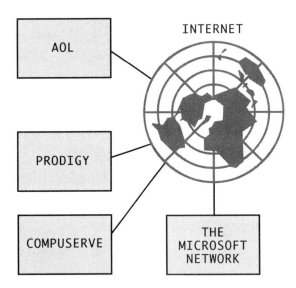

Figure 5-1. E-mail can be sent to members belonging to different online providers through the use of the Internet

Because electronic mail messages may pass through many UNIX nodes en route to their recipients, they can be read by people other than their documented recipients, and e-mail and other communications can be almost tracelessly forged, so no one receiving a message can be sure it came from the apparent sender in the "from" field, one of the standard fields in electronic mail.

What Is TCP/IP?

TCP/IP is what Internet computers use to communicate with each other. TCP/IP is a collection (or suite) of data communication protocols, period. These protocols permit the routing of information from one UNIX node to another, from one user's PC to a node, and from one of these entities to thousands of others.

TCP/IP stands for two distinct protocols: transmission control protocol and Internet protocol. In addition to these, there are other protocols that deal with how this information is handled at the user or computer level (say, the application level).

The History of TCP/IP

TCP/IP began its use on ARPAnet, which in the 1970s was mostly a modest collection of point-to-point-connected institutions. By 1983 all the computers connected to ARPAnet were running TCP/IP, along with many other military and academic institutions not permanently connected. Initially ARPAnet was restricted to a select group of agencies and government departments; the National Science Foundation created the NSFNT, which also used the TCP/IP protocol. NSF computers added high-capacity network backbones connecting major computer centers and a series of smaller networks in a mesh all over the country.

Over the years many interfaces adapted gateways into TCP/IP networks. Multiplexer protocol converters, routers, and personal computers all needed interfaces to TCP/IP networks if they were to remain competitive.

Since the late 80s TCP/IP drivers have been available for Ethernet LAN cards and routers, and this combination of technology has caused a sharp increase in the use of TCP/IP and the number of connections to the Internet.

Concept of a Global Village

The best example of the Global Village is the story about the man in China who saw O.J. Simpson's famous low-speed freeway chase in June 1994 on CNN. When he called his relative in Los Angeles, he told them to look out their window, and the Bronco passed by just at that moment. I myself was talking to my agent on the phone that night, and after he urged me, I drove a block away and saw O.J. pass by a nearby freeway overpass. With the Internet, you can communicate with people all over the globe at the same time, making separation less inhibiting to human interaction.

There are no real doors in cyberspace (save lots of trap doors), no walls or windows; what separates everybody else in cyberspace from you? Small online service providers make up most of the 30 million Internet users. Suspended in cyberspace, these virtual communities collectively make up the global village.

The only walls in Cyberspace are virtual, existing only in the absence of knowledge of your user id, your Internet address, your service provider's node address.

What joins you with other members of the cyber-world? Common online communities, common occupations, location, interests, activities, profit.

How to Set Up a UNIX Node: Ordering Data Lines and Registering as an Internet Node

To establish an Internet node site in order to set up a Web, ftp, telnet, or other server, you need a computer and server software. CPU, disks, router, and other hardware will cost about $15,000 minimum. You will need a 56KB or faster line. Cost for the leased line may range from $750 per month for a 56KB leased line (depending on how far from the provider, it could be half this cost) to $4000 per month for a T3 connection (which would be large enough to support hundreds of simultaneous connections). Nodes can be connected with either a leased line or a full-time SLIP connection.

To get an IP address, you must contact an Internet provider such as Netcom or the World Software Tool & Die Company. Many companies want to establish their nodes as a name, such as *davespizza.com*. The provider can actually provide you with your own domain name through the use of mailboxes or alias names. So, if Dave's Pizza wanted to use *davespizza.com* as its node address, it could without actually being a real Internet node. At that point, all you would need to do is determine what services to offer.

Once you are a regular user of the Internet, or a business operating on the Internet, you'll learn very quickly that, despite the incredible surge in popularity, cyberspace can be a cold place. With so many thousands of dishonest people online, and with so many computers lying vulnerable, if a node on the Internet is not secured, it will probably be violated.

The Internet Can Be Perilous

The Internet is an now the fastest place to get the latest news before it hits the streets, stock market reports before they're in the journal, the mail, multimedia entertainment and Web action, romance, commerce, commercial endeavors, professional sports, political discussions. You can even get financial or emotional help (you can get a loan or a therapist). There is no doubt that the Internet is the future, and that its benefits so outweigh its disadvantages. The economic realities and overhead of the material world will cause most of us to escape to seek economic survival and a competitive edge in cyberspace, but there is a potential dark side of the cyber-universe: It is the same dark side that we all have as flawed humans.

And as flawed humans, we are all subject to imperfections and tendencies that cause us to covet power for selfish motives. Just possibly, we are all potential hackers. An example that best illustrates my point is a story told by a former chief of a big city police department. He tells how he used his police spies to check out his daughter's fiancee because he was concerned about her welfare. Certainly, critics were correct to criticize the chief's spying on law-abiding citizens. But I wonder how many of us would have done the same thing to protect our own children—especially if we were in a position of public stature. If there are 30 million users of the Internet, could it be that there are 30 million potential hackers? Too unbelievable?

Let's look at another hypothetical situation and examine a typical phenomena of the Internet that also takes place in U.S. mail or "snail mail." I'm talking about hate e-mail, sometimes referred to as "flames." "Flaming" can fill up a individual or company's e-mail box, effectively shutting off all communications to that party. What if Exxon Corporation had a Web page during the Alaskan oil spill, would public rage not have resulted in enough angry e-mail messages to shut down their Internet facility? There were certainly a lot of letters sent, and it's not hard to see how a computer attached to the Internet could be both a valuable business tool and a difficult technological liability depending on the situation and how you have prepared for it.

In my almost twenty years' experience in data processing and telecommunications, I have seen the inhibitions of many mild-mannered professionals undergo almost Dr. Jeckel into Mr. Hyde[Endash]type transformations when they go online. Sometimes all it takes is a little provocation, a bit of anger, malice, or mischief. Unlike face-to-face communication, or even written correspondences, e-mail is seen but not touched, but its impact can be profound, since one person can send e-mail to hundreds of thousands in just a few minutes. If the communication is negative, damaging, or host to dangerous viruses or *cyber-worms*, the Internet becomes a serious weapon of "electronic warfare."

The Internet: Woes in Cyberspace

Because the Internet has so many attached computers and millions of subscribers, the ability to attack from complete darkness exists to almost a greater extent than just on the telephone. Internet computers are attached to corporate computers (not a good practice, by the way) that contain millions of dollars of proprietary software. Proprietary or confidential data are also stored in computer systems foolishly attached to the Internet and other publicly accessible networks, permitting penetration by unauthorized sources. But business won't learn.

Internet Hacking Techniques

The phone phreaks and computer hackers adapted easily to cyberspace—taking their knowledge of technology to the deepest realm in the Info-Superhighway—the Internet. Just as phone and computer hackers came from all backgrounds and mind-sets—from teen pranksters to sophisticated network geniuses.

Internet vulnerabilities were exploited and discussed like science, often coupled with an amazing level of disrespect for all authority, order, and government. Phreaks would do outrageous things, such as get an FBI or Secret Service agent's home phone and post it on a BBS, just to impress other Internet hackers. Here are some of the online hacking techniques unique to the Internet.

- **Stolen Access**—The technique used to gain access to the Internet through somebody else's account, using stolen user ids and passwords.
- **Stolen Resources**—Once on the system, Internet hackers can search the Internet for nodes to store their stolen software and databases on.
- **Worm or Internet Virus**—A worm is like a software virus, only designed to roam through the network, from node to node, either passing confidential information back to the author or doing damage to the system or storage resources.
- **E-mail Counterfeiting**—Faking the "From" field is extremely easy in electronic mail for an Internet hacker.

  E-mail traverses the Internet, allowing people at every gateway to look at its contents. People who think that their e-mail is secure and use e-mail to send extremely sensitive or valuable data are risking the security of their communications.

- **Vandalization**—Some Internet hackers like to leave their mark by erasing disks, or planting viruses that make the user think the disks are damaged or erased.
- **Internet Agents** (worms)— Software programs are designed to search, retrieve, and update information and programs in computers throughout network environments. Agents can be "good" or "evil."

White-Collar Crime

Carlton Fitzpatrick, branch chief of FLETC's Financial Fraud Institute, says, "Virtually every white-collar crime has a computer or tele-communications link."[3]

For instance, there was a book-keeper at a bicycle store who fre-quently entered incoming checks as returned merchandise and then cashed the checks. Even more dam-aging are cases involving skilled

Satan in Cyberspace

In 1995, a software programmer was fired by his employer after releasing a program called Satan— not just on computer store shelves but in cyberspace—to attack every computer connected to the Information Superhighway. Programmer Dan Farmer of Silicon Graphics Inc. of Mountain View, California released the program on the Internet as a way to force lazy companies and administrators to confront the threats to security in many installations. The program was designed to use a variety of tried and proven methods of hacking its own way into Wide Area and Internet-attached networks. Several parties made anti-Satan detection software available by the time Farmer warned of Satan's release. Some people did admit that Farmer's unique method of marketing helped to shape up a good number of lax computer administrators. Silicon Graphics was placed under considerable pressure by the industry to discipline Farmer, so he was soon fired. (This and other hacker programs and tools were discussed in detail in Chapter 2). The fact that Satan was launched into attack on the Internet is significant, and it emphasizes the fact that Internet-based hacking may in fact provide the most cost-effective way to hack into a system.[4]

computer consultants who embezzle millions. One of the problems with wire theft—many institutions have refused to prosecute when thieves are caught, if they agree to return a portion of the money. They never admit to the public when they thieves get away. One of the oldest British banks was bankrupted in 1995 when a 28-year-old securities professional engaged in high-risk trading and then transferred hundreds of millions of the bank's funds to cover his losses. The senior banking executives were completely oblivious to the improprieties of this "go getter"—they waited until they were insolvent to ask the technical questions they should have asked before they allowed their bank to be the victim of a white-collar thrill seeker.

Industrial Secrets
The new generation of hackers are pilfering industrial secrets. In November 1994, someone infiltrated Internet-linked computers owned by General Electric and stole research materials and passwords.[5]

Stolen Services
Writing down or stealing and then reselling long-distance calling codes is a big business, says Bob Gibbs, a Financial Fraud Institute senior instructor. Also hackers are breaking into private phone networks and using long-distance access to establish "black market telephone companies." One university found a phone bill for $200,000 and realized a mole was in its PBX—a mole from the cyber-nether world.[6]

Smugglers
Smugglers money-launder their revenue electronically and use the Internet to pass messages. Moreover, they cover up secret communications by cracking

into corporate voice-mail systems and by operating their own "underground" cellular-telephone networks.[7]

Child Pornography

Terrorism

Computers are allegedly the basis for the communications systems being used by a number of terrorist groups to pass messages and also gain access to top-secret sites, such as FedWire, the Federal Reserve's electronic funds, or to control the vital telephone switching stations.

The New York phone systems did go down in 1992, and though the

Jefferson County, KY, Police Lt. Bill Baker busted a major kiddie-porn ring in England from his home base—in Kentucky.
An e-mailed tip from a source in Switzerland led the FBI to an actual Internet site in Birmingham, England.
Their three-month investigation involved downloading many pages of files related to child pornography and 400 photographs or digital images.
The FBI agent, Baker, then called Interpol and New Scotland Yard to arrest the distributor in Birmingham.

event was attributed to a load of untested software, some cybercops still suspect a hacker may have been involved.[8]

The FBI Uses Anticrime Software to Trace Misdeeds

To combat wire crime, FLETC's Financial Fraud Institute has 14 software programs engaged at all times, regularly updated to help agents record and analyze data and other evidence, and track credit card fraud. Then they supposedly follow legal search and seizure techniques to obtain evidence from computer bulletin board systems, or BBSes.

ORDERING BOOZ ON THE INTERNET

A transcript from ABC World News Tonight reported that one news organization ordered a bottle of vodka on the Internet to make the point: Internet is used to order booze. They inferred that the liquor manufacturers were appealing to children by advertising on the Internet and by allowing people to freely order through the World Wide Web. But the 18-year-old (who was unsupervised) admits that he was lying on the order form:
REPORTER (George Wallace. NBC News.):
"How old did you say you were?"
TEEN: "I said I was 23."
Makers of the distilled wine and spirits steadfastly deny that they are using the Internet to target consumers under 21 years of age. Congress is said to be considering legislation.

FBI instructors note that cyber-cops don't have a paper trail like previous generations of law enforcement. But the vast number of computer and telecommunications professionals fear that intrusions of police or government will destroy intellectual freedom, creativity, and interaction in ways never before possible with mere phones or televisions.[9]

The mainstream media have adopted a somewhat hostile attitude toward computerists, viewing their culture as "counter-culture" and "threatening." The public has lost the important lesson in the process—that computer crime almost always exposes terrible negligence. Law enforcement has an extensive record of electronic abuse, but in the area of cyber-sleuthing, they have been characterized as conducting investigations like bulls in a china shop.

The Internet buzzes with stories of cops who "arrest the equipment" by barging into BBS operations to haul off all the electronic gear, as if the machines possessed criminal minds.

Internet User-ID or Screen Names

You don't use your actual name on the Internet, you use a user id or screen name (also called a handle), which either you select or is assigned by the online service provider. Depending on the service you subscribe to, screen names can be letters, numbers, or a combination of each. Of course, alpha characters are far easier to remember. Here are some examples of e-mail addresses:

Bill Clinton	president@whitehouse.gov
Author Tom Clancy	tomclancy@aol.com
National Enquirer publisher Ed Sussman	70317.410@compuserve.com
Santa Claus	santa@north.pol.org
Noam Chomsky, the famous linguist and speaker	chomsky@athena.mit.edu
Tom Brokaw	anchonightly@nbc.com
Comedian Paula Poundstone	paula@mojones.com

Since remembering a person's e-mail address is necessary to send him or her mail, always having your address on the tip of your tongue can make the difference between your getting mail or not. Services with less members have more letter combinations available. The right address can be a major benefit on the Internet, just as a vanity 800 number (such as 1-800-PLUMMER) helps customers remember you long after they see your number in print. E-mail addresses are usually 10 characters long or shorter. Some services permit longer addresses, but they shouldn't, since long addresses are hard to remember, unnecessary, and subject to more typographical errors than shorter addresses.

The Internet Advantage

The one thing about the Internet, unlike other portions of the Information Superhighway, is that it provides a common, simultaneously place for millions of users to carry on efficient, inexpensive interactive communication. Using e-mail, chat, online forums, conferences, newsgroups, BBSes, and other almost instant forms of communication, people can exchange words, information, conversation, pictures, sounds, and video clips.

Typically, the three major online services may have from ten to thirty thousand users online in a busy evening. With the online providers on a busy day, it's conceivable that as many as one million users could be online at the same time, able to send e-mail and to participate in online chats, conferences, and forums simultaneously.

Internet Culture

Before a company starts to depend on the Internet for its future profit and competitiveness, and before students jump on the Internet-education bandwagon, they had better become aware of their surroundings and look at the security record of other parts of the international communications infrastructure.

The Internet culture, combining the worlds of both computers and telecommunications (telephone systems and equipment), has opened the door to a new breed of crime, with a diverse and intellectually equipped criminal population: *phone phreaks*, hackers, wire thieves, PIN number snoops, "data thieves, defense secret spies, and vandals. There are many more specialists, but most violators are experts in a variety of technology disciplines. Engineering oversights are rank throughout the relatively new data communications technology, and hackers learned early about exploiting the access points in information systems.

Something about the cyber-world seemed to captivate these electronic scavengers, who quickly realized how little in the computer world was secured. The culture began with crude and then sophisticated acts of 1) finding a dial-up modem line—anywhere, then 2) finding the password into the attached computer or network through trial and error, dial and redial, 3) exploring the computer environment, 4) downloading, transferring, or corrupting files, or 5) laying in wait in core memory, seeking passwords, attempting to pose as a regular user, making regular secret transfers, and so on. It was only later that hackers discovered that they could locate and transfer money. Other hackers were demented vandals, deleting files and programs to satisfy some power trip—like psycho arsonists and bombers.

Many hackers crossed over from computer hacking to become more sophisticated "phone phreaks" so that they wouldn't have to pay the long-distance calls at their favorite pillage sites. When the Internet came into existence, hackers were presented with a new universe in cyberspace, one in which the potential for potential exploitation, fraud, deceit, theft, and abuse eclipsed the former limited world of phone phreaks and BBS addicts.

The UNIX operating system is the software running on the computers in the Internet. An understanding of UNIX, its structure, organization and features, will give the Internet user (even casual users) an understanding of how it works, its security features and limitations, and how implementing TCP/IP at the top UNIX sites around the nation created the Internet as we know it.

UNIX Security Primer

The Internet was built around mini, mainframe, and personal computers running the UNIX operating system, licensed by AT&T (but now owned by Novell). There are versions of UNIX for IBM mainframes, Hewlett Packard, Digital Equipment VAX, Unisys, AT&T, Motorola, Convergent Technologies, Sun Microsystems, Sparks, IBM, and Macintosh-compatible PCs. With over 20 million computers attached via leased lines to nearby Internet facilities in a mesh-like fashion (see Figure 5-1), this network is by far the largest data network in the world. Still, depending on who or what you run into, and where—it can sometimes seem like a dark labyrinth of danger, and in the darkness of cyberspace, your computer can be raped and ravaged of its essence.

Most of the new software being offered for the Internet provides beautiful color graphic point-and-click user interfaces for ftp, telnet, newsgroup reading, Gophers, and other more popular Internet applications. But even these easy-to-use programs (such as AOL or Prodigy's Web Browsers and Internet tools) still refer to themselves by their original names and are functionally identical to their command-line equivalents. In the context of these items will be discussed security considerations and remedies and safeguards for potential and real security threats to data, identity, even your system while doing business or just surfing the Internet.

The UNIX Operating System: Its History and Structure

UNIX is the official operating system of the Internet. Computers attached to the Internet are running either compatible versions of UNIX or a communication subsystem, sometimes called the "TCP/IP stack" to convert data from computer ports from UNIX-compatible form into the native format of the computer for processing. In these cases, the computers are said to have "UNIX front ends."

Directory and File Structure

UNIX is the perfect operating system for the Internet, and for hackers too. More than DOS, all UNIX system and file resources are similar, no matter what machine they're running on. Hackers (like normal UNIX users) have grown very familiar with UNIX structures and commands. This removes the first protection, the unauthorized user's unfamiliarity with the system, from the equation.

Because of its openness and the ability to use its integral capabilities to search the Internet like a huge computer and not millions of connected ones, in terms of resource visibility and availability, UNIX is possibly the most powerful operating system in use. UNIX has also proven to be especially vulnerable to hackers and viruses. The ARPAnet virus invaded Digital Equipment Corporation VAX systems and Sun microsystems running Berkeley UNIX version 4.3.

The Root Directory

Everything in UNIX is hierarchically structured like a tree, starting with the root directory (Figure 5-2). Root privileges allow system administrators to set up all accounts, passwords, permissions, attributes, and directory and file access.

UNIX DIRECTORY STRUCTURE:

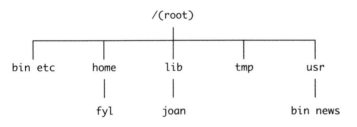

Figure 5-2. Basic UNIX Directory structure

Root directory privileges are the highest level of authority in UNIX systems, and one must restrict this level of access to system administrators. More than one person should have root directory privileges, and the passwords for these individuals should be guarded with the highest level of secrecy possible.

Internet Addresses

Internet addresses take several common forms.

E-Mail Addresses

E-mail addresses have three parts. Consider this example:

john@compuserve.com

john   The user's online name or user-id (mail name)

@compuserve   The domain *(Assigned by the Network Info Center, the closest thing to a central authority in cyberspace)*

com   The extension, preceded by a dot (not period) *(To verify the validity of an e-mail address, send a message. Most mail services tell you immediately if the destination address is valid. Otherwise you will get an undelivered mail error message back from the Internet.)*

Internet Host Addresses

Int.host.address

Int   domain

host   subdomain

address   first-level domain

Domains

Listed below are the major first-level domains in the Internet:

Address	Organization Type
edu	Educational and research institutions
com	Commercial organizations
gov	Government access
mil	Military agencies
net	Major network support centers
org	Other organizations

Internet Protocol Addresses

An Internet computer recognizes other Internet computers by their Internet Protocol Address (not by their host address, which is a translation of the IP address). This address is a part of every message to and from a given host. Every host on the Internet is assigned a numeric address that looks like this:

144.160.0.0

144	160	0	0
first-level domain	subdomain	subdomain	host name

   As shown here, the four portions are divided by decimal points. The Internet IP address consists of two parts: The network portion describes the network, and the host portion describes a particular host belonging to that network. A central agency is responsible for all new Internet addresses. There are four classes of IP addresses: classes A, B, C, and D.

All four address classes use four portions of 32 bits; each portion is referred to as an *octet,* giving an IP address four octets, each having a value of 255. Some values have reserved functions.

In Class A the first octet represents the network portion, and the remaining three octets are available for the host. This permits a large number of hosts in that network.

Class B networks use three octets for both the network and the host portion, allowing far more networks than in class A.

Class C networks have three octet sites reserved for the network and one reserved for the host, allowing many network addresses but far fewer hosts for a Class C network.

Class D networks are unique, with unique addressing schemes.

Here is an example of class c address:

1   9   17   25   31

| | | 1 | 0 | net id | host id | |

123456789012345678901234567890123456789012

Subnets

Every host has a specific IP address to enable other hosts to communicate with it on the same network (as opposed to outside the network) There can be millions of hosts on a class A network. It would not be practical for class A or B to be restricted to one network with millions of host, so *subnets* were developed. A subnet is derived from the host address by using what is called a *net mask* that moves the dividing line from one place to another within the address. This increases the number of available networks but reduces the number of hosts that can be on the network. Even World Wide Web URLs (such as http://info.cern.ch/hypertext/DataSources/bySubject/Overview.html) have corresponding Internet addresses.

Types of Internet Connections

Internet connections are basically of two types, through an office local area network (Ethernet, token ring, or other) or through a modem connection. Ethernet connections are the most efficient, and there are many utilities that make the Internet services faster and easier, like TurboGopher, Fetch, NCSA, and Telnet (not telnet). Modem connections are made on either dial-up or leased lines, using either voice grade or digital service.

Internet accounts are either dial-up shell accounts or SLIP/PPP accounts (Serial Line Internet Protocol and Point-to-Point protocol, used by Netscape, Mosaic and other Web Browsers). The most efficient Internet performance comes on SLIP/PPP lines at speeds of 14.4 kilobits per second or faster. Modems running at this speed and faster are required if one is to use the World Wide Web effectively.

Cable companies are experimenting with extremely fast cable modems, capable of transmitting about a half million bits per second, allowing lightning-fast performance and downloads in seconds that previously took minutes. Their test customers seem to be extremely happy, but with heavy downloading, these lucky users quickly run out of unused disk space!

Internet accounts are offered by the major online services, like CompuServe, America Online, Prodigy, and Microsoftnet; but most of the 30 million users access the Intenet through direct-feed accounts on small Internet providers, such as Netcom and Earthlink. Many BBS providers also have Internet access, as do Freenets offered by local municipalities and other public institutions.

UNIX Shell Prompts

UNIX computers will always display a prompt before accepting a command or call. Prompts can be typical or site-specific. Tables 5-1and 5-2 show a few examples of UNIX prompts:

Table 5-1. UNIX Shell Prompts

%	UNIX, Xenix, A/UX
:	UNIX
>	UNIX
$	VAX/VMS

Table 5-2. UNIX Application Prompts

ftp>	FTP host
telnet>	telnet host
>	Standard prompt
BIGBEN:	Customized prompt

UNIX Security Features

UNIX is armed with a number of built-in security features:

● Passwords

● File access (and visibility)

● Directory access (and visibility)

● File encryption

● Security on password files (after initial releases of UNIX)

The UNIX operating system provides protection for users, telephone connections, terminals, files, directories, and mail. The first level of security in UNIX is to the user. Password security provides eight-character password security to all users. Longer passwords can be used, but UNIX evaluates only to the first eight characters. Punctuation marks can be used with passwords, but you cannot use character or combinations of characters that serve to delete characters or whole lines (such as Control-S or Control-H) during the logon. The password is not displayed on the screen as it is being typed, preventing others from reading it.

Newer UNIX releases encrypt passwords. This prevents hackers from reading the file even if they manage to find the password file (usually the /etc/passwd). UNIX uses the DES or data encryption standard algorithm to encrypt the passwords (using the hash calculations). Once the password has been encrypted, it can never be reversed. Using this technique there is no way to decrypt passwords.

In UNIX a user can change his password at will. He is responsible for the maintenance of this password, and in some cases system administrators can utilize password aging, which causes the system to force users to change their passwords on a regular basis.

Assigning Passwords in UNIX

When establishing UNIX user accounts and passwords (for the password files: /etc/passwd and /etc/shadow), the system uses /etc/passwd to identify every user. It contains 1) the user name, 2) the user id number, 3) the group ID number, 4) the home directory assigned this user, and 5) the user's logon shell. You have space for comments about the user and assign the following characteristics to each account:

- **PASSLENGTH**—For minimum character length of the password
- **MINWEEKS**—The minimum number of weeks password must be maintained without change
- **MAXWEEKS**—For the maximum number of weeks a password can remain unchanged before the user is required to change it
- **WARNWEEKS**—To send a message warning a user of this number of weeks before expiration

System administrators can establish files and programs accessible to a logon account called "guest," which is designed for temporary employees of a certain group. Administrators can also block a user account: 1) by using an administrator's system menu or 2) by using the shell commands shown in the adjacent sidebar.

To assign a new account:

$usermod -e 6/5/95

An input of usermod -e" " cancels the effect of the expiration date.

To block an account:

$usermod -e 8/5/94

Removal of a user logon account and group when a user no longer needs access to the UNIX computer is accomplished by:

$find / -user paul -ok rm -rf -{}\ ;

The above command removes the user and the user's home directory from the system.

To remove user accounts and groups:

$find / -user paul -ok rm -rf {}\;

-ok in the find command will prompt a system confirmation.

To delete an account:

$userdel -r peter

To delete a group:

$ find / -group project -print

To check which users have access to the system, and the authorizing accounts, and which accounts are blocked or deleted, or password protected:

$grep `^[^:]*::` /etc/shadow

You get a list of the /etc/shadow file, which has an empty password field.

Important Commands and System Calls

The following commands, entered at the UNIX prompt, are helpful for anyone concerned with security in the UNIX environment, essential for administrators and network management or for anyone concerned with these commands' potential for abuse. Gaining a basic working knowledge of these commands will give needed insight into how the UNIX operating system provides unique visibility to the critical system functions, files, and processes, and how it allows users and operators elaborate control and access to the UNIX system resources—no matter where those resources are physically located.

UNIX	**Commands**
at	Execute commands at designated time
cat	Display file contents continuously
cd	Change working directory
chgrp	Change group id of a file
crypt	Encode and decode text with encryption
cu	Call UNIX—connect to another UNIX system
find	Search directories
ftp	File transfer program
last	List last user or last terminal login
ln	Create a reference to a file (link)
login	Log on to the UNIX system
ls	List contents of a directory
man	Get specific help on these commands by typing: "man command"
mail	Send or receive message using UNIX mail package
mkdir	Create a directory
passwd	Enter or change password and password attributes
ps	Process status
pwd	Print working directory (current directory)
rm	Remove files
rmdir	Remove directories
rsh	Execute a shell on a remote UNIX machine
telnet	User interface for TELNET protocol
uucp	UNIX-to-UNIX copy (one computer to another)
who	Display current system users
write	Write to another user

System	**Calls**
access	Ascertain access permissions on a file
acct	Enable or disable process accounting
chmod, fchmod	Change mode of file
chroot	Change root directory
exec	Execute a file
exit, _exit	Terminate a process in UNIX
fork	Create a new process
kill	Send a signal to a process or group thereof
open	Open a file—prior to read or write
read, readv	Read from a file (plus read verify)
write, writev	Write from a file (plus write verify)

These commands and calls typically require entry of the command (or call) followed by required parameters or filespecs. But the exact format of each command can be displayed by the specific UNIX system after you type either **help** or **command /?** or **/h** for online help on commands and calls.

Enhanced UNIX Security

Enhanced UNIX versions have features that prevent terminals or PCs from being presented with spoofing logon prompts. Spoofing logon prompts ask users to provide user IDs and passwords and in fact capture those passwords to be used at a later time without permitting users to know they are being spoofed. Enhanced UNIX versions featured trusted path protection of host-to-terminal sessions. The user of a terminal or PC or with this feature will have to enter a certain combination of keys before he gets the logon prompt. Using a modem to connect to a UNIX host, you use the command CU rather than log on. You then enter a telephone number, and the terminal will print online when the connection has been established. Otherwise, you would get a busy or no answer if a successful connection was not possible. Once you have established the connection, press XX to be given the logon prompt. From this point on logon is the same as with a locally attached terminal or logon computer. Since access is via telephone, the same considerations must be made as otherwise.

When a user is finished, he must log out by pressing Control-D (that's holding down the [Ctrl] and [D] keys simultaneously); until a user has logged out successfully his session will be active.

Files and Access Permissions

System data and user data are stored in files. These files can contain both program and data files and are stored in hierarchical sets of directories. The access permissions in UNIX determine which users are allowed to access and take action on which files. The access permissions in UNIX allow three levels of actions:

1. Read access
2. Write access
3. Execution access (only when a file is a program or shell procedure)

UNIX Disk-Full problems

No computer should permit its disk drives to become full. Disk directories should be saved with every backup, and drives that become nearly full should have their data transferred to another mass storage device. UNIX computer systems often experience serious system problems when disk drives (especially boot drives) become full. Not permitting regular users to save to certain critical drives is an easy way to eliminate this problem.

UNIX User Categories (Permission Assignments)

1. The owner of a file, who determines the ultimate accessibility for all other users, except system administrators. The owner of a file is the person who created a file. This person has the ability to establish or change the access rights to that file for any other user or any group of users on the system.
2. The user's group
3. All others

Access permissions for directories determine which owners, groups, and others have access to those directories just like those for files; the permissions over the directory apply to the directory only and not to its member objects, so that once permissions have been restricted, files contain only the restrictions granted by their creators.

CRYPT

Through the crypt command UNIX will encode and decode text that need to be confidential. Crypt uses a simple need that is relatively easy for a hacker to crack. For this reason files that are extremely important should not be encrypted using the embedded UNIX crypt command.

System Files

It's important to use very restrictive permissions on shell scripts and system initialization files. Make sure critical directories are accessible only by authorized system administrators. Since viruses attack system files and object files, all programs should be scanned for possibly suspect code. Do not permit the execution of software from unknown sources unless it has been tested. A program called COPS is available by anonymous ftp, which can check a file or system permissions. The following UNIX files should be protected with the highest level of security:

profile—which is the users' logon directory, /etc/profile

CSHRC in the user's login directory

login

logout

KSHRC

Internet Provider Evaluation and Selection

Selecting an Internet provider is a critical decision, whether you are a customer or trying to set up a business on the Internet. When selecting an online provider, you should remember that there is a wide range of monthly costs, services, access line speed options, and so on. There are four types of online providers—large, medium, small, and free. America Online, CompuServe, and Prodigy are the top three and charge about between $10 and $12 per month for about five hours, and if you use more time, they charge by the hour. The new Microsoft Network (starting in August 1995) offers Windows 95 users one-touch connection to the Internet and will run under $5.00 per month (for basic service). Many new users can wind up paying from $200 to $500 the first month, since it's somewhat addictive. The majority of the tens of millions of Internet connections are made through small online services using publicly available software. It's important to select an honest, reliable provider with good support. Because it's necessary to always have a backup e-mail address, it's recommended that you establish two or three online e-mail address at two or three Internet services. This will give you a backup e-mail address and a backup service provider in case your primary provider's lines or computer are temporarily down when you need to send mail or access the Internet.

The small providers offer Internet connections at vastly lower costs than the online services, and many offer the advantage of having a more local subscribership. Internet access is practically free through certain municipal services available in dozens of American cities (see Appendix D for a list of Freenet providers and how to contact them).

Chapter 05: Security on the Internet

Here are some of the main factors to consider when selecting an online service:

1. Local access number or 800 number available?
2. Minimum monthly charge (generally five hours max)
3. Charge per hour
4. Uniform or varying rates (impossible to calculate varying rates)
5. Number of people in support
6. Wait time on support line
7. Interests of members, prevailing environment, and culture(s)
8. Degree of censorship
9. Objectivity of online censors ("guides")
10. Mail delivery or sending charges?
11. Internet services available (SLIP/PPP lines for Web available?)
12. Database space storage charges?
13. Higher line speeds available, higher rates for them?
14. Charges for instant messages (IMs)?
15. Redundant mail server and backup sites?
16. Too many variable charges to calculate?
17. Sufficient pages per mail message?
18. Easy point-and-click graphic user interface?
19. Always busy at critical periods of the day and night?
20. Integrity of service organization
21. Free or low-cost Web page with account?
22. Free software?
23. Business account available?
24. Support quality, availability, and hours (third party?)
25. Redundant, diversely routed, fault-tolerant network?
26. Insist on a port per customer ratio of 20 to 1 (20/1) for consumers and

4 to 1 for business-oriented services (America Online has an excellent 20 to 1 ratio, but they have had frequent system maintenance shutdowns in 1995 with little advance notice).

Some services are too busy, making it difficult for you to get through. Other services have excessive down periods for maintenance. When you establish business using e-mail, you must plan on always having access to e-mail, so as a professional, you should establish accounts at more than one service. With two screen names at two services, you have essentially four e-mail addresses, providing you with ways both to back up your mailbox (you get a new mailbox with every name) and to organize your incoming mail. It also provides redundancy at the service provider level and at the account level. A suggested strategy would be to 1) use one screen name for regular business mail, 2) use one at the other service as a backup business e-mail address, 3) use the third as a primary e-mail address for personal business, and 4) use the last address as a backup for the third.

What Information Not to Give Online Providers

When you do sign up, you will be asked to provide information about yourself. Find out what information is required by the provider, and ask what information will be made available to subscribers. Also ask if credit card records are stored on online nodes (like Netcom did), and how long they have been in business. Ask if they have any reference customers who are happy with their service. If you want some degree of privacy and anonymity, don't provide any more information than you have to. Here's some information you may consider *not* giving out:

Chapter 05: Security on the Internet

1. Middle name (if possible)
2. Street address (provide mailing address instead if possible)
3. Phone number (why would an online provider call you anyway? You call them.)
4. Social Security Number (large providers don't ask for this, don't give it to anyone)
5. Long distance telephone company or credit card number (they don't need this)
6, Family member names (they don't need this)
7. Household income (This is your business and the IRS's, don't give it out.)
8. Race (right, so they can segregate the network!)
9. Political party (unless you want them to know)
10. Religion (unless it's required that you be a certain religion to sign up)
11. Age (you can tell people later, as with the next eight items)
12. Sexual orientation
13. Line of business
14. Employer
15. Work phone
16. School or college
17. Make and license plate of car
18. Other suspicious questions that are unrelated to online service and usage.

Selecting a Screen Name

As mentioned above, some services allow you to select your own screen name, or several names. If you want privacy and some degree of anonymity, you should not use anything similar to your real name. Don't even use your initials. If you do want recognition, use something that is between six and seven characters in length, similar to a name of a person, place, or thing. Experiment with what is available (the system will reject user ids that have already been taken.) Finally, select as many letters as possible and as few numbers as possible. If you must append your alpha characters with numbers, put the numbers at the end, and make them either the same two or three numbers (if possible no more), or numbers in sequence (like those in the user id *JBond007@well.com.*)

The Online Services' New Internet Gateways

The three big commercial services—Prodigy, CompuServe, and America Online—all have Internet access, including access to the World Wide Web. This is the easiest way for new users to familiarize themselves with newsgroups, ftp, telnet, and Gopher by just using the easy point-and-click "front-ends" provided by the major online services. They all allow you to look up other users on their systems only. CompuServe and Prodigy allow you to search by the names of users (real name and screen name); you must then search forums and message boards to find out about your friends, their interests, or the organizations they are associated with. Once you become comfortable with the Internet, use your subscription to a smaller, less expensive online provider for Internet access (you can get a whole year of access for under $20 on the Freenet. See Appendix D.)

Compression, Uploading, and Downloading

We have already discussed compression in the chapter dealing with computer security. If you intend to upload files attached to mail or to download files from newsgroups, software download libraries, anonymous ftp, or telnet servers, you will need to use file compression.

There are also compression programs that convert data files and programs from binary data to hexadecimal equivalents, effectively reducing their size by up to 75 percent (eight bits in binary code can be converted into two bits in hex code). Compressed files look like random plain text (garbage), so they provide an added level of security and privacy to both stored and transmitted data.

Encryption

Encrypting data on the Internet is an important topic today. Encryption is becoming more recognized as the most secure way of hiding the contents of electronic data. Financial institutions, communication software companies, and credit card companies are now developing products based on current and developing encryption standards. We will discuss encryption in detail in the corresponding chapter on that topic, but it's important to understand that it is a necessary element in assuring security and privacy on disks and in data and voice communications.

As will be explained in the chapter dealing with encryption, it is considered the best way to protect your disk files and transmitted data, be they voice, data, sound, or image. To bust one well-encrypted message may take as much as a year using the fastest computers on earth—and that's if there's only one algorithm used. But even if a message is encrypted, how do you know it is not forged?

Authentication

Authentication is the way that a message postmarked from an individual is actually from that individual. With a PC and an e-mail program, what's to prevent somebody who finds out the password from sending phony e-mail to his bank and stealing money? Many e-mail programs (like PEM and PGP) guarantee or authenticate that a mail message is actually from the person whose name appears on the "From:" field. One technique used to achieve assurance of identity is the digital signature.

Digital Signatures

Why do you need digital signatures when you have encryption already? To prevent the unauthorized person from transmitting a message—authentic or not—from a computer, phone, radio, or wherever.

Simply put, digital signatures provide assurance that the person sending the message actually is that person by providing a serious of verifiable numbers at the top or bottom of a message, with an indication of whether that message was sent from a specific person.

Without digital signatures, problems can occur. The accompanying sidebar lists a couple of examples.

Digital signatures are a unique, algorithmically generated numeric identification that is created by combining your signature's value with a number that is based on the calculated value of the contents of the file to which the signature is being applied. As a result, digital signatures are almost impossible to replicate, and unless a digital signature is verified at the other end, the message is rejected.

The digital signature provides both identification and authentication, something that assures the party

Forged Messages

In 1993, a student at Dartmouth University forged e-mail from his professor, saying that his course was canceled because of a family emergency. Only half the class showed up for the exam the next morning.

In 1994, an out-of-work janitor gave false radio commands to pilots at the Roanoke Regional Airport in Virginia ordering pilots to abort landings, change altitude, and alter their flights. He did so from an unsecured transmitter and caused many pilots to actually follow his orders.[10]

receiving the message (or even a hard copy of the message), that the sender was in fact not an impostor. The signature is generated on the sender's computer, with a program that is protected by a secret password. Some UNIX systems will generate a digital signature for all their subscribers. Unless the signature pass phrase or password is divulged to anther person, the digital signature (along with other measures) of the sender's mail is more reliable than a signed and notarized document. The digital signature will be one of the primary foundations of electronic commerce and communications (including electronic voting). Without the digital signature, e-mail is really nothing more than a collection of electrons displayed on video monitors, which generally reflect what the sender transmitted—most of the time, but not always.

E-Mail

As mentioned earlier, E-mail is and will continue to be the most important property transmitted over the Internet (Figure 5-3). E-mail attachments will contain "fax-type" photographic images that will permit it to displace much of the fax communications being conducted today at a level never expected. On my Macintosh computer, a high-quality fax at 9.6 or even 14.4K still takes over one minute, but an e-mail message with an attached GIF image at 28.8K takes about a minute and can be broadcast to hundreds of locations simultaneously! Sending the equivalent number of faxes would take over a hundred minutes at a significantly higher cost.

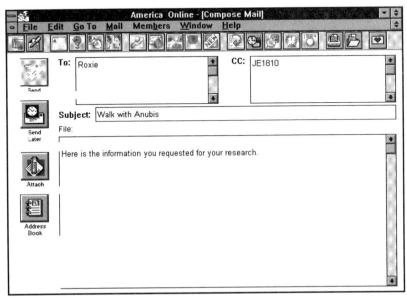

Figure 5-3. E-mail through America Online

So, it only makes sense to anticipate an extreme increase in the amount of e-mail traffic being sent over the Internet. But beware, the e-mail box must be properly cared for and managed. If it becomes too full, the recipient's local node will shut off delivery, and the sender may believe your account is terminated or invalid (so messages should be saved to your word processor and deleted from your mailbox as soon as possible). If an account is not kept active, e-mail won't be accepted for the associated e-mail address, and your address may be removed from important mailing lists.

E-Mail is sent to your user id or screen name, and many providers permit you to set your mail to be permanently forwarded to another Internet address. Each provider can determine how many pages can be sent in each mail message, but nodes throughout the Internet do not normally restrict the size of the message (or attachments).

Let's look at the basics of e-mail and discuss some of the security issues and solutions.

Using the standard UNIX Mail and Mail X, users can send messages to other users on the same node or on different nodes. There is a potential security problem in that the sender in the Mail and Mail X commands does not have to be the actual user who appears at the head of a message, if it comes from another system. And the receiver has no way of establishing who the actual sender is. It could be a problem. For this reason, it's probably best to avoid using Mail or Mail X. Instead, use one of the many secure popular commercial programs available, such as cc:mail.

Netiquette

Good manners on the Internet are more than putting up with the anticommercialist. Bad netiquette is a security issue, because a mailbox that is filled no longer accepts messages. This effectively shuts down the recipient's communications. Usually, bad netiquette results in flames—or cyber-hate e-mail.

Good manners actually serve everyone on the Internet, if for no other reason than to prevent it being critically overcongested with flames, or hate mail generated from people *not* following basic netiquette. That's not to say that following netiquette will prevent you from getting flamed, there are too many people who seem to use the Internet to do nothing more than flame, even for petty things like misspellings on postings.

1. Avoid language that relies on emotion, that is joking, angry, sarcastic, or otherwise emotional; remember that in text media, where people have no graphics or video to see your facial expression, they may misunderstand your meaning.

2. Don't post to a newsgroup (or other group) articles that are commercial in nature, or solicitous for e-mail when your posting has nothing to do with the general theme or objective of that group.

3. Don't ask questions whose answers are probably in FAQ (frequently asked questions) files. These files are everywhere in the Internet, like help files in computers.

4. Don't send or request others to send chain e-mail letters as a way to subtly exploit your product.

5. Never send unsolicited e-mail. If you ask before sending the letter, you should identify yourself, state your objective for the inquiry, and include

a polite request to send e-mail. (You still may get flamed, but don't worry about it, just remove the flamers from your mailing list. Use a "?" character before the subject in the subject line.)

6.   sending e-mail regarding another person's e-mail and posting, put a copy of the person's text in your letter. Indicate that is what they said, and comment on it underneath.

Composing Mail

Composing mail is simple. There are only four things necessary to compose— send address, return address, subject, and message. Most software supplies the return address, and some don't require text in the subject box. Basically, all you need to compose is to put in the send to address and a message. The message can be only one character or up to several pages long.

When finished typing the message, type message termination keys or click whatever button the program uses to complete composing.

Sending Mail

Sending mail is accomplished by filling out the three main parts of all e-mail. You need only put a "To:" address, a "Subject:" and the message text itself. You have the options of sending copies to others people and selecting return receipt. This will automatically generate e-mail messages from the recipients' mailboxes when they open the mail.

You also have the option of attaching files; any type of file: 1) data, 2) program, or 3) virus. It's recommended that you *do not download* anything unless you are very familiar with the sender. Viruses can't be sent through the mail alone, only on attached files.

All business correspondence should be marked for return receipt if possible. It time/date stamps when the letter was read by recipient, making it impossible for them to claim they didn't see a particular document.

To receive mail, a user need only open it. He will see text, up to so many pages (depending on the mail service). If there is an attachment, the user can download it if he wishes. The text of the message cannot be changed by the receiver. This is part of the X.400 specification.

Copy List: This is for other people who you want to receive mail (like carbon copies of a letter). Depending on the software you are using, you can put from one to several hundred names in this field at the same time. To avoid allowing everybody from seeing who else received this mail, put the names in parenthesis, and nobody will see the other recipients except the primary person in the "To:" field. [for example, "[CC: "(john@aol.com" or "marry@compuserve.com)]."

In certain business situations, you would never want parties of the first part to know that other parties exist, and vice versa. That's why it's important to make a habit of using this feature, and to be sure, test it (and all mail functions) by sending e-mail to yourself. Yes! It works, and it allows you to send time-stamped memos to yourself.

Since certain declarations document a known event or phenomenon, they can corroborate its occurrence. The event can be immediately documented by an e-mail memo to yourself—it could have the force and weight of law if a reference was needed to establish possible time ranges for an important event. For example, if you witnessed a man rob a bank on the ground level of a high rise, and you witnessed it from the top floor while entering e-mail. If you send an e-mail message to yourself—it establishes a time stamp on the event because it puts a time-date stamp on the letter. Always use *return receipt* when the e-mail is important or dealing with a legal matter or issue where there may not be consensus or agreement.

To *ignore* mail, the user simply selects the "ignore" option, and the mail will be deleted from the box.

Forwarding mail allows the recipient to forward it to another party. When forwarding is used, the original message is preserved exactly, so that the party can have some degree of assurance that it is the original message. If you receive e-mail from a party, what was sent is documented, and if the original message is forwarded to another party, X.400 e-mail specifications provide that it is the exact same message as the original—that is unless it was intercepted.

Deleting mail is the same thing as *ignoring* it.

Replying is easy, simply select "REPLY" and you will get a new screen with the sender's name in the To box. Supply the message and send it to destination user.

Saving mail is something supported by all systems. It's probably best to save in ASCII format, so that a message can be loaded into a word processor later. Saving your mail is important when it is important. Sending mail to yourself is also a good way of time/date stamping communications to anther person.

Attaching files is easy with e-mail; simply use the attach option with the e-mail program and identify the file needed to accompany the e-mail. Remember that all attached files should be scanned with antivirus software, since this will probably become the most popular way for hackers to send viruses through cyberspace. Virtually everybody who uses e-mail must take responsibility to keep the Internet virus free—just as highway travelers often pull over and remove obstructions from the highway. Even attached data files have been known to contain hidden viruses. The destructive nature of viruses is potentially so damaging, and scanners are so easy to use (and free), there is no excuse for not scanning before attaching files. Telling a person whose computer disk is destroyed that "you didn't know you sent a virus" won't make them feel any better. Computer and Internet viruses will be in cyberspace forever—safeguards must be taken before and after every network, floppy disk, or other media transfer of files.

Graphic signatures are text-character designs that personalize your e-mail message like a letterhead. They go a long way to warm communication up but can also be a distraction if too elaborate. Here is an example:

TO: JOHN
FROM: JOE
SUBJECT: PAPERWORK

➤➤➤➤➤➤➤➤➤➤➤➤⊂

➤➤➤➤➤➤➤➤➤➤➤➤⊂

➤➤➤➤**JOE**➤➤➤➤➤➤⊂

➤➤➤➤➤➤➤➤➤➤➤➤⊂

➤➤➤➤➤➤➤➤➤➤➤➤⊂

MESSAGE:
JOHN,
Wanted to let you know I'll get
it shipped to you at close of
business tomorrow.
-Joe
(END)

Automatic Mail Reader/Sender Software

There are many PC and Mac programs that automatically log you onto your online service and send and receive your e-mail automatically (many also download and upload files, read and post messages to specific areas and more). Most of these applications save users much time, trouble, and money, because there are no keystrokes or prompts needing human attention—the programs go into mail and then receive and send messages to and from the hard drive. These utilities allow PC users to store their passwords inside the program, so that users need only click on their program icon and walk away. But this feature can be used by anybody who has access to the PC, so it shouldn't be used on PCs used by more than one person. If there is any question about the security of your PC desktop, users should refrain from storing their passwords in their mailer programs.

Group Passwords

Some services allow users to have multiple screen names on the same account at no extra charges. This feature permits a user to establish a screen name for business, personal, special interests, or other purposes (each screen name can have a separate password, but only one screen name can use an account at the same time). For those services who do not allow users this option, many subscribers—particularly family members—share the online user id and password. Even if family members don't mind other members having access to their e-mail, it could cause some problems. Parties receiving mail from that screen name never really know who sent the message, and if they find out that the sender is not the expected one—they will forever question the source of all mail from that address in the future. It affects the perception of credibility and reliability and should be avoided. (I don't know of too many families who would even consider reading each other's U.S. Mail, and before families decide on this arrangement, they may consider if it will cause a breakdown in trust).

One thing parents should watch for—children using parent's user ids and passwords or auto-logons to gain access to online chat rooms. If parental restrictions aren't set on parents' accounts, children and teens often go into adult rooms (some of these rooms have very adult conversation topics) and pretend to be adults. If adults think that minors are adults, they may engage in conversations that could be inappropriate or even traumatic for children or minors. Parents should also make sure that kids don't remove any software restrictions on accounts used by an entire family.

If more than one person uses the same user id/password pair, legal problems could also result. If one party in the group does something illegal online, the entire group using that user id/password could be hauled into court to account for their activity on the account. In a civil suit where there's no requirement to prove absolute fault, and principles of "deep pockets" often overcome issues of absolute certainty, all the individuals in a password group may be held financially responsible for damages caused by only one member. In settings where instructors provide temporary passwords for classes, the password should be changed with each new class. If organizations do elect to use this most dangerous (and not recommended) type of password, it should be changed every time a member of the group leaves the organization. For more on online liabilities, refer to Chapter 2.

E-Mail Violations

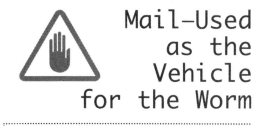

Mail–Used as the Vehicle for the Worm

Failure to recognize the dangers in cyberspace is like walking on the highway with your back turned against traffic. E-mail, one of the net's most basic services, sets the tone: An electronic letter consists simply of a text file containing a header specifying the sender, addressee, subject, date, and routing information, followed by a blank line and the body of the message. Although mail programs generally fill in the header lines accurately, there is little to prevent a whimsical or malicious person from inserting whatever infor-

In November of 1988, the Internet worm took advantage of the D-bug option of send mail. After the program was completed, the trap door was never removed, so that it was possible to gain access into any system from a remote machine without having to give the user name or password. As a result the entire Internet was taken down by a sniffling brat. The best way to prevent back doors and trap doors is to not permit users to run programs that compromise security and to restrict the execution of all programs until they have been properly tested.

mation he pleases. A message from "president@whitehouse.gov" could as easily originate from a workstation in Amsterdam as from the Executive Office Building in Washington, D.C. Forging e-mail is "trivial," Farber asserts; what makes such forgeries a problem as the Internet grows is that the incentive for successful forgeries does so, too, as do the dangers of being taken in. Companies and individuals have already begun doing business via e-mail; real money and goods change hands on the basis of electronic promises.

The "Sendmail Bug"

Another class of security problems comes not from misplaced trust in domain name servers or IDENT daemons but rather from the same versatility that makes networked computers so useful. Perhaps the best example of this is the "sendmail bug," a disastrous loophole that has reappeared time after time in the history of the Net.

The bug arises because most mail programs make it possible to route messages not only to users but also directly to particular files or programs. People forward mail, for instance, to a program called vacation, which sends a reply telling correspondents that the intended recipient is out of town. Many people also route mail through filter programs that can forward it to any of several locations depending on sender, subject matter, or content.

But this same mechanism can be subverted to send electronic mail to a program that is designed to execute "shell scripts," which consist of a series of commands to perform system functions, such as extracting information from files or deleting all files older than a certain date. This program will then interpret the body of the message as a script and will execute any commands it contains. Those commands could cause a copy of the receiving computer's password file to be sent to an intruder for analysis, fashion a subtle back door for later entry, or simply wreak havoc on the recipient's stored data. Mail sent to certain files can have similar effects.

Some fixes for the latest incarnation of the sendmail bug have been published on the Internet and presumably have been implemented by most system administrators who saw them, but many systems remain vulnerable. Furthermore, other programs that process electronic mail contain analogous holes.

Even more ominous is the fact that e-mail is by no means the sole way to plant uncontrolled data in a victim's computer. Steven M. Bellovin, a researcher at Bell Labs, points out that Gopher and other information-retrieval programs also transfer large, potentially ill-identified files. A hacker would have to go to some trouble to set up a corrupt Gopher server and would even have to stock it with useful information to entice people into making connections to it. "I won't be surprised when it starts happening," Bellovin says.

Virus contamination by e-mail uses not the text of the mail message but attached files to spread viruses.

E-mail Security = No Security

Since e-mail is routed through at least two nodes for normal delivery, and possibly hundreds of intermediate nodes before being delivered to the destination user, it is subject to fundamental reality—node and network administrators have the ability to see the originator, the destination address, and contents (Figure 5-4). *Tanya Harding's e-mail was inspected during the last Winter Olympics.* Administrators have access to mail since they sometimes need to manually process mail or resolve address problems on outbound or inbound e-mail. If either the outbound or inbound data are being tapped at the line via modem facilities, private e-mail can be tapped until the parities at either end are convinced of each other's betrayal.

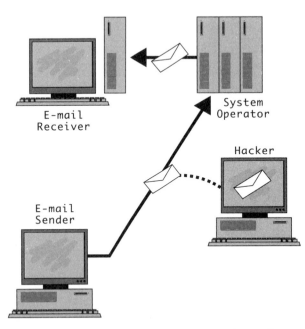

Figure 5-4. E-mail can be read by hackers that tap directly into business'
network communication lines

Tracking E-mail

Even if the e-mail eavesdropper can't bust the contents of your encrypted
message, he can bribe some administrator at a node site handling your e-
mail. That person could supply the eavesdropper with copies of your mail,
allowing him to see the destination of all your messages. The nature of your
communications could be interpolated to some extent by determining the type
of persons and communications associated—attachments, frequency,
personal or business, etc.

Eventually, one of the contacts receiving your mail or its contents could pass
it on unencrypted—available to whatever or whoever wanted to see it. This
phenomenon is one of the most ominous and frightening to users of the
Internet and truly threatens the senders of even secured communications.

Online Service Interception of E-mail and Virus Distribution

There is a threat in the online world more serious than viruses or regular hackers. This threat comes from malicious hackers within the time-sharing service. I experienced a most frightening problem when preparing this book for publication.

When I sent this manuscript to my personal editor, it was in text format so that she could pull it up on her own word processor. It was attached as a file to her mail message, with the subject titled "Chapters 1&2."

In addition to being a fine editor and writer, she is also a very popular online personality with many friends on AOL that know her in person and online. On a previous occasion, her online popularity caused her to be attacked by some petty individuals, who actually spoofed her screen name in a chat room—while she was there. Her screen name was producing chat text that she wasn't even typing, and the spoofer was saying negative things that reflected badly on their victim—while my editor watched and protested. The spoofers mocked her and then typed nasty insults to her friends. When my editor reported the spoofing, she sent a copy of the complaint to the other chat room participants—including the suspected perpetrators. She warned them (impetuously, yet indignantly), indicating that she was working for an author of a book on Internet security and that she wasn't going to tolerate the replication of her user id. This apparently provoked the hackers even more; they apparently had a way (or a person) to monitor all e-mail sent to and from my editor's account.

I uploaded an e-mail message with the following subject title: "Chapter 1&2"; when my editor opened the attached file and later booted up her system—her desktop appeared for a few seconds and then faded away with a "mist" affect (as seen in computer programs, like fadeouts on video). The apparent virus rendered her Macintosh Performa unusable and prevented her from editing my material. She wasn't able to purge it using antiviral Disinfectant 3.6, and then Sam and Virex both also failed to catch it. The FBI was called, and they asked her to not discuss details of the case with the online service until they were able to arrest the perpetrators (they already suspected several staff members responsible for the spoofing and virus interception of mail).

The virus attack raises some extremely serious questions about the security of e-mail and the integrity of the online service. It presents the possibility of a very serious threat to all subscribers on the Internet, not only because it involved e-mail interception and viral contamination, but because was possibly introduced by an online employee. The loss of ability to e-mail my editor during a 24-hour period resulted in my losing her services for weeks, and her losing income. I called the FBI instead, and the official I spoke with suggested that I not report the e-mail contamination until they put the known suspect under electronic surveillance. I suggested that if I send out additional chapters (I would send garbage telecom-babble passing for manuscript), the hacker may be baited into another violation. At the time of this writing, no arrests have been made.

Normally viruses are only put in programs, since data file–based viruses must "crawl" out of their text-formatted files into a program—in this case the Macintosh Finder program (system file) was affected. Since the virus was attached to a text-data file, the virus may have easily been broadcast to

Chapter 05: Security on the Internet

tens of thousands of Macintosh users, jeopardizing billions of dollars and even the lives of innocent individuals on a mailing list. It could have prevented the availability of critical medical-related or research data, or even national security data.

I thought about the extent of violation that had occurred, and it seemed too bitterly coincidental to be funny. I spoke with an inside source and found out that on a wide-spread basis, hackers secretly obtain:

1. Personal files on subscribers
2. Credit information on subscribers
3. Password files for subscribers, getting access to all their mail and use of online account time ($)
4. E-mail, intercepting, monitoring, and saving it

If my sources (which included a report by an unnamed employee) are correct, several of the above acts took place in the interception of my mail and data, and in addition, someone very skilled in programming viruses attached one to a text file containing the first two chapters of this book. I had never heard of such a specific, almost "programmed" trapping, interception, saving, viral contamination, and retransmission of subscribers' e-mail messages.

There were apparently no audit trail records of violators intercepting and corrupting my mail, and days later in the same Star Trek chat room, certain members talked about a "back door" and "death" and "revenge" while the victim of the virus was present in the room. Then they kept typing her password in middle of a esoteric poem. She was terrified and even though she changed her password, she didn't know if someone else would get it. This is an extremely dangerous security situation.

Indeed, this type of backdoor could give a bitter ex-employee means to penetrate e-mail and password files, to send global mail to every person online—mail perhaps labeled "Free Software Worth $1000" but really infected with a virus.

Online services can broadcast e-mail to about three million potential recipients; most who saw a free software offer would probably execute the "free software" and unwittingly launch a virus, even if it were only a test file. The one that hit this book attached to the manuscript text file en route—somewhere between the online service and the editor's PC, most likely a staff member or former staff member.

If only 300 of those one million users were infected with a virus, users who were performing critically important scientific or medical work on the Internet—it could effectively shut down their systems and their work, and it could also shut down the Internet (effectively, since dead disk drives from viral ravaging can't typically be used to sign on the Internet).

QUIZ: What should you do if you get unexpected e-mail and a download file?
A. Ignore it.
B. Download it then run a virus scan on it.
C. Download it to a floppy disk, then write protect the floppy disk quickly.

The proper answer is "A," ignore it. Do not download it. You should set your automatic mail-reader program *not* to download files automatically. If you accidentally download a file, run all known virus scans on the entire disk. The reason for this is, many good antiviruses are free, effective, and fast. They can often be integrated in your Windows or Mac environment, so that every floppy disk inserted is prechecked before inserting in your disk drive.

Most online services recommend that you don't download anything from anybody unless you trust them, but with hackers developing new viruses directed towards specific computers, to perform at specific times on specific applications—it's often hard to detect viruses until it's too late (as with time bombs).

E-mail Security Measures

Computer scientists have developed protocols for verifying the source of e-mail messages, but spoofers are also improving their techniques. Correspondence on Usenet discussion groups such as "comp.security.misc" illustrates this evolution: Some security-minded system administrators have advocated the use of "IDENT daemons." If a spoofer connects to a mail server and offers a false identification (the first step in sending a forged message), the mail server can query the IDENT daemon on the spoofer's machine.

Others disparage IDENT; they point out that the name returned by the daemon is only as trustworthy as the computer it runs on. Once hackers have gained control of a machine—either by breaking in or because they own it—they can configure the IDENT daemon to respond to queries with whatever name they please.

One Solution: Limit Connections

Some system administrators are meeting the threat of such deceptions by barring connections to their computers from untrustworthy parts of the Internet. Each range of numbered addresses on the Internet corresponds to a particular organization, or domain, and so it is simple to refuse connections from computers in a domain believed to serve as a vehicle for hackers.

Can Hackers Still Find You and Rape Your System?

Even this step has a countermeasure that hackers can use to gain access. Most machines rely on "domain name servers" to translate back and forth between numbered network addresses and domains such as "xerox.com" or "umich.edu." But the name servers are just ordinary computers. They are vulnerable to deception or intrusion, and so the road maps they provide can be rewritten to serve deceitful ends. A cracker can modify the name server's database so that it tells any computer querying it that the address belonging to, say, "evil.vicious.hackers.org" instead of "harvard.edu." A computer that accepts connections from Harvard University will then allow the hackers in as well. Indeed, it is almost impossible for any program to know for sure where the data packets reaching it over the Internet really come from or where the packets it sends out are going.

The Ultimate E-mail Security Solution: Anonymous Remailers

There are two types of anonymous remailers: those that hide your return address, but not the destination, and those that provide complete anonymity for both sender and destination.

The first variety accepts standard readable text messages (or plain text) in the subject field of the message, so when a message is sent to a remailer, snoops may be able to see the destination address, but the sender's address is stripped from the message.

The second type of anonymous remailers accept only encrypted destination addresses and requires that you obtain their public key in order to hide the recipients' and senders' identity, but also the contents of the message itself. This type of remailer is the only type that can provide total anonymity in that the eavesdropper cannot determine the person sending the message nor determine its final destination. But the recipient can reply to the sender—with complete confidentiality maintained.

Anonymous remailers can prevent a person who intercepts mail from knowing who you send mail to, frequency, contents, and the sizes of the messages sent by sending your mail to a third party set up to remail your messages, swapping the destination return address for yours. Also called untraceable mail, this provides a system for sending and receiving mail without risk of being traced.

The sidebar on this page lists the addresses of some anonymous remailers.

Anonymous Remailer Addresses

hh@pmantis.berkeley.edu
hh@cicada.berkely.edu
hh@soda.berkeley.edu
nowhere@bsu-cs.bsu.edu
re-mail@tamsun.tamu.edu
ebrandt@jarthur.claremont.edu
hal@alumni.caltech.edu
[Fwd:hfinney@shell.portal.com]
elee7h5@rosebud.ee.uh.edu
hfinney@shell.portal.com
re-mailer@utter.dis.org
0x@uclink.berkeley.edu
[Fwd:hh@soda.berkeley.edu]
re-mailer@rebma.mn.org
re-mail@extrapia.wimsey.com[11]

Totally Anonymous E-mail

There is a service that provides an added level of security for mail; based in Finland, it provides encryption of both the destination address and the contents of the message. It is accurately referred to as: anon.penet.fi.

Here is an example of how to use this service.

If you were to send anonymous E-mail to:

John@compuserve.com

you would specify the following *modified* address:

John%counterpane.com@anon.penet.fi

(instead of John@compuserve.com)

The owner of the service charges a small amount for the forwarding of every message, and although hackers have violated his credit card files once or twice, he has an excellent record of keeping complete confidentiality for users of the service. Two exceptions—a case involving alleged private intellectual property of the Church of Scientology being posted from e-mail forwarded by anon.penet.fi, and another involving a violent European criminal. In both cases, their names were released by the order of a judge.

But since the e-mail leaves the U.S. to get to the Finnish remailers, it's probable that the NSA monitors it, and if someone were to send quite a bit of mail to the remailers, traffic analysis of the key sites could still produce enough data to allow reasonable guesses about who was receiving the mail and how many recipients there were for each message. Remailers actually prevent traffic analysis from arbitrary places but don't prevent the tracking of mail—even from the anonymous remailers. With standardized message sizes, however, snoops wouldn't be able to distinguish message sizes as a way of isolating certain messages, also preventing the determination of where certain messages were being delivered (since associating the recipients with the comparative sizes of a forwarded e-mail message would no longer help in this deduction).[12] For more information on encryption and encrypted e-mail, please see the last chapter.

Anonymous FTP

Anonymous ftp (ftp stands for *file transfer protocol*) is one of the primary utilities for downloading and uploading files to and from Internet servers. . The password for access is typically the word "anonymous." Most of the point-and-click Internet software packages make ftp very easy to use; but it is basically a simple task of identifying and specifying an ftp address, locating the directory and file you need, and then downloading it to your computer via ftp protocol. Many software packages offer intelligent ftp search utilities, so that you don't need an address, just specify a topic and you can select sites located on their system. Ftp sites are one of the primary sources of Internet viral contamination. Even if online services and many Internet sites scan all their software with antiviral software, viruses are out there—and there are new viruses being developed every day that will most likely park themselves in files located at popular ftp sites. For this reason, it is important that all software downloaded should be immediately checked for viruses. If possible, until this is done, download to floppy disk and write protect as soon as you save the file.

When a user specifies the ftp command together with the name of a remote ftp machine, if the machine is configured for anonymous access (access by users who do not have logons at the ftp machine), they won't be required to enter a separate user id or password. The anonymous ftp machine is accessible because it maintains an active user id actually named ftp, with privileges assigned permitting users to read, write, and execute permissions in a certain directory.

For non-anonymous ftp sites, the local .netrc file is checked (it must be in the home directory of the user's local machine and must have access permissions), and the password obtained. The user is then auto-logged on, with no need to actually type in a user id and password for that site. Otherwise, if the ftp site requires a password, users can be forced to supply a user id and password. The login is recorded in the remote machines /usr/adm/wtmp file for a record of all who accessed the machine. Restrictions can be placed on certain directories, files, and user accounts.

Telnet

The telnet utility is a remote terminal facility, which can work in conjunction with ftp once users have logged onto a UNIX system and found their file. Most sites limit the capabilities of telnet commands for subscribers. If this is not done, telnet can be used to gain access to most parts of the system. Administrators should test telnet functionality on their own systems—before someone or something like SATAN does for them.

Usenet Newsgroups

Usenet newsgroups are a collection of interest groups with message boards where users can view and post short messages, articles, discussions concerning the topic of the group. Another set of discussion groups is located on ClariNet, which is similar to Usenet Newsgroups, only not free.

There over 15,000 newsgroups, with more being added all the time. Here are some examples of newsgroups:

- **alt.blues-music**   A group discussing blues
- **comp.music**   A group discussing comparative music
- **k12.ed.music**   Music for children, grades kindergarten to 12th grade

Newsgroup subjects seem almost unlimited, and to give order to the Usenet cyber-universe, newsgroups are divided into categories, dealing with the industry and topics. The accompanying table (Table 5-3) lists all the newsgroup categories.

Table 5-3. NEWSGROUPS

Category	Description
comp	Computer hardware, software, and programming languages
misc	Topics that don't fit other categories
news	Newsgroups about Usenet developments and administration
rec	Recreational activities and hobbies
sci	Discussions about science, from simple to complex research
soc	Discussion about cultures, current events world-wide
talk	Debates on controversial topics
alt	Alternative, or controversial, topics
bionet	Biology discussion
biz	Business and commercial topics
de	German Usenet newsgroups
fj	Japanese Usenet newsgroups
gnu	Discussions about Free Software Foundation software
k12	Pre-college students and educators
vms	Users of the VMS operating system (DEC and VAX)

A Flaming Encounter

A married couple in California who were immigration attorneys posted advertisements on every Usenet newsgroup and got over $100,000 in business in just a few days. They hired a programmer to write a posting program that would automatically post to over 5,000 newsgroups. They were kicked off their service and received thousands of flames, but the book they wrote about the exploit made the couple even more profits. In addition to doing something that nobody else had ever done (to this extent), they appeared on TV and magazines openly challenging Internet conventions. They posed an important question—doesn't freedom of speech include freedom to conduct commerce on the Internet, and is the restriction against commercial postings a violation of the First Amendment? Another man successfully advertised his business and netted $30,000 in profits from newsgroup "spamming" (as it's now being called). He intends to do it again. Such postings are a direct violation of most online service provider rules and soon get subscriber accounts terminated. But with the economic benefits of this type of "junk postings" being so huge, it's likely that we'll not hear the end of this debate for a long time.[12]

Holding online discussions using newsgroups helps reduce overall e-mail proliferation on the Internet, since everybody can read and post at a central location. Unlike dial-up BBS systems, there is often strict "moderation" (censorship) of newsgroup postings, and it's entirely up to those in charge to accept postings and uploads. The moderators have the responsibility of keeping unrelated, sophomoric comments off the newsgroup, without censoring and influencing the slants and opinions put up by subscribers. Some of these moderators are very dedicated to keeping the level of discussion at a certain standard; sometimes they take their jobs very seriously. Some go a little too far and send flames to those whose posts don't conform to certain guidelines.

But you can also subscribe to a newsgroup mailing list simply by requesting that you be added. If it is a popular newsgroup and you are added to their mailing list, you would be send every posting made to that newsgroup—problem: It may eventually contribute to completely filling up your mailbox in just a few days.

Internet users are still used to the anticommercial culture of the Internet, so when posting to newsgroups, it's important to follow netiquette, where you read the types of messages before posting your own and refrain from posting commercial messages unless it's permitted by rules posted on the newsgroup.

Newsgroups are probably the most well-known common area in the Internet for the exchange of information, software, and the discussion of issues. Major authorities world-wide participate, contribute, and are often involved in online conferences organized by newsgroup participants. The culture of the Internet is very brutal. Initially, Newsgroup culture isn't too friendly; it's anticommercial, antinewbie, antidissent, antienquiry. It's advised that before posting questions or comments on newsgroups, users read frequently asked questions (FAQs) typically posted on every newsgroup with helpful information on the group's objectives and focus of discussions. It's also not advisable to brag about being new, since you don't get that much sympathy, but you may get helpful tips (may). It's also advised that you not use newsgroups to solicit commercial ventures, but to provide information freely. This is because there are so many Internet users who have become accustomed to getting stuff free, not only is posting ads typically a violation of Newsgroup guidelines, but it may result in making many people very angry (no—they shouldn't get that angry—these people have too much time on their hands). If you ignore these and other conventions, you will be the recipient of another Internet innovation—the flame.

Flames

A *flame* is a nasty newsgroup or message board posting or e-mail message sent from somebody who is angry about your newsgroup posting—its content, its commercial nature, or simply because the person is mean. Flames have a dual effect—they serve to provide a type of cyber-social pressure in cyberspace, and they can be quite upsetting and fill up your mailbox, shutting down your e-mail (and possibly your business). It's best to ignore people who send malicious flames (you can tell real quick, if it has four-letter words or petty stupid objections), even if they send you lots of mail. But if you should respond to an objection, don't post it on the newsgroup, send it by e-mail. When in doubt, don't respond—it's just what busybodies want—you can tell who they are—they often seem to care more about your posting than the national debt, crime, and pollution. The effect of looking too closely at video monitors may be producing cyber-trolls, who angrily search for people to flame, threaten, and harass. If they become a problem, report them to their Internet provider (found in the second part of their e-mail address).

Newsgroup Privacy

Newsgroup postings can be read by anybody, and it's against the rules to use public- or private-key encryption, so how does one post messages for certain people to read—but that may be offensive to others? rot13. It's not an encryption code, but just a simple offset code of the standard English alphabet.

The rot13 system of encoding is a simple coding scheme that assigns a number to each letter of the alphabet (1 for A, 2 for B, etc), adds 13 to each number, and then converts it back into a letter, so that A is now M, B is N, C is O, . . . , Z is L. Although the message is unreadable, virtually anybody who recognizes rot13 can decode it—either with the free rot13 utilities available or by writing a little program themselves that converts a message to normal alpha characters (or of course, decode it on a piece of paper).

EXAMPLE of rot13 MESSAGE:
SUBJECT: HI
MESSAGE: HI BILL
SAME MESSAGE *IN rot13*
MESSAGE : TU NUWW

Discussion Lists

BITNET started a network of e-mail based discussion lists, devoted to academic, research, and now commercial discussion of just about every topic you can imagine.

The groups grow daily, with thousands in existence, and can be subscribed to using the UNIX list management program called LISTSERV. To join a group, send an e-mail message to the list server:

TO: listserv@csncs.com
SUBJ: [always leave blank unless told otherwise]
MESSAGE: subscribe htmarcom Meg Jones

This will subscribe the person to High Technology Marketing Communications magazine

The above message will be sent to the LISTSERV server at the destination address, and you then receive every piece of e-mail associated with this particular area of discussion. Use LISTSERV with caution; your disk drive only has room for so many mail messages.

Publicly Accessible Mailing Lists

There are more than 500 mailing list available. This list is printed in the Internet Reference Guide together with a description of the list and a contact e-mail contact, sometimes a person, other times a LISTSERV server. The list is available on the Internet and should be referenced to determine how to join a particular list.

Providers can install e-mail deflectors and/or e-mail readers, which trigger preprogrammed set of messages designed to fill up the mailboxes of all the employees of that company. This could effectively overflow the e-mail providers' mailboxes, the PC hard drives, even the LAN and CPU buffers. Then, at that point, nobody could send e-mail to the company, either from outside or from within. The garbage e-mail messages could take days to clear from the organization's hard drive, and if they were infected with unchecked viruses, the messages (if downloaded files or attachments contained these viruses) could serve as hosts to wipe out or damage hard drives throughout the PC population.

If false or slanderous information is posted on a newsgroup or any message board, contact the newsgroup moderator or manager—not the person who posted the message. If you know the statement is false, contact the newsgroup moderator. Don't post a personal attack or retaliation on the newsgroup. If the posting is that inaccurate and irresponsible, you probably won't be able to reason with the author; plus the author can't remove it, only the newsgroup manager or moderator. Unless you want to expose yourself to possible retaliation, let the manager do his job. Node administrators and newsgroup moderators may be held civilly responsible if they contributed to the slander through negligence or recklessness. There is more discussion on antislander law and about online provider liability in Chapter 3.

The World Wide Web

If you are equipped with a modem that operates at 14.4K to 28.8K, you are in for a treat. You possess the vehicle for the most exciting surfing of cyberspace—on the World Wide Web. The Web provides multimedia capabilities to the Internet, using the HTML formatted pages to provide full color brochure–like screens or Web pages. But when a cyber-surfer clicks on one of the pictures or highlighted words, he is taken to a new screen or Web page—which could be in the same node or located anywhere else in the Internet. Many entertainment, publishing, communications, and computer companies have Web pages, and some are incredibly popular. For instance, Time/Warner's OJ Central Web page received over 250,000 visitors in a day. The quality of information seems a cut above newsgroups, and Web pages feature the ability to leave mail, offer user-friendly help, and send you to another place without having to go back to an initial screen. Figure 5-5 shows America Online's Web brower home page.

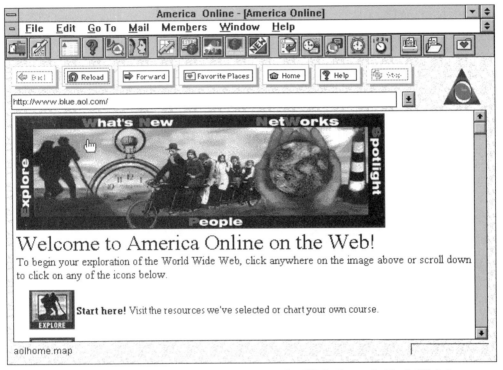

Figure 5-5. America Online offers access to the Web through their Web browser

In addition to providing text, Web servers have the ability to access pictures, sounds, and even video files, so that Web surfers can experience multimedia information online. But because the impact and effectiveness of these new pages can attract thousands of surfers to a particular site—security and accuracy is a very important factor.

Web Site Security

Web Sites are UNIX nodes, connecting visitors to HTML formatted files, often offering multimedia sound file and even video clip support. Web pages are protected by the UNIX system security environment at the particular node.

Password protection can restrict access to a specific Web site, or page (by restricting directories and/or HTML-formatted files). The guidelines for posting messages on Web pages and e-mailing others who post are similar to those for newsgroups, but because Web pages serve as storefronts for many commercial operations, there will be far more delinquent and criminal behavior directed towards nodes that provide Web pages. Web pages are created using Hyper Text Markup Language, or HTML. This relatively easy formatting language allows Web authors to designate where text, photographs, video clips, sounds, and graphics go—and how to arrange them so that it's easy and attractive for the Web surfer to access what he needs. Most Web cruiser software programs permit viewers to save the source code of the Web pages they view: the source code, capable of recreating the fancy text (but not the graphics, videos), displaying the designations and filenames of the graphic, video and application programs that would be executed by selection of menu items.

If a hacker working for your competitor were to save a Web page and access the associated files, he would be in a position to modify text, reference other Web pages, redirect orders to his bank account, redirect your e-mail and postings, essentially stealing the business at the owner's expense. If law enforcement could not tie the hacker to the competing business, you may not be able to even prosecute him. For this reason, it's important to remember that Web sites—even if they are not commercial—should offer file security on their computers. The Internet surfer would have no way of knowing the real Web page from the phony.

Netscape, developer of the most popular Web browser, supports connection to Netscape Commerce Servers, which run transparent encryption between the PC and the host node. If the little key symbol in the corner of your Netscape software screen is complete, the server you are connected to is running encryption. Hopefully, Windows 95 will offer encryption for its Internet and Web software (I don't have information on this feature at this time).

The Netscape Commerce Server provides security based on public-key cryptographic technology from RSA Data Security.

Security features include data encryption to ensure the privacy of client/server communications; server authentication, which uses certification and a digital signature to verify the identity of the server; and message integrity, which verifies that the contents of a message as they arrive at their destination are identical to what was sent.

Netscape is also offering comprehensive services for businesses interested in gaining more security for financial transactions over the World Wide Web.

Netscape is offering a merchant system for online mall tenants, a startup

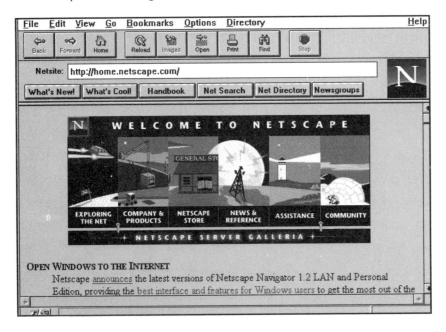

business package, a system for online publishers, and a software package for those who want their own Netscape Commerce Servers. All are protected by Commerce Server secruity, and Bank of America, Apple Computer, DEC, First Data Corporation, IBM, MasterCard, and MCI (among others) have all endorsed the SSL protocol for Internet security. Other companies are also offering support for those who want to operate Internet businesses in a secure environment for credit card, debit, and digital cash transactions.

Finding People, Places, and Things on the Internet

When it comes to surviving in cyberspace—forewarned is forearmed. The Internet allows people to contact people and find resources that may otherwise take days, weeks, or longer to find. Some information is exclusive to the Internet or one of its on-ramp adjuncts (online services, BBSes, and the like). This can provide extreme time and cost savings, bring people together around important issues, causes, and crises affecting our society—something very good. But the power to use the Internet's search resources is available to all cyber-surfers, including hackers, stalkers, phreaks, and other thieves. There are thousands of them in cyberspace, and although you can't see them, they're out there waiting for you.

UNIX's structure, portability, and features are perfect for the Internet. Far more than with any other operating system, the UNIX architecture offers a command structure designed to be open, available to both local and remote users. UNIX allows many other UNIX and non-UNIX machines to function as one large seamless virtual computer. UNIX is equipped with a number of local and global search features that are both convenient and powerful. They can also be used to locate password files, system files, or confidential data files that should be out of bounds for unauthorized users.

Several commands are designed to help the user roam from domain to domain, or node to node, searching for directories, files, UNIX hosts, and people—electronically!

These commands have specific formats, like DOS; but it's not necessary to learn most of these commands because of the new point and click, mouse-oriented Internet client software (Mosaic, Netscape, Prodigy, AOL, and others). Refer to a UNIX command reference for command format information. This section offers an explanation of the functions of the major UNIX research searching tools.

Finger

The finger command finds people on the system, displays their real names, files, and directory, even the name of the access device. It works on both local and remote computers. It can also find a node with a specific name. Finger can reveal large amounts of information about a machine if applied systematically, including a machine's disk structure, account names, and hosts users commonly connect from.

Last

The last command allows the user to find out the login times and logout times of all users on a system or a particular user. It even tells what station the user has been on (PC or terminal), and if the user session is still active.

Archie

Archie helps to find information about an Internet server, or files of a particular name, on the Internet. Once a user finds the file, he uses ftp to transfer it, so Archie and ftp are often used in conjunction.

A file by the name of "PC Diagnostics" may exist at the NYU server, and a user in Ohio could find it by using Archie. Archie could match exactly or by a "subsiding," a similar but not exact match. Archie could be used to find servers located at NYU and then asked to search for directories, files on the famous high-speed roadster.

Gopher

Gopher is an Internet search tool designed to let you *cruise* the Internet's resources across the globe. There are many Gopher servers on the Internet, and each client has a default Gopher that will get the user started on a cruise through cyberspace, which automatically uses telnet and ftp to connect to remote systems and download files.

Who

The who command lists information about a user of a system; including logon name, PC or terminal, and time that the user logged on. If a user can access other nodes, he can use this command to check out active users of other systems.

Whois

The whois command is designed to search for literal names within the same provider service. To check a different service, you can use whois.intemic.com. Internet users can often use "whois" just by typing "whois" at the prompt, followed by the name you're looking for.

When you telnet this site (whois.intemic.com), a set of brief instructions tell how to search.

whois-h *whois.internic.net first-name lastname* connects to a specific whois server, looking for one person.

Whois was really designed to search for military personnel by name (initially the military was a heavy user of the Internet). Whois may be available via your Internet access provider; if not, telneting to whois.internic.com will suffice.

Brief instructions appear when you connect, and you can be very general in your search criteria or be very specific (for less hits).

For example:

whois **-h whois.internic.net Colin Powell**

This connects to a specific **whois** server, looking for the former military chief of staff. If you use only the last name, be prepared to be overwhelmed with too many names unless the last name is very unique.

Netfind

Yet another way to find people on the net is to use a tool called Netfind. It searches for a name and a key. If you telnet to eis.calstate.edu and log on as netfind, and then at the search prompt type the name and the place or domain where your target is located, you may locate the person immediately.

Using Netfind, you have to know where your target is because you can't use Netfind by e-mail. But it's quick and easy to use, so it's possible to search millions of users in thousands of Internet domains in a few days.

The Netfind system can be found at the following sites: bruno.cs.colorado.edu (University of Colorado, Boulder), ds.internic.net (InterNIC Directory and DB Services, South Plainfield, New Jersey), eis.calstate.edu (California State University, Fullerton, California), monolith.cc.ic.ac.uk (Imperial College, London, England), and nic.uakom.sk (Academy of Sciences, Banska Bystrica, Slovakia).

You telnet to the address, enter **netfind** as the login, and enter your search terms after you select Search from the menu.

X.500

X.500 is the Internet equivalent of the white pages. For a directory of locations where it can be retrieved, ftp to nic.merit.edu and retrieve documents/fyi/fyi_11.txt.

Knowbot

Another method used to find an Internet e-mail address is to message or visit the "knowbot" site. If you were searching for three individuals, you would e-mail kis-cnri.reston.va.us with the following:

> *query Robert Redford*
> *query Billy F. Kennedy*
> *query Oprah*
> *quit*

You can also telnet directly to sol.bucknell.edu or info.cnri.reston.va.us port 185, and query Redford at the prompt. For help, use the "man" command after connecting or in the body of your e-mail request.

It was formerly know as the Knowbot Information Service, and it relies on a standard called X.500, which links many Internet address lists. Relatively few Internet sites or online services are part of Knowbot now, but MCI Mail is, as are various "whois" databases covering many telecommunication industry contacts.

Usenet Addresses Server

If you suspect the person you're looking for has posted a message on a Usenet newsgroup in the past, you may be able to find his or her address by searching the usenet address database on the pit-manager.mit.edu server.

Simply send an e-mail message to mail-server@pit-manager.mit.edu and type **send usenet-addresses/*name*** in the subject line and the body of the message. The name is either the first or last name of the person you're searching for. For example, to find someone named O'Brien, you'd type **send usenet-addresses/o.brien**.

Searches are not case-sensitive. The only format fussiness is with punctuation in names, such as apostrophes, which should be represented by periods, as shown in the example.

Multiple search requests can be sent (on separate lines) in a single message to the mail server, but each request will be answered in a separate reply.

Network Navigator Gopher, Also the Cyber-Pirate Ships

Many benefits come from programs such as Gopher, World-Wide Web or Mosaic, which help people navigate through cyberspace in search of information. A single menu selection or click of a mouse may take a researcher from a computer in Minnesota to another in Melbourne or Zurich. Files containing U.S. census data, pictures of the aft plumbing of the space shuttle, and lists of British pubs or of artificial-intelligence software are available free for the finding. Such tools, many of them just a gleam in researchers' eyes a few years ago, are drawing tens of thousands of people to the Internet.

Yet that rapid evolution may have leapfrogged steps that could have contributed to security. Cyber-surfers are relying on "the first or second version" of programs originally written to test ideas rather than to provide industrial-strength services.

The popular Gopher program, according to CERT advisories and other sources, has security flaws that make it possible to access not only public files but private ones as well. ("It's only insecure if you configure it wrong," insisted one informant who will return to his job as system administrator for an online service in New York City when he is released from prison.) Running Gopher initiates a dialogue between a client program on the user's machine and a Gopher server somewhere on the Internet. The server presents the client with a menu of choices for information, along with a set of "magic cookies"—shorthand specifications for the location of additional information.

Searching for Members on America Online

Online Services Provide the Fastest Searches

AOL, CompuServe, and Prodigy are the major online providers in America. Subscribers of one network service can get the latest sports and news, do shopping online, post messages and ads, chat, and e-mail people on the Internet. They can use name or profile search to find others on the same net, but it's a little bit trickier to find people on other online services. People on the online services conduct business, hobbies, and fun activities, and they often develop online friendships, clubs, organizations, and groups. A cyber-community of sorts develops between the users of each service (from big to small), perhaps because of the simple common proximity in cyberspace.

The America Online Search Member Directory feature allows you to search every word in the profile, so that if you wanted to contact every person interested in boating, you would get hundreds or thousands of people. If you wanted to find online lawyers from San Diego, you could search for profiles by searching: "Attorney AND San Diego" in the search criteria. If you wanted to contact someone at a TV station, you could type the call letters of the station and see if they solicit e-mail from viewers or press releases. This is probably the most powerful search tool on the Internet, since it allows you to find people by name, city, interest, occupation, hobbies, sex, age, and even computer used. Here is an example of a profile of an individual who is most likely online to meet people socially:

SAMPLE USER PROFILE (name and certain items changed)

Screen Name: MaribeeGood

Member Name: MARY

Continued

The services usually require a credit card to sign on, but many (like AOL and CompuServe) allow you to use your checking account for immediate logon. Smaller online services allow you to pay in advance or pay by the hour or day.

Online Screen Name and Profile Searches

Location:	NEW YORK CITY
Birthday:	69
Sex:	Female
Computers:	Powerbook 170
Hobbies:	music (creation and consumption), healthy life, Noam Chomsky, hip hop, bluegrass, Sir Stewart Wallace as himself
Occupation:	music biz, freelance writer
Quote:	every wall that i face is of my own design

If a person wants to look up another person but doesn't subscribe to the same service, he can simply e-mail someone he knows with your service and ask them to look up your name. Prodigy allows you to search by a fellow member's name. CompuServe allows you to search by name, address, city, and state. America Online's search facility is the most powerful in cyberspace. It's extremely fast and easy, allowing multiple simultaneous key words to search. If you know someone's screen name, real name profile, city, interests, and place of work, finding someone takes about five minutes max. Obviously, knowing about this capability causes one to think about what to put in the profile. But most AOL members aren't even aware their profiles can be searched by keyword. The following illustration has some suggestions for what to supply and what not to supply in your profile.

America Online (currently America's largest online service) permits you to search by anything in the users "profile," a short biography of interests. Only those individuals who complete a profile have it available for others to read. But many users are unaware that their interests may attract individuals who are interested in you for business, whereas you use the Internet for personal reasons, or vice versa.

America Online's users can actually scan thousands of users by real or screen name, sexual preference, race, occupation, interests, company, even religious beliefs—if that is in a profile. And many people put the most revealing information about themselves in their profiles. It is an extremely powerful tool that many AOL members aren't aware of, but that AOL can use for marketing research.

America Online and many other services permit subscribers to create profiles or mini-autobiographies about themselves. If you don't supply a profile, people can't search for it, but they can find your screen name when you are online. The questionnaires typically don't ask users for addresses. The sidebar shows a sample of a profile screen:

But if you don't want e-mail from folks interested in your profession or interests, you should probably not supply a profile. If you are conducting business on the Internet, provide only what's necessary, not what could compromise your security. For example, if you supply what type of PC you use, someone can design a virus just for your system and send it to you on an e-mail attached file. If you are in a competitive industry (who isn't), you probably don't have to put your phone number, you can supply that after the inquiry. Let people e-mail you to request information and your phone number. Other things to consider *not* supplying are detailed in the following example, which shows the profile input screen:

AMERICA ONLINE SECURE PROFILE RECOMMENDATIONS:

Screen Name:	**SCREEN NAME ONLY (MEMBER NAME IS SUPPLIED): FULL NAME IF DOING BUSINESS City,State,Country:P.O. BOX ONLY NEVER GIVE STREET ADDRESS**
Birthday:	**DO NOT SUPPLY, COULD BE USED TO FIND YOU**
Sex:	**MAY CONSIDER OMITTING IF ONLY DOING BUSINESS**
Marital Status:	**OMIT UNLESS YOU ARE INTERESTED IN MEETING FRIENDS**
Hobbies:	**PROVIDE IF YOU ARE INTERESTED IN MEETING FRIENDS**
Computers Used:	**DO NOT PROVIDE UNDER ANY CIRCUMSTANCES**
Occupation:	**PROVIDE IF NOT DOING BUSINESS ON NET**
Personal Quote:	**AVOID IF YOU NEED ANONYMITY**

COMPUTRACE

Using COMPUTRACE from CompuServe, you can research recent and historical city, state, and zip code of residence for over 100 million living and deceased U.S. citizens.

COMPUTRACE will normally provide name verification and the city, state, and zip code of the last reported residence for living individuals. For deceased individuals, COMPUTRACE will also provide the year of birth, partial social security number, the state that issued the social security number; information on over 40 million individuals whose death occurred after 1928 are included. Individuals contained within this file were United States citizens residing anywhere in the U.S. or in one of 14 foreign countries at the time the individual's death was reported.

Other Directories

Michael Santullo and Larry Dreibes of Palo Alto founded the 4-1-1 Online User Directory. It's a kind of an online Internet white pages searchable by e-mail, World Wide Web, or text browser.

They began by recording names of people on newsgroup postings. Then they set up their own Internet node so people could list themselves. So far, they have a database of more than 500,000 entries. To get on the database, you simply send e-mail to Info-four11.com.

Once you enter yourself in their directory, you get a password allowing unlimited free searches.

Universities

If someone is trying to find a person who works or attends a university, they could employ Gopher, an Internet multilayer menuing system. If one were to begin the search by selecting the local Gopher at the University of Southern California, they could use cwis.usc.edu, which is at the University of Southern California. At a menu prompt, they would select:

● Additional Gophers and Information Resources
● Name and Screen Name Directories (names, phones, addresses)
● Phone Books for other Institutions
● North America

With these selections, you will get a long list of institutions, and you page down until you find the correct university or group of universities you are looking for. After pressing [Enter], you get a search field, where you supply the name you want to search, and possibly get the person's e-mail address, phone number, and sometimes even postal address. Since so many colleges and universities provide all registered students with e-mail, and since professors have been using the Internet for such a long time, it's often extremely easy to find people in higher education. Other "wired" industries are military/aerospace, TV and radio professionals, computer and telecommunication industry professionals, publishers, engineers, sales and marketing professionals, social scientists, and survey professionals.

By e-mailing radio and TV stations and subscribing to media mailing lists, you can request staff e-mail addresses for just about every major station in America; they're all going online. By e-mailing someone you know in the phone, computer, or telecommunication industries, you can request the e-mail addresses of administrators in key companies, who may be able to send you e-mail lists of certain staff members in certain departments (don't expect entire lists; they won't give them to you). you may not get an e-mail address (many companies have a policy of only letting the employee give the e-mail address out). The same general rules apply to every industry, and when all else fails, it may be safe to conclude that the person who's hard to find may have chosen to be unavailable. Privacy, although sometimes more difficult in cyberspace, is possible—if you know how to cloak yourself properly.

Other Internet Search Resources

For high-speed searching on the Internet, a powerful search engine is available on the World Wide Web:

> ***http://www.biotech.washington.edu/WebCrawler/WebQuery.html.***

This is the WebCrawler that searches the Web for other crawlers. If you type in keywords, it will list Web sites pertaining to many subjects, listed thoughtfully. You can search by anything, and it will provide other sites and search engines that you can Cyber-surf to.

Web site

> ***http://guinan.gsfc.nasa.gov/K12/StarChild.html***

is called the StarChild Project, and the home page features free files, pictures, movies, and messages, NASA information. It has connections with schools in France to Japan, so kids can meet other citizens and learn about space flight.

Scott Yanoff: the Man with a Thousand Lists

Scott Yanoff, a widely known Internet address authority, maintains the Special Internet Connections, one of the best resources in the Information Superhighway.

The list is posted on the first and fifteenth of every month to newsgroups on Usenet: alt.Internet.services, news.answers; it is also at several ftp sites under Internet-services/list categories. Yanoff has many interesting and informative sites, with instructions on how to get there.

To receive the list, type **finger yanoff@alpha2.csd.uwm.edu** from your Internet connection. There are other places in the Internet to find the list:

- ftp: ftp.csd.uwm.edu (get/pub/inet.services.txt)
- E-mail: Send message to inetlist@aug3.augsburg.edu (server automatically sends a list.)
- E-mail: Send a message to listserv@csd.uwm.edu, and in the body of the message type:

gopher: gopher.csd.uwm.edu (choose Remote Information Services at menu)

- URL: http://www.uwm.edu/ Mirror/inet.services.html (for World Wide Web users)

When you e-mail a request to be on the list, put this text in the message: "SUBSCRIBE INETLIST" followed by your e-mail address.

Other Search Methods

1. Send e-mail inquiries to other online services and organizations or people that you may interact with (Sysop).
2. Use a program that shows how often a person has been on the net (checks logon and logoff records and creates a report).
3. Universities, entertainment, communication companies
4. Associations, newsgroups, message boards
5. Examine boards that reflect the subject's interests, either professional, or, ah, personal
6. People who may have received mail from the party
7. Organizations that may have done business, etc.

Password Stalkers

Computer "password-stalkers" still watch until someone logs on to a privileged account, then they read the password out of memory. Some are smart enough to have the computer deliver the secret information on e-mail. Once they have passwords, they can act as system managers, altering or destroying data, selling it, and even shipping it to competitors or hostile parties. Hackers have even found ways to "cover" their intrusions by altering system logs.

Internet Ignorance in the Media

Even if newcomers to the Net try to secure their systems, they do not always have an easy time finding the information they need. Computer hardware and software vendors are often loath to talk about security problems. And CERT generally issues netwide advisories only after manufacturers have developed a definitive fix—weeks or months later, or sometimes never. Most advisories do not explain the security flaw in question; instead they name the software and hardware involved and specify the modifications that should be made to reduce the chances of intrusion.

This policy keeps potentially useful information away from those crackers who are not well-connected within the illicit community. But it also keeps many novice system administrators in the dark. Experts estimate that between half and three quarters of the security holes currently known to hackers have yet to be openly acknowledged.

LAN Access to the Internet May Compromise Operation

For the last 15 years, an evolution has transformed most computer environments in administrative offices, big and small. Computer terminals have been replaced by personal computers. Many American businesses connect all their employees' personal computers in local area networks. Internal boards connect to cables, which in turn connect to network control and routing equipment. The employees can thus easily communicate with other computers, storage and printing resources, other employees— regardless of location. This metamorphosis of American business has dramatically widened and improved the way American business communicates, and e-mail has dramatically reduced the over-reliance on voice communications. But if an employee uses a floppy disk that contains a virus, everybody within that corporate network may be vulnerable to great damage to their disk drives or other erasable media.

But if a company's Internet-connected resources are also connected to their other computer and network resources, there is the potential for trouble. Cables connect their precious computer and network devices to every other ARPAnet user, unsupervised by any government authority, since ARPAnet has never been understood by Congress. (Few even publish their e-mail address— probably the most cost-effective way to keep in touch with their constituents.)

Thousands of PC file servers, minicomputers, and mainframes are the hunting grounds for hackers from cyberspace searching for security breaches in every computer they come upon.

System administrators for corporate local area networks also control the connections with the company's wide area networks and the Internet. They set up their file systems to be accessed by friendly network users, but other people can often see their directories, and soon the entire world can be snooping into their company's confidential secrets, technical, financial, and often even personal. As most corporate stockholders understand, most of the violations go unnoticed, are unreported, and often occur repeatedly for extended periods of time before anybody notices anything abnormal.

Computer companies often ship their systems preconfigured so that each machine automatically shares resources with all its peers. This happened to the customers of Sun Microsystems, whose microphone-equipped console workstations were audible to other Sun workstation callers—without the subjects' knowledge! Any hacker who could gain network access the specific models of workstation could listen to computer room conversations. The oversight triggered an alert from CERT (the Computer Emergency Response Team), a clearinghouse for security-related problems based at Carnegie Mellon University. One can only imagine what might have happened had the problem been on video-equipped workstations.

Another CERT alert warned about memory buffers that stored images displayed on workstation screens, being preset to world-readable mode—as clearly as they might appear on a screen.

Internet Firewalls

Internet firewalls are the most comprehensive tool to implement an organization's network security. A firewall is usually implemented on a strategically positioned node with attachment to both its internal users and the Internet. The firewall is a set of software and hardware tools, programs, and diagnostics that allow the organization to scan all incoming (and outgoing) messages to ensure that they are from authorized parties who have permission to use the system.

Internet firewalls are able to screen at virtually every one of the seven OSI modem standard levels for communications: 1) application, 2) presentation, 3) session, 4) transport, 5) network, 6) data-link, and 7) physical.

INTERNET INPUT AND OUTPUT

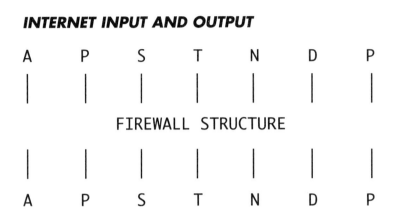

With firewalls established between corporation and public, activity at every level can be monitored, greatly reducing the chances for infiltration, vandalism, theft, or unauthorized use of the system.[14]

Customer LANs or CPUs

Some LAN routers, such as those from Cisco Systems, actually have the ability to "filter" packets in and out, discarding those from unknown people, computers, or organizations, or ignoring specific organizations, computers, or people.

There are many who will argue against attachment to the Internet, that all corporations who attach their computer systems are asking for disaster. But if these organizations allow their employees to dial the Internet from their desks, rather than going through a LAN or modem pool, they may be even more vulnerable. If the employee's downloads are ridden with destructive viruses, and the viruses are spread by internal e-mail, floppy disks, and file transfer within the office—the policy of "no attachment" has been completely compromised by an employee who just did what he does everyday at home. A virus can be "customized" or designed to attack certain computers and companies.

Proposing a firewall and constructing it are two different matters. Users would like to have access to all possible Internet services. But that desire encounters a harsh reality: "Some things you can't do securely," maintains Marcus J. Ranum of Trusted Information Systems. Ranum, who helped to install the firewall for "whitehouse.gov," names Gopher and Mosaic as two programs whose trusting nature defies the attempts of a firewall design to provide safety. In such cases, he argues, security experts must be content to minimize risk rather than eliminate it entirely.

At a minimum, a firewall must allow users to pass mail in and out (even though mailers may be insecure). Beyond that, users want to safely log onto machines elsewhere on the Internet and to retrieve files from public archive sites or from the directories of colleagues at other institutions.

To accomplish this goal, AT&T developed a firewall consisting of two dedicated computers: one connected to the Internet and the other connected to the corporation's own network. The external machine examines all incoming traffic and forwards only the "safe" packets to its internal counterpart. In addition, it will accept outgoing traffic only from the internal gateway machine, so an attacker attempting to transfer information illicitly out of AT&T's domain would be unable to do so without subverting the internal gateway. The internal gateway, meanwhile, accepts incoming traffic only from the external one, so that if unauthorized packets do somehow find their way to it, they cannot pass.[15] Pilot Systems in California became the first company providing safe access to the Internet, with a 24-hour-per-day manned service already available in many major cities.

The Internet the Final Frontier–the New Crime Scene–Cyberspace

But the new frontier for electronic piracy is the Internet. Initial funding for this network came from Department of Defense's Advanced Research Projects Agency. Ironically, security was not a concern. ARPAnet veteran David J. Farber says that in the beginning, only scholars and researchers used the Net, and they shared a community of interest. Since that time, over 20 million users have gained access from every walk of life—including the shady side of cyber-culture.

Other Methods

Other, less automated services are less effective. Employees want to log onto their office computers from anywhere on the Internet, for instance. But any intermediate computer relaying traffic over the Internet may have corrupted files, and a hacker could be reading packets (including those containing passwords) as they go by his data-scope. In two incidents in 1993, hackers gained access to Panix, a public-access Internet site in New York City, and to BARRNet, an Internet carrier in California. They secretly installed "packet sniffers" that automatically recorded all the data going by and recorded user names and passwords as people logged in. The hackers got passwords for accounts on over a hundred computer systems, according to sources at Panix.

Such attacks render conventional passwords "obsolete," Ranum asserts. Instead safe connections to machines inside a firewall require a different kind of authentication mechanism, one that cannot be recorded by a sniffer and then replayed to gain unauthorized access. Two methods are already in limited use: the "one-time" password and the "challenge-response."

To use one-time passwords, a worker simply carries a list of them. Reuse indicates that an intrusion attempt is in progress. Challenge-response systems have no list of passwords; instead, they require an answer to a random query before allowing access. Most often the query consists of a number that must be mathematically transformed by a secret key known only to authorized users. Most people cannot multiply 100-digit numbers in their heads, so commercial challenge-response equipment usually employs a "cryptographic calculator," primed with the key and activated by a shorter sequence that a person can remember.

Chat Rooms

Chat rooms are virtual. These cyber-conference rooms allow users with a variety of interest to chat in groups ranging up to a maximum of 25 to 50 people. Public rooms on America Online are always monitored, but private rooms (which are created by individual subscribers) are not—courts have ruled that they are protected by the First Amendment, since consent is implied when a person enters a private room. Rules govern chat areas, and the online providers have a right to establish their own standards. The rules generally discourage 1)"name calling, beratement, or personal attacks," 2) threats, 3) shouting [typing in ALL CAPITOL LETTERS], 4) scrolling or *spamming*, and 5) chat room disruption. (The term "spam" came into use after people—in boredom—used to type the word "spam" followed by the return key, causing the word to be printed and scrolled up on everybody's video screen in the chat room. This of course, makes it difficult to conduct chat and can interrupt the conversation. The term scrolling is also used for this practice. Some users create nice character art and transmit it during chat sessions. Even though they are cute, they are also against the rules and can get you kicked offline if your service's Chat Cops are watching).

There are no precise definitions of these terms, and the online provider has the discretion to determine if a violation has actually taken place. Sometimes enforcement of online rules is dependent upon the censor, sometimes upon the person lodging the complaint. America Online seems to be the most harsh enforcer of chat control (who have been accused of throwing people off who simply dissented with others and got them angry), with Prodigy being less strict, and CompuServe hardly monitoring its rooms. For a listing of the America Online chat and other guidelines, see Chapter 2.

Chat and Trust

Because on the Internet you meet people online whom you've never met in person, there's a necessity to establish trust and confidence between yourself and a person, and you can learn about that person through your own experiences or through communication with that person. But you see only text on the network, not people. If you engage in a business or personal relationship with someone, certain precautions are in order.

Before you divulge any information to anyone, it's important for you to understand that unlike a family relation or a friend that person may not feel any great degree of loyalty towards you. Many adults send sexy pictures to chat-pals they meet online. But if you send sexy pictures to someone who is collecting them for later publication or sale to *Penthouse,* you may learn the hard way that people can be dishonest in cyberspace just as in the regular world.

Chat Spoofing and Replicating

A program called AOHell allows people to replicate another America Online subscriber's screen name while in a chat room. This is used when a person wants to hurt another person's online reputation; going into rooms and insulting the friends of the person they are impersonating, behaving in an unfriendly way, and so forth. The results can be emotionally quite harmful, with possible legal consequences and account termination for those caught using it.

The same program could also be used to implement collusion (see the next section)—or even to harass a person. Imagine going from your favorite room and finding a member you didn't like, then going to another area and finding that person still there. You then leave all rooms and decide to write a letter, when you are bombarded with three IMs (Individual Messages) from the same screen name. Before you can respond to one—you are bombarded again—this time by more angry messages than one person can possibly type. This is what it is to be a victim of AOHell, or online replicating. (It is normally not possible for more than one person to sign on with the same user/id and password or even on the same account at the same time. If you log on and someone is already logged on your account, contact the Internet provider or Online service immediately!)

How to Treat People on the Internet

Often, experienced users taunt and ridicule newbies for petty and almost esoteric reasons, often going out of their way to condescend, without much consideration of whether their communication is effective. If communication does not result in the exchange of useful information, but instead generates and propagates useless, hostile messages—it is not effective communication. It's best to keep the Internet clear of garbage data; there's enough of that already.

Here are a few words and cautions on how people should relate to the new technology, and what computers and the Internet are doing to us. The quote is from Clifford Stoll, an astrophysicist and best selling author.

I love computers. I love computers. Computers are great. It's the culture of computing that gives me the *heebie-jeebies* that we are being sold down the river. It seems to me that important things are being lost by going online. We are being told that if you don't have an electronic mail address, that if you don't go online you are a nobody. Where is this computer problem? It's so addictive that it can easily swallow the most special thing in your life . . . your time. I would suggests that it might be that computer networks, instead of saving you a great amount of time, cause you to waste a great deal of time. Lots of people spend hours a day downloading files that have no meaning, sending pictures across the network that have no value at all. . . . Maybe this information superhighway is doing a similar thing that the car highways are doing. Rather than bringing us closer together they isolate us from somebody else—stop us from getting along with other people. These are the very things that you can never learn from the computer; you cannot download the ability to get along with somebody else. I am not saying throw your computer away. I am saying understand it. Appreciate it, and occasionally question it.[16]

Spying, Collusion, Conspiracy, Online Watchdogs

There is a related area of cyber-hackery worthy of mention. Online "collusion" is defined an effort by several participants who cooperate to deduce the identity of a chatter, a sender, or a receiver, or to break a cipher.

Most cryptosystems are sensitive to some forms of collusion, but when people are online, other users can check your presence on the system (anywhere on the Internet and other online services, as described earlier in this chapter).

If a person is in a chat room, a controversial forum, or an online conference about a sensitive topic—they may not want other individuals to know. For this reason, it's advisable to use a second user id or screen name when you intend to conduct sensitive or highly private sessions online.

Positive efforts are being made to lure and search for online stalkers and pedophiles and are producing surprisingly successful results. Many online services provide e-mail addresses to report such crimes.

Other Techniques

In addition to an e-mail imp's monitoring traffic to determine who, when, and where you are sending your e-mail to (and what it is if it's not encrypted), other techniques exist to determine whom you are communicating with

E-mail

E-mail, as discussed earlier, is the most popular and important application on the Internet. When military and academics began using e-mail on the Internet (then called ARPAnet) in the early 1970s, its functionality was immediately appreciated. Discussions of engineering problems, specifications, military documents, research, and news could be sent freely from one UNIX terminal or personal computer to another.

E-mail Security Issues

Network privacy and security require reliability and availability of network facilities. You would never hear about a long distance telephone company or a local carrier denying service to a customer based on their words on the phone. You wouldn't expect them to disconnect customers whose families were considered "filthy" or "obscene." That's because what's stated on the telephone is considered (but not assured to be) private. As long as a person doesn't regularly discuss violence, crime, and bombs on the telephone, phone companies are all too happy to let people use whatever language they want as often as they want, with one person or on a conference call. (I've been on some pretty heated business conference calls where four-letter words were used by very successful and respected people.) The same is true of a letter sent through the U.S. Mail, since a letter is sealed in an envelope—which has intrinsic verifiability—since the recipient can see the envelope hasn't been opened (in most cases). Wouldn't it be absurd for the U.S. Postal Service to remove someone's mailbox—even if they committed mail fraud?

As ridiculous as these suggestions may be (terminating phone and mail service over moral value judgments made on the content), e-mail is subject to not only widespread viewing along its path but also censorship and even termination of online services if a user doesn't like the contents of the e-mail, or e-mail sent under certain seemingly harmless circumstances. Even if e-mail has been solicited, its contents may cause the sender to be liable for slander, copyright, or software piracy charges, or termination by the provider's online services.

E-mail Tips

E-mail not to send: unsolicited, commercial, illegal, obscene, copyrighted, to people on the Internet

If you do elect to send unsolicited e-mail, put a ? in the Subject box before the subject text. ("?SUBJECT")

E-mail to send: $ in Subject Box when sending commercial e-mail ("$SUBJECT")

Target your market, don't send e-mail to people who may not have an interest.

Do not forward someone's personal e-mail to you to another person without permission.

Do not e-mail someone's posted messages without their permission

E-mail Costs

Some services charge nothing for e-mail, only time on the system. Other online services charge for outgoing e-mail, but not incoming. Some services may charge only for Internet e-mail, and not for mail to and from local subscribers. Since e-mail costs can add up quite quickly when you send hundreds or thousands of messages per year, it's important to select an e-mail strategy that is the most cost effective. Since so many services send Internet e-mail instantaneously, it's important that e-mail users not put services that delay mail in the path of their personal or business communications. Online e-mail users should avoid services that are not capable of delivering mail to all Internet and Internet accessible e-mail addresses. Table 5-4 shows the e-mail charges for five of the online services.

E-mail Charges

SERVICE	E-mAIL CHARGE
1.AOL	FREE*
2.MCI	$35 per year, plus charge per outgoing message**
3.CompuServe	FREE
4.Prodigy	FREE
5.Freenets	$20 per year

*FREE mail, but normal online time charges
**MCI mail outgoing charge detail
1. 0-500 characters, 50 cents
2. 501-1000, add 10 cents
3 additional 1000 characters, add 10 cents
4. after 10,000, add 50 cents

Junk E-mail

Like newsgroup spamming, sending unsolicited commercial e-mail can destroy your online reputation fast. If you are the recipient of a lot of junk mail, it can fill up your mail-box quickly and possibly render it useless—so users can't send mail to you anymore. When this happens, you can do one of three things: 1) Ignore or delete the junk mail and risk another bombardment at a later time, 2) send a response demanding to be removed from the list (do not use profanity or insult the junk e-mailer; this may set off an e-mail war—not fun), or 3) report the junk e-mail to your own and the sender's service provider (check sender's address and send mail to "sysop@*network.com*." There are many junk or bulk e-mail services already online. They must remove you from their list when you request. Remember to mark return receipt to your mail to the firms, and let them see whom you copy the message to so they know you are serious.

If your company is attempting to establish a corporate presence on the Internet, the only way to get away with junk e-mail is to offer the recipient something free, or actually send it to him (like a free program on floppy disk or a free report). Companies should refrain from the hard-sell online, instead adapting to the culture of the Internet, and establishing a reputation of leadership and authority in a given industry or field of endeavor. Internet business seems to gravitate almost automatically to companies who have built up Internet public relations credibility. Other companies irritate potential customers so much with junk e-mail that they poison a market they would have otherwise potentially sold to. Charities can get away with unsolicited e-mail if they don't come on too strong.

Concealment of the Insidious, Protection of the Whistle Blower

The Cybernet's plain-text communication, by its nature, gives the impression of anonymity; more than the telephone—where a voice can be heard; more than video—which lets you actually see the person you're talking to. Video conferencing is available through MCI and other providers, and most PCs aren't currently equipped with cameras and cards.

Whistle-Blowers

For whistle-blowers and citizens to express unpopular views electronically— anonymity on the Internet is an absolute necessity. But the FBI contends that anonymous remailers are used by hackers to bombard targeted recipients with thousands of gibberish messages, flooding mailboxes and disrupting personal lives and business. Mail systems, even computers have been taken down when e-mail bombardments, which fill up mailboxes and the disk drives that store them and possibly cause the host computer to crash.

The FBI's main argument, its most emotional argument against anonymity on the Internet, is that child pornographers use anonymous remailers.

Lance Hoffman points out that "no legislative act can stop the spread of cryptography." He claims that rules can be created to safeguard free speech and also determine what kinds of transmissions should be outlawed.

The computer-security authority and professor at George Washington University's Computer Science Department continues, "There are 394 foreign encryption products; over 150 use DES—strong encryption . . . and all are legal to import."

There have been some interesting discussions about this subject. I've included a few articles and online postings. Generally, attitudes about anonymity seem to reflect the personal experiences of individuals, often reflecting a glaring lack of appreciation for the need for both personal responsibility and anonymity.

Cyberspace Hides the Bogey-Man, but Parents Use It as a Baby-Sitter for Children and Teens

The Internet is not a safe baby-sitter for children or even teens. Online pedophiles exist, and lascivious photos (in GIF and JPEG format) for the downloading are often used to lure children into involvement with sick adults.

Experts say that computer and modem children are not in great harm, unless you have negligent parents and curious children who are unsupervised, don't receive parental control, and often seek out precisely what their parents forbid them to seek. But the media tend to focus only on the problems, not the solutions.

Peter Banks of the National Center for Missing and Exploited Children says that "parents ought to teach some basic safety skills." Children, Banks says, shouldn't be left unsupervised to "surf the net."[17]

Others say kids should be taught the rules of the road in cyberspace: never give out personal or family data, like phone numbers or addresses, and never respond to suggestive messages. All kids should be told to report such instances to parents.

America Online, CompuServe, Prodigy, Delphi, GEnie, and other online services provide parental advisories and controls to restrict access to certain areas of their network. One company offers a product (Surf Watch) that specifically blocks all adult areas on the Internet and Web. The National Center for Missing and Exploited Children offers a free booklet for kids, by the Interactive Services Association and the National Center for Missing and Exploited Children, 800-843-5678.

Parental Control

The Internet has no official cops, supervisors (overall), ombudsman, arbitrators, or negotiators. It has become the de facto electronic town hall to discuss and disseminate information related to just about every area of human thought and endeavor. But it is also a place where sick people reside, using the voiceless, faceless medium of plain text to deceive, manipulate, and seduce minors (and a surprising number of adults) into doing things they may not otherwise do, and in some cases harm those whom they snare in their cyber-jacking ploys.

It usually stars with chat, that's where the stalkers hunt for naive youths. I didn't have the patience for Prodigy, so after being a subscriber to CompuServe for almost 15 years, I tried America Online. After trying a couple of harmless chat rooms, I was just about to leave an auto-parts-oriented chat room when another AOL member asked me, "Do you like to talk about having sex with boys?". I probed the pervert and verified he was serious, but he became frightened and quickly logged off. Many other friends (all adults) have had similar experiences on all three online services, and in 1995, there was a rash of cases in which minors ran away from home after conversations with adults in chat rooms. In one case, a Seattle teenage boy was persuaded to visit a new "friend" he met on AOL. When his terrified parents looked at his e-mail a few days after his disappearance, they found his male "friend," and were able to contact him online. But he was no help, he only taunted them, describing in detail what he had done to their previously virgin son. Since their son claimed he wasn't harmed, the "friend" was not even charged. But parents were justifiably concerned, and well they should be. In all the cases of teens running away into cyberspace, they had been left alone by their parents with no parental control restrictions on their access software (available from the online services). Although federal and state legislators are passing laws to lock up online stalkers, no law can protect your child better than parental supervision.

There is a software product distributed by a California company called "Surf Watch" that includes a program that automatically blocks adult locations on the Internet from access by children. It probably still doesn't allow adults to leave their children unsupervised with the PC, but they won't have to worry as much about their kids "accidently" winding up the in adult-oriented chat rooms, bomb-recipe newsgroups, and other locations where the words, Web pages, and GIFs may not be acceptable for young ears. Surf Watch's developer is constantly surfing the Internet, updating the growing database of locations that parents dread their kids visiting. Considering this relatively low-cost and straightforward solution, it's difficult to understand why some in Congress would prefer a huge federal censorship bureaucracy, as is being proposed (in the Exon Amendment, attached to current legislation).

The following text is taken from AOL's Parental Control information screen:

The Parental Control feature can only be used by the master account. The master account is the permanent screen name that was created during your first sign-on to America Online.

Parental Control enables the master account holder to restrict access to certain areas and features on America Online. It can be set for one or all screen names on the account; once Parental Control is set for a particular screen name, it is active each time that screen name signs on. Changes can be made by the master account holder at any time.

The master account holder can set any or all of the following four Parental Control features to block access for any screen name on the account:

BLOCK INSTANT MESSAGES: turns off Instant Messages-the immediate, person-to-person conversations that can only be viewed by the sender and receiver.

BLOCK ALL ROOMS: blocks access to the People Connection-the live, interactive chat area of America Online.

BLOCK MEMBER ROOMS: only blocks access to the member-created rooms within the People Connection.

BLOCK CONFERENCE ROOMS: blocks access to the special-interest rooms found throughout America Online, such as the classrooms in Learning and Reference, the technical forums in Computing and Software, and the NeverWinter Nights role-playing game in Games and Entertainment.[18]

After about five cases of cyber-runaways, the major online services stepped up the public relations effort, declaring to the public that they were committed to increasing their monitoring efforts to prevent the widespread stalkers. All three services set up special programs to report those who stalk minors online and warned potential abusers that their accounts would be immediately terminated and they might be subject to prosecution in some jurisdictions. A few news reporters illustrated how easy it was to find the pedophiles online by simply indicating they were 13-year-old teenage boys who were confused. Stalkers started bombarding the journalists with propositions to meet for sex, and the meetings were arranged on camera. They caught one church organist (male adult) and a school teacher on video attempting to meet the fictitious teens. Instead of meeting the "teenagers" they had been communicating with online, they were shown on the evening news thoroughly incriminated. Even though the parents admitted not knowing about the parental protection on America Online, the news media focused on them and made AOL look like they were hiding the seducer just because they followed the law and waited for a court order to turn over the name and the address of "Dameon," the S.F. "friend" who had adopted a boy. Nobody in the media asked these parents why they hadn't used parental control—none were aware the feature existed.

One analyst criticized the media's anti-Internet hype; the seeming knee-jerk reaction by the public, and the uneven media coverage, pointing out that if the molestation had not involved the Internet, it wouldn't have received the attention it did. But the fact that the crime takes place in the comfort of one's home may do more to account for the singular terror of parents faced with new technology that now enables strangers to reach into their homes and steal their children's minds, childhood, and innocence—sometimes even making them run away and reject their families.

The products and programs designed to protect children are effective and inexpensive, certainly more than an army of bureaucrats censoring everything that goes on. But the Information Superhighway's fastest lane—the Internet—will never be a baby sitter for children and teens. Parents must study what is happening on the Internet and keep tabs on what their children are downloading and viewing and who they are talking to.

GIFs

GIFs are graphic interchange files, whose format was developed by CompuServe to permit the transmission of pictures, drawings, and graphics to all computers and PCs. JPEGs are in the other popular graphic file format that can be sent over the Internet via e-mail, or postings on message boards and newsgroups and then uploaded by ftp at other UNIX computer sites.

Just as with data, GIF files can sent by the owner through the Internet; every day, thousands of GIFs are posted on hundreds of message boards, newsgroups, and Web pages, sent to hundreds of thousands of other e-mail users, even collected by some users. This could be good, if you are an actor who gets jobs when people see your face. But if the GIF is a sexy picture and it's sent to someone you don't know very well, it may wind up as an embarrassment later. The element of personal loyalty seems to take longer for people who meet on the Internet, so it's advised that adults refrain from sending pictures to other people unless they have known them for some time (just as it's advised not to download files from strangers).

Subliminal Messages

Subliminal messages are screen messages flashed across the monitor at speeds too fast to notice; they are rumored to be used on one or more of the online services; but there was no opportunity to investigate this. With high-resolution full-color screens, they could be something to exploit for advertising. Of course, none of the service providers admit using them.

Online Service Integrity

Just like the local and long distance telephone companies, online services are capable of giving their employees access to information about your name, number, credit card, employer, social security number.

The largest online service, America Online, once allowed their employees to access password files, to help change passwords. According to the billing department, America Online employees can now only change user passwords and view the last four digits of credit card numbers, and there is supposed to be a "fingerprint"—or audit trail of every transaction, together with why the record is being looked at. There are indications, both from inside sources and documented accounts to the FBI, that secret back doors still exist at AOL.

America Online, CompuServe, and Prodigy all advise cyber-surfers to download only stuff from trusted, sanitized sources (this holds for e-mail, ftp, the Web, telnet, or any other Internet resource). Otherwise, the only way to remain virus free in Cyberspace is—don't download any file—not from e-mail, not from ftp, not from newsgroups or any Internet resource.

The services are supposed to be 98 percent virus free (approximately) because of their continuous scans on all software they offer. But the other two or more percent of the time, the viruses get through. New viruses are introduced all the time, and it's important to follow strict antivirus procedures whether you think you are infected or not. It's also important to remember that before we upload anything to the Internet or an online service, we should scan it first so other users won't catch your techno-sickness.

The Hackers' Legacy

Without the hacker attacks, on every computer, from Department of Defense, to NASA, to the Federal Reserve Bank, to IBM—valuable transmissions would have probably been far more at risk of being corrupted, compromised, and possibly exploited. With each hacker attack seemed to come a new consciousness of how vulnerable the Internet was.

The entire national treasury of some small country might have been sacked if a hacker named Rifkin hadn't had a little trick of stealing a password and $10 million from Security Pacific Bank in 1988 hadn't shown the industry the weakness of static passwords (he then wired the $10 million to NYC and left the country). Every few months, I hear about electronic thieves relieving banks of millions—but banks don't generally send out press releases. The Internet Worm provided immediate incentives to fix a flaw in e-mail that could have caused a much greater disaster. Until password pirates began pilfering the Internet, sites were still storing unencrypted password files on Internet-attached nodes. The technical-type crimes often ultimately saved the victim potentially more harm (in the long term) by showing people how to protect themselves. But the FBI has elected to take a more comprehensive approach—make everything on the Internet completely visible to law enforcement; including the monitoring of e-mail, ftp, file transfers, and all other communications.

This would be the equivalent of opening every letter and package sent through the U.S. mail, reading every word, researching and probing into the meaning and importance of those words, and then obtaining a search warrant to open and read it after you knew what was in it. Sound like something you would want to live under? With this capability, there might not be one secret passed on e-mail that they couldn't read. One must ask, "Where does the government's natural lust for more information stop?" History shows us that governments who have either sought or come close to getting this type of information advantage have always oppressed their citizens and hastened the decline of their societies. One must ask if catching a few hackers and wire-criminals is worth sacrificing any degree of privacy.

The hackers have only used the access that was left open to them. If systems were designed properly, phone and data abuse could be drastically cut down.

The necessity to violate everybody's privacy in order to catch less than one user in thousands is hard to fathom. But if the FBI says it's necessary, well then, it must be okay. It defeats the purpose of the FBI in the first place. They are supposed to guard federal law, and what law is higher than the Constitution?

Digital Cash—the Key to Booming Internet Commerce

Cryptography is expected to grow the most with the growing use of digital cash, which is a way of passing real money—or actually the electronic equivalent—over the network. The digital cash resides in a computer protected by a multitude of passwords, access restrictions, and encryption.

David Chaum, founder and developer of DigiCash, (a Dutch-owned company), says his creation combines the benefits of anonymous legal tender with the speed and convenience of online commerce. There is no risky exchange of credit-card information.

DigiCash needs cryptography—theft- and counterfeit-proof—asserts Chaum.

DigiCash even prevents consumers' names and personal habits from being diverted to noisy databases, designed to "capture" records usable by commercial customer-tormentors (advertisers and solicitors).

Economists say that digital cash will be good for society, helping to reduce the cost and delays in commerce, providing cheaper goods and services to consumers. But it's said that "criminals will love digital cash. Anybody can use it to transfer money for legal or illegal purposes."[19]

Political theorists believe the widespread use of E-cash will empower citizens—as they see fit—to use Internet to regain control of democracy from the central government. The discussion of what may happen when people have the ability to communicate and trade completely without government intrusion, regulation, and restriction has many people excited, others fearful. But the energy behind the discussions seems to acknowledge the preexistence of perhaps an unrealized level of societal and government censorship. It raises the obvious challenge to every American, "Are we too advanced, is the government so hated, are there too many criminals for us to retain our privacy, our intimacy, our secrecy—the things that help us develop and expand our individuality, creativity, and productivity from our intellect? Is modern civilization incapable of letting private citizens have private thoughts, conversations, commerce, exchanges?" When you really listen to the FBI, they are saying "Yes!"

Online Banking

Some online services offer online banking, which permits subscribers to view account status, transfer accounts, even pay credit card bills, utilities, and mortgage payments.

Visa and Mastercard have now announced that they will be working together on a mutual standard for providing secure encrypted credit card transactions. They have also reached agreement with the developers of Netscape (and Mosaic) to permit credit card purchases for Web shoppers. The agreement reinforces the positions of industry authorities who predict that the Web will replace a significant piece of the mass commercial media, and with the two leading credit card companies establishing a standard, that prediction now has a lot of validity.

Security on the Internet: Merging Full-Speed

It seems certain now that the Internet will be an important and critical on-ramp to the Information Superhighway. With so many important jobs and activities heading at full speed for cyberspace, it's crucial that both private individuals and companies not forget the privacy and security considerations before suffering a head-on collision with disaster on the Internet.

WAN AND LAN
SECURITY

It's a
Small World

WANs (wide area networks) make up America's enormous data communications infrastructure; with hundreds of thousands of businesses connecting to hundreds of thousands of remote sites all over the globe, the nation's business computers rely on WAN connections to accomplish the movement of their life blood—information. Banking, real estate, transportation, retail, accounting, manufacturing, aerospace, engineering, mining, and agricultural data are being constantly transmitted to and from computers and massive data banks containing billions and billions of gigabytes of information.

Within the American office, LANs (local area networks) began connecting millions of personal computers in the early 1980s. LANs now connect millions of PCs to each other, to file servers with large drive capacities, to printers and mini and mainframe host computers. Coax cable and fiber deliver high performance throughput (speeds of 10 megabytes per second and higher), enabling PC software to reside on LAN servers so that PCs can share programs instead of each requiring separate software installation. Offices have begun to warm up to LAN servers such as those made by Novell, Banyan, 3Com, and Ungerman Bass; these NOSs (network operating systems) provided centralized user and resource administration (LAN administration). This chapter will deal with both WANs and LANs (Figure 6-1), their security considerations, their vulnerabilities, examples of security problems, and guidelines to prevent exposure to the woes of networks—hackers, viruses, and system failure.

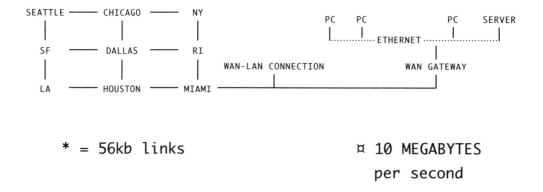

Diagram of Wide Area Network*

Diagram of Local Area Network¤

* = 56kb links

¤ 10 MEGABYTES per second

Figure 6-1. Examples of LAN and WAN connections.

Perhaps you don't have responsibility for a wide area network or need a sophisticated understanding of wide area networks, configure equipment, and software, but virtually every network user should have a basic understanding of the fundamental concepts. This section will discuss WAN characteristics, equipment, and security problems, along with guidelines and procedures to address those problems.

The Evolution of Wide Area Networks: from Analog to Digital

Data communications is the movement of computer-encoded information from one location to another, by means of an electrical transmission system. As text, voice, video, and image converge onto a PC platform, the role of data communications is expanding. Digital technology has now enabled customers a more accurate, reliable, and cost-effective mode for the transmission of voice, data, and image (still and full motion).

Digital communications between devices use established codes based on the binary number system, or "zeros" and "ones," to represent the absence or presence of an electrical charge. To a computer, zeros and ones are considered "on/off" conditions, and in various combinations, they are capable of representing any character or digit. Wide area networks connect PCs (Figure 6-2), larger computers, terminals, and local area networks (Figure 6-3) to elsewhere. People in other locations, near and far, can trade stock from home, transmit sales orders, or send stories to a newspaper on dial-up or leased-line connections.

PC-modem —— data —— data —— data —— modem-HOST

Figure 6-2. A typical PC-to-host connection

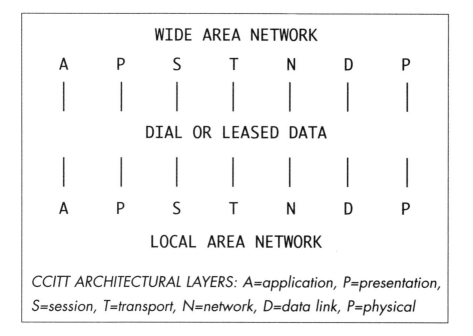

Figure 6-3. LAN-to-WAN connections

WAN to LAN connections link America's business environment to the Internet, and since LAN and WAN security can be directly affected, it's important to understand the basic elements of each, and the important security issues and solutions.

Transmission Speeds for a Movie
relative difference in downloading file

Plain Telephone	2.4Kb	5 days, 19 hours
X.25	64Kb	5.2 hours
T1	1,544,000Mb	13.3 minutes
ISDN	2Mb	10 minutes
T3	42Mb	28 seconds
SONET OC9	466Mb	2.58 seconds
SONET OC48	2,488Mb	0.48 seconds
DS0	64Kbps	5.2 hours
DS1	1.5Mbps	13.3 minutes
DS3	45Mbps	30 seconds
OC-3	155Mbps	7.8 seconds

SECURITY STARTS WITH RESILIENT DESIGN

Network security starts in the design phase. Redundancy, high performance, alternate routing strategies, direct access, application and data base distribution should be implemented when and where ever possible; disaster recovery plans should be a mandatory part of every LAN and WAN design. Obtaining the services of an experienced network design consultant and implementation specialists can provide support for small and large businesses who lack this skill in-house and help an organization avoid making million-dollar mistakes (or worse). Without a reliable network, security problems are often difficult to distinguish from hardware, software and network failure.

Network Basics

A data *bit* is the smallest unit of information, consisting of one binary digit: either a zero or a one.

- A *byte* is a group of bits, usually eight bits, but byte sizes can be anything above two bits.
- A *character* is a group of bits that can be translated into a letter, a number, or a punctuation mark.
- ● *Baud rate* is sometimes confused with bit rate, but is actually the number of signal transitions per period of time over a communication link. Older 300-baud modems actually operated at 300 bits per second because there was exactly one bit per baud. Baud rates on a normal phone line can't exceed 2400 because of bandwidth limitations. But with advanced analog modulation techniques permitting multiple bits per signal transition, modem and line speeds are more often referred to by the number of bits per second.
- *Bit rate* is the actual transmission speed in bits per second (bps); data are typically transmitted at speeds from 300 to 1.5 million bits per second.
- *EBCDIC* is Extended Binary Coded Decimal Interchange Code developed by IBM. It was one of the first transmission codes and is no longer in broad use outside mainframe environments.

- *ASCII* is the American Standard Code for Information Interchange, the most commonly used transmission code for data communications.
- *ANSI* is a set of standards for keyboards, permitting special functions and screen graphics via combined character sequences.
- *Parity* is a method of checking the integrity of data after they has been moved or processed in some way. Parity bits are added to the code being transmitted so that the total value is either even or odd; *odd* parity produces an odd value, *even,* an even value. Parity is checked inside computers to assure integrity and also in asynchronous communications— where users have the option of odd, even, and no parity. With parity, the parity value of the original data can be compared to the data sent, to determine if an error occurred.
- *Protocols* are agreed-upon methods forming the basis for information exchange. Network protocols take encoded data (alpha, numeric, and telemetric) and transport messages from one communications device to another, for example, from a PC to a host. Below are the major network transmission modes and network protocols:

Network protocols

Asynchronous transmission, also called "start/stop" transmission, is a common method of attaching dial-up modems to WANs and to both corporate and public online services. It is a relatively inefficient protocol, only transmitting one character per set of start/stop bits; but it is widely used, and asynch software is very inexpensive. Most asynch connections are point to point, but multipoint asynch is sometimes used for automatic teller networks.

Asynch transmission
ISTART BIT I CHARACTER ISTOP BITI

Synchronous transmission relies on synch characters and timing, not on framed start and stop bits. Synchronous communication permits faster speeds and multipoint connections, and it can provide connections that service multiple asynch sessions. Synchronous communications have older and newer implementations with vastly different performance characteristics.

The term *bisynchronous* or *bisync* stands for Binary Synchronous Communication Protocol, developed by IBM in the 1960s. It is a half-duplex protocol dependent upon special control characters to determine when to send, receive, reject, and acknowledge data transmission.

Bisynch
ISYN ISYN ISYN IADDRESS IDATA BLOCK IEDB IBCC IBCC I

HDLC stands for High-Level Data Link Control procedures, and it is the basis for most of today's more efficient bit-oriented protocols. SDLC, X.25, IP, and many other proprietary and nonproprietary protocols follow the HDLC model, making translation of internodal communications a simple matter of converting certain address and control values. The HDLC standard is code transparent, serial-by-bit (not byte) which means that it will carry other protocols inside its envelopes without problems. The following protocols have similar implementations:

SDLC and X.25:

IFLAG IADDRESS ICONTROL   IINFORMATION IFLAG I

BYTEI BYTE IBYTE I 256 CHARS IBYTE

TCP/IP:

IHEADER IIP HEADER ITCP HEADER IFTP COMMAND/REPLY ITRAILER I

Wide Area Network Security

WAN backbones, which tie major locations together via leased lines, connect major sites with other locations in other areas. WANs gain alternate routing capability with multiple links in the same location, permitting multiple routes to virtually every other node in the network. The speed or bandwidth of these backbone links are typically 56Kb to T1. WAN protocols include asynchronous, bisynchronous, synchronous. Higher-speed WAN connections include ISDN, FDDI, and frame relay services, which can carry from dozens to hundreds of lower-speed data or voice links within a single connection. Using frame relay in Asynchronous Transfer Mode (ATM), data, voice, video, and the like can be transferred inside of high speed digital packets.

Dial-Up lines

The majority of end-user communications connections come from dial-up devices—PC to host communications established by dial modems (from 300 to 28.8 bits per second analog, or digital data sets (switched 56Kb digital has become extremely popular in recent years).

Dial-up modems are very common, and most PC users have used modems at some point to connect to a host computer. CCITT standards have created international uniformity and compatibility among modem products, so most higher-speed modems will connect with their lower-speed counterparts (for example, 28.8 modems will attach to 14.4 modems) and vice versa. Although performance degrades with poor dial-line quality, most new modems (14.4 to

28.8) have extensive error correction and compression features, allowing remarkable accuracy and efficiency even under poor line conditions. Coupled with error correction at the host (data line and application levels), WAN communications achieve a reasonable amount of accuracy.

Digital Data Service (DDS) is the most accurate of all data services offered by telephone companies. This full-digital service, by law, must achieve a level of accuracy equal or better than 99.5 percent (up time), making it suitable for critical links that can't endure the problems of voice-grade lines. When DDS modems (DSUs) are connected via clear-channel T1 access (ESF), network management systems can obtain instant status on the condition of ESF-DSUs.

Dial Network Security

The field of data communications used to involve the transmission of data only, but now data communications permit voice, video, telemetry on digital links. It's now possible to have videoconferences, send and receive high-fidelity music and video clips, and have digital quality phone conversations through your personal computer with a modem and a dial-up communications device.

Management of Dial Nets

Corporate dial-up networks are the most vulnerable to damage by hacker. Even when telephone numbers are not published, demon dialers find modem lines and hackers begin the password busting process, followed by either skilled targeting, novice exploration, or viral contamination. When hackers attack modem banks, it's possible to determine who they are and where they are calling from with the new caller id services now available in many areas of the nation. When there is a limited and known group of users, all other phone numbers can be locked out. Dial-back systems are available through Codex/Motorola, AT&T, Racal Communications, LeeMah (Figure 6-6), and others.

The other method to reduce the problems related to dial-up hackers is through dial-back security, where the user first calls the modem rack and inputs his user id and password. The system then calls back a telephone number corresponding to the name.

LeeMah Systems

LeeMah systems have the most comprehensive call-back network security systems. LeeMah has a more advanced call-back system with the choice of either call-back dial security or direct logon to the computer, using one to three "secure devices" that are needed to sign on to the host.

Hackers love challenges, and dial-back security is one that is extremely difficult (but not impossible) to crack. Much of the security is dependent upon the discipline of both administrators and users to not compromise security with their mouths or written documents. The accompanying sidebar offers a summary of dial-up security options (with and without management):

Leased-Line Management

Leased-line networks include both voice-grade and digital communications links that permanently attach two or more sites. Management systems from AT&T, Codex/Motorola, Racal Communications, and other manufacturers utilize sub-channels on specially equipped modems and DSUs so that line failures or prob-

Procedures for Dial-Up Security

- *Keep a confidential dial number—don't publish it, keep it confidential.*
- *Limit access to systems users as assigned.*
- *The dial-back phone number should already be stored and available.*
- *Provide a time window for logging on.*
- *Provide port restrictions.*
- *Provide account restrictions.*
- *Provide a max session time for those who gain access to the system.*
- *Provide a network control center, monitoring, remote diagnostics.*
- *Provide password protection*

lems can be acted upon quickly. Line management systems detect voice-grade problems such as phase jitter, harmonic distortion, frequency shifts, hits, and other impairments. These systems also report on the signal levels and signal-to-noise ratios of voice-grade facilities. Since signal levels are affected by tapping, management reports can provide some of the first signs of violation of data lines. Digital line interruptions, retransmissions, and other failures are also detectable with line management systems, and since digital service is normally reliable, management reports can tell managers specifically what DSUs are experiencing prob-lems and provide technicians with instant information on the location of the problems. Modems and DSUs can be disabled, reset, reconfigured, and used to control other electrical devices at the remote end—such as burglar alarms, lights, or auxiliary power equipment.

Network Management

Network management tools provide security, configuration, performance, resource, and accounting management to private corporate networks. *NetView* is IBM's high-end network management software, and it permits network control centers to have end-to-end visibility on all active devices, users, configuration, operation, and management capability. But again, physical security is vital, so it's recommended that terminal access be restricted. AT&T's Accumaster Integrator allows heterogeneous systems powerful centralized management.

Another management system is available for many computer platforms and is now considered a standard for network management—SNMP or Simple Network Management Program. SNMP is a standard UNIX-based management package, but both Hewlett Packard and AT&T (Accunet) offer more feature-rich UNIX-based packages for computer network management. Candel Corporation's *Omegomon* and similar third-party products monitor the MVS and OS operating systems in all IBM, Amdahl, and other plug-compatible systems. Disk usage, user activity, erasures, and other key factors are visible to network control, allowing action to be taken upon unauthorized access to a system.

High-Speed Circuit Switching

Switching of high-speed links from one pair of locations to another is now possible with products such as switched T1 and switched T3. This capability is extremely useful when one site's building has failed and a backup site is ready to go into operation, but doesn't have permanent links. Configuration control software for these products is often integrated into Netview and other network management systems. Password protection is extremely important to maintain security on switching, since a malicious attack, connecting the wrong locations, could disable a network for an hour or more (since many times switching takes several minutes).

Defenses to Hacking

Because WANs are susceptible to most of the same hacking methods as telephone and computer installations, most of the same procedures for assuring security should be applied to wide area network facilities. Here is a list of network procedures and equipment that can enhance WAN security:

1. Connectors, cables, jacks, taps: protect or conceal
2. Physical restriction of communications equipment rooms
3. Confidentiality whenever possible, everything on a need-to-know basis
4. Line management to detect failures and possible line tampering
5. Network management to examine, troubleshoot, configure, and operate remote devices on a wide area network
6. Tempest protection for the prevention of eavesdropping on EMR
7. Protocol analyzers can be set to record and save messages before they reach the host computer; with special trap features, these devices can filter and protect hosts from unknown network addresses and even monitor hackers as they attempt to break into the system (before host access).
8. Bit error rate test sets determine the number of errors on a link, often a sign of line problems or tampering.
9. Transmission test sets can determine the quality of the line, if it's conditioned, signal levels, signal-to-noise ratios, noise, and so on. Changes in these conditions could be caused by hackers tapping the line.
10. Bug detection (see Chapter 4) equipment detects hidden devices attached to phone lines.

11. Passwords and phrases at every juncture of a network are the best way to maintain a secure installation.

Local Area Networks

local area networks, as their name suggests, tie local PCs and terminals to adjacent workstations, providing mail, shared resources, and peer-to-peer communications (Figure 6-8). LANs operate at speeds of 10 megabytes per second and higher, permitting the efficient storage and transmission of data along with the ability to operate shared programs within the server CPU—providing performance equal to or better than single-user mode operation.

LANs connect personal computers, terminals, shared printers, file servers, mail servers, and network

ATM Crime

All hackers needs to duplicate your ATM and to steal all the money in your bank account is your ATM card number and your PIN. Hackers can get this information if you discard receipts or if they can videotape you using your ATM (and see your PIN). Cover your hand as you enter your PIN number at ATMs that aren't protected. Banks have been somewhat lax, considering the number of counterfeiters, jackers, and muggers victimizing their ATM customers.

Eighty percent of all armed ATM robberies occur at night. Almost all ATM robberies occur in the open, where there are no protective enclosures for the bank customer (required in only some states). One hacker positioned a homemade depository in front of the real ATM, and directed customers to place their deposits in "the slot." Many ATMs record pictures of those making withdrawals, but this really doesn't protect customers before they are robbed. State and federal governments have yet to realize how simple enhancements such as panic PIN numbers could improve safety, so that if customers were forced to extract money, they could put their number in backwards (for example) and alert the authorities as they withdraw funds (without letting the gun-bearing crook know).

Logging In And Out

After Logging into any session, whether on a WAN or LAN (including the Internet), make sure you properly log off; DO NOT TERMINATE YOUR ACCESS SOFTWARE YOUR MODEM, OR PC (don't reboot). If you disconnect without terminating your host session, it might allow a hacker to inherit your session; at your expense, and possibly to your data's destruction.

gateways (including Internet gateways). LANs also store multilicense software, for use by everyone on the LAN (typically much less expensive than purchasing separate programs for all PCs). By making these devices and resources available to all users, companies save enormous expenses on hardware and obtain security and control they wouldn't have otherwise. But most importantly, LAN users can interact instantly with one another.

LAN networking allow users to go beyond providing shared resources, applications, and e-mail messages. Programs such as Lotus Notes, cc:mail, and other server-based applications allow professionals to trade and develop ideas (brainstorm) as well as share messages, schedules, images, faxes, and documents via e-mail, with the sender never having to worry about the recipient being authorized to see these things—that's all figured out by the system. LANs are literally transforming the way the modern office does business.

LAN Security

Most of us who still commute to work are familiar with the endless ranks of cyber-cubicles enclosing identical-looking PCs, lined up in formation, ready to go to war, in the bloodless, paperless battle with the competition. Even if it's a public agency, you are still battling—only a shrinking budget. In millions of offices, personal computers are linked by local area networks, which allow hundreds of users instantaneously and simultaneously to access programs, data, printers, and mail from their coworkers—both local and remote. LANs also provide links to mini and mainframe computers—both local and remote. The LAN is typically the glue that binds the other elements in cyberspace (using network interfaces, gateways, routers, bridges).

Corporate LANs typically link personal computer users to minicomputers, mainframes, remote networks (including the Internet). By sharing and "pooling" disks, printers, modems, host-gateways, and LAN-to-LAN routers and bridges, LANs permit universal access to resources that would otherwise require individual dedication to each PC. This saves businesses on hardware investment and also reduces the hardware and software maintenance and support overhead and responsibilities. But the wide availability of services and resources leaves companies more vulnerable to hacking—from without and from within (85 percent of the attacks come from within).

Apart from the hundreds of millions of financial and record transactions, LANs also connect people. LAN workgroups are in a real way a co-located network community. Employees in the same office can use e-mail to send messages and attach files and fax documents. Workgroup-oriented software permits brainstorming sessions to take place in cyberspace—either in real time or through multiple e-mail messages, chains of ideas are sent simultaneously to many people.

American workers have become very much at home with the new technology, and they have learned to "network" within the "networks," forming formal and informal workgroups, mentor relationships, administrative contacts, research, and info-exchange.

When failure occurs, whether it is in the personal computers, the LAN, or the telecommunication link, an entire company's operations are affected, and the losses and damage can even put a company out of business.

LAN Primer

There are several types of local area networks: 1) bus, 2) ring and 3) star.

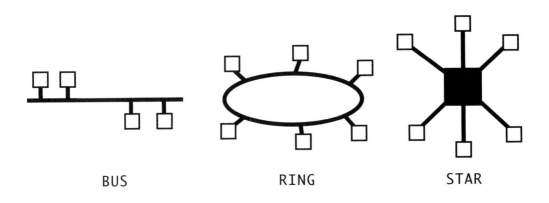

BUS   RING   STAR

Figure 6-4. Typical LAN topologies

The most popular technologies are Xerox's Ethernet (bus) and IBM's token ring (ring). Ethernet is designed to operate on a bus at 10 megabytes per second, and IBM's token ring is

LAN Failures

Cable problems	*60–80%*
LAN hardware failures	*10–20%*
Server disk drive failures	*10–20%*[2]

designed to operate in a ring of PCs at a slightly slower rate; but both Ethernet and Token Ring have been adapted to operate from third-party star-type controllers. Mesh topologies can adapt to any topology; by attaching to both peers and multiport network interface units, they provide the most versatile attachment options for customers.

Ethernet LAN connections are based on protocol standards for high-speed transmission of data through coax, fiber, twisted pair, and other media. The 8023 standard defines CSMA/CD transmission standards that make it impossible for any two users to broadcast on the same cable at the same time. LAN standards deal with the speed, interface, message and error-handling capabilities of the various protocols so that products work across manufacturing lines.

Ethernet LANs are the most popular, offering three cable options: 10 Base T (fault wire), thin, and standard Ethernet cables. All achieve the same 10 megabytes-per-second performance available through standard Ethernet.

With so many cost-saving and efficient applications available to business LAN users, LAN connections are critical in a large percentage of American businesses. Employees know all too well that high-performance applications are expensive, as are full-featured laser printers, plotters, scanners, and other peripheral devices that might not be available to them if not for the LAN. But as is the case with most high-technology improvements, there are a host of new security issues associated with LANs.

Cable Flaws and Breaks

As noted in the adjoining sidebar, cable problems are regarded as the number one contributing factor for LAN failures—between 60 and 80 percent of them!

Businesses with LANs should incorporate cable inspection in their security procedures, regularly checking for broken, excess, split, or failing cable. This will ensure that the network operates properly (cabling problems represent 60–80 percent of all LAN hardware failures; compared with repeater failure, 10–20 percent; and server disk drive failure, 10–20 percent. As mentioned in a previous section, all cables should be enclosed in conduit, concealed, or tie-wrapped tightly so that visual inspections can expose tampering. LAN cables (Ethernet especially) are easy to tap and give off enough EMR to feed any hacker's appetite.

One note about non-cable media—wireless LANs. Surprisingly, infrared transmission seems to be fairly secure. The two types of infrared transmissions are called *line of sight* and *diffused propagation*. Line of sight simply directs an unobstructed beam from one point to another—making it difficult to extend a LAN to more than one room. Diffused propagation makes use of reflective surfaces—like walls—to bounce the signal to the next reception point. Diffused propagation is more vulnerable to interception, since the hacker need not obstruct the light beam to tap the LAN.

LAN Cable Monitoring and Tapping

Monitoring devices are an excellent way to view the data-link level characters traversing Ethernet, token ring, twisted pair, and other LAN media. Programs like Lanalyzer permit complete visibility of address and control information enveloped in the Ethernet data packets. As mentioned previously, each LAN card has a unique hardware id, and this is embedded into the source address of even outgoing and incoming message. Managers, technicians, and LAN administrators can use hardware LAN monitors and PC-based LAN monitors—like Lanalyzer—to verify every station using the LAN, view the data they are transmitting, and even see the screens and key selections they are making. This is very useful for testing, but there is no way for users to know that their keystrokes, traffic, and screens are being monitored.

Unfortunately, LAN analyzers can be used to spy on the network, to view and record all data from all stations on a particular LAN segment (which can be one to several hundred stations, depending on the topology, protocol, and population). This is why all cable taps, inserts, and access points in the LAN are secured, so that unused ports can't be easily used and used ports can't be quickly removed. The procedures for securing cable plant should be followed so that LAN-snoops do not have the opportunity to install access hardware on exposed cable plant.

LAN cables utilize metal, fiber, and light-beam media, of which fiber is the most secure.

A Discussion of Topologies and Security Considerations

The most critical component of the LAN is the file server itself, but unsecured or unconcealed cable plant connecting the server to PCs, peripherals, and other networks allows hackers access to your network.

Bus, ring, and mesh topologies allow universal access to all or many devices connected to a given LAN segment (coax, fiber, telephone wire, and so forth.). This makes them slightly more susceptible to tampering where a person could attempt to tap into a cable and monitor the LAN traffic. The way to avoid this is, of course, by securing cables in conduit, behind walls, or underneath the floor and having some means to detect cable tampering.

A star LAN topology reduces the opportunity for a hacker to gain access to the entire LAN network from one cable, since each device is connected by a separate wire. So "star-type' LAN controllers gain the advantage of not having media that carry traffic from all PCs on a single segment.

LAN Server Substitution

After installing local area network servers during the late 80s, I was amazed at how file servers were often placed out in the open, or under unsecured cubicle desks, or even in an area accessible by nonemployees. These same organizations might spend ten million dollars securing the same data on their mainframe resources, not realizing that their oversights compromised every security measure taken to protect the mainframe computer room.

If a single server is running in an unsecured area, whether it be Novell, Windows NT, Banyan, or 3Com, it would be possible to replace the real file server with a duplicate (with the same name and "appearance") in order to "spoof" users into typing in their user ids and passwords. All the server-swapper has to do is to remove the LAN connection from the real server and replace it with an unsecured user workstation acting as a server. If this server had full access to another LAN server or a large host (which was not set to monitor), it could not only serve as a "spoofing" mechanism to steal user ids and passwords also be used to monitor, intercept, collect, and deliver sensitive data to unauthorized computers and parties for eventual sale to the highest bidder.

Obviously, this would require some trouble and expense, but when you consider the value of the information on the server, it's not hard to imagine competitors or vindictive employees investing what was necessary.

Security in Redundant Design

Safeguarding against unauthorized swapping, or introduction of unautho-rized devices, or other similar LAN violations can be augmented in any of several ways: 1) multiple servers, all equipped to monitor all other servers, 2) restricting server access, 3) restricting workstation access (see "Keyboard Protection" in Chapter 4; this technique is effective when a thief uses an authorized station), 3) securing cables and wires connecting service with PCs, and 4) monitoring by network control center staff, watching for missing or added devices.

Using multiple servers not only adds redundancy to a business computer/networking system, it also provides a mechanism for constant network monitoring, so that if a node is removed, an alert or alarm will be triggered. With just one node swapped out from an unsupervised and unsecured area, there is no way to determine if the new server is authentic, since hackers could easily give it the same name and use the same Ethernet cards. No matter what safeguards are taken, there would be no way to prevent this. Thus, not securing a LAN file server is a major mistake that is unfortunately being made at thousands of businesses as this book is being written.

Security in Popular Local Area Networks

This section deals with security features in popular LANs available from Novell, Banyan, Microsoft, and other vendors.

Novell Netware

Novell's Netware is by far the most popular local area network. Netware offers file sharing, print sharing, and host and modem pool access, as well as system monitoring, analysis, and password protection. It supports PC applications and communications for workgroups that would normally require standalone software and hardware. Novell's network operating system or NOS is called Netware; Netware version 3.x works for 250 users, and Netware 4.x supports up to up 1000 users and is a global, distributed, and replicated database of network system resources.

There are an estimated six million local area networks in the U.S. alone, and Netware accounts of about 70 percent of the new local area networks sold.[3] The company provides an online staff of support technicians through CompuServe. Netware has long been regarded as the fastest and most reliable network operating system, but administration has been tedious, by contrast to Banyan's Vines; which has long enjoyed enthusiastic regard by its users, who tout its ease of administration. One aspect of Novell's support infrastructure—the certification of CNA and CNE—has established professional standards for administrators and engineers. But some critics say that Novell has made support overly complex, often making it hard to get information on features (they have an 800/900 number that charges $25 per question for non–product owners). Other popular networks discussed later in this chapter are 3com and various implementations by Microsoft, Ungerman Bass, IBM, and Apple.

Netware 3.x supports the following features:

- *Disk mirroring,* a feature that duplicates all file writes on two separate disk drives. (Using disk mirroring, if one disk fails, the secondary disk switches over automatically.)

- *Disk duplexing,* a feature that not only duplicates a second hard drive but does so on a separate channel simultaneously. (If the original disk fails, the second disk takes over automatically and is not dependent on the primary disk's channel. This provides even greater security than disk mirroring at only the cost of an additional hard drive controller.)

- *Software record locking,* which prevents two or more users from simultaneously using the same file record. This is a standard feature on all serious NOS systems, and is fully supported in DOS. This is a standard feature on all shared LAN systems and all DOS-compatible LANs.

- *Write verification,* which checks the integrity of all data writes to the hard drive

- A *hot fix* is a feature that allows write verification and rewriting of a file to a new location where bad data has been detected.

With a hot fix, if the uninterruptible power supply attached to the file server (or UPS) fails, the monitor will alert the user immediately, and the transaction tracking system will make sure that the communication failure will not result in an incomplete data transaction. Moreoever, the directories from all possible harddrive failitues FAT contains the file addresses. Duplicate copies directory are in separate areas of the hard drive the backup copies are used.

Directory Security Features

Directory verification is a feature that protects all data files from failures resulting from network hardware; it does this by performing consistency checks on the duplicate directory and file allocation tables to verify that they are identical (FATs define file locations and sizes on an entire disk).

These are hardware, not software, features that can't be used without the Netware administration authority and access rights to directories and files in Netware 3.X. Users only view directories and files; when they have been give access rights in Netware 3.X as supervisory, they can change subordinate users read privileges, right privileges, create privileges, modify privileges, file scan privileges access control to grant rights and erase privileges for directories and files. Netware 3.X is installed in many C2 security-type sites (DoD required government trust level).

These are hardware, not software, features that can't be used without the Netware programming instructions access rights to directories and files in Netware 3.x users only view directories and files..when they have access rights in Netware 3.x are supervisory, read privileges, right privileges, create privileges, modify privileges, file scan privileges access control to grant rights and erase privileges for directories and files. Netware 3.x is certified at C2 security (government trust level).

ATTRIBUTES CONTROL

The attributes controllable on files are the following read and write, shared, system, hidden, read audit, no copy, no rename, execute only, for .EXE and .COM files (this prevents any other file extension s from being used to trigger programs) read only, transactional, mark as archive. needed purge on delete, write audit, no delete indexed. The designations are self explanatory and in case of read audit and write audit all read actions and write actions are recorded respectively. Program file attributes are usually read only..and shared the X or execute only attribute..prevents future change of that attribute once set.and programs marked with this designation cannot be backed up or even updated also data file attributes are usually read write, shared, and possible archive needed or transactional.

As an example of how restricting directory access can help solve problems, if users could use software through their menus but not have access to the directory where it resides, companies could cut down on software piracy in their offices.

Directory attributes override access rights and limit a user's ability to access and process in that directory. Directory attributes are DI, H, P, RI, and SY (for no delete, hidden, purge on delete, no rename, and system, respectively) Netware 4.x is an enterprise-oriented LAN NOS that supports multiple remote nodes and the integration of WAN network connections. NDS allows LAN administrators to have easier visibility to users, groups, servers, volumes, directories, computers, and printers, globally. Using a system of objects, properties, and values that is the main advantage over version 3.x, additional security features the ability to support up to a thousand concurrent users. Most large organizations are choosing to adopt Netware or other LAN

NOSs as their global network design strategy. This is quite a change from the day in which IBM's SNA was the primary corporate communication solution.

Security Features for Netware 4.x

1. There is no longer a *bindery;* it has been replaced by the NDS system, which greatly reduces the possibility of compromise.

2. Public-key cryptography has been added to Netware 4.*x*, with every single private-key assign on log on.

3. Write security, which previously existed for users, directories, and files, has now been added for objects and properties. This enables security to be established for entities defined by the system administrators.

4. An audit monitor tracks all system events and maintains secure records.

5. An intruder lock-out is supplied to the entire enterprise LAN.

Other Changes in Netware 4.X

There are minor changes in inherit right mask NW Ad men and the new fire phaser. The new fire phaser now emits a very loud alarm from the designated workstation to call attention to security violations and major critical errors.

The new *Fire Phaser* now emits a very loud alarm from the designated workstation to call attention to security violations and major critical system errors.

Access Control Software

Boot locks protect PC LAN workstations from being booted from either the floppy or the hard drive without users entering the correct password. This feature comes built into Novell DOS version 7.

Screen savers blank the screen so that unauthorized people can't view LAN and PC workstations.

3COM

3Com offers a large-office LAN that is very popular; all models feature standard disk, print, and network resource sharing, complete with multilevel user privileges. Single and multiserver networks can be linked with bridges or routers, or with modem connections.

Password protection is standard, but the new 3Com LAN security architecture (LSA) is designed to allow each hub to act as a management and security node, permitting closed user groups, improved password protection, and automatic disconnection of unauthorized users.

Banyan Servers

The Banyan Vines 6.0 local area network is considered the "gorilla of LANs." It is a high-performance LAN with advanced UNIX-based software operating on a IBM-compatible platform (including on Pentiums). It is the top-selling LAN for networks with over 50 stations, and its UNIX-based peer-to-peer and node-to-node networking makes it a top performer among large multisite enterprise data networks.

Vine's Streetalk naming/addressing system has three parts (username@sitename@org)—just like the Internet naming structure; in fact Banyan has offered their Streetalk search engine to CompuServe and Prodigy—free of charge. Banyan Vines offers server-, organizational-, group-, and user-level security, with comprehensive control over shared resources and gateways, including server-to-server WAN, SNA, and TCP/IP gateways. It has an excellent e-mail system and DOS, UNIX, Windows, and Macintosh user interfaces. Security features prevent anybody but the super-adminstrator to access files that have been hidden by their creators. The password file is encrypted, and administrators can change the password file, but they can't see the old passwords.

The Banyan Vines LAN software product has a unique installation feature, which aids in the installation of a new file server in a multiserver network. When configuring the new server, the installer is asked if it is to be a stand-alone server. Unfortunately, if a user answers "yes," the server will function with no administrator, allowing the very first PC that attaches to that server to become the super-adminstrator (having total user and service administration and access privileges). If this person happens to be a hacker and gives the server a similar or identical name to an existing server, unwitting users might mistakenly begin to store files and programs and send data to attached computers and networks—all of which could be replicated phonies made to look real. The hacker could "spoof" passwords, steal valuable files, and damage or modify other files. The result—temporary or prolonged security violation, possibly causing permanent damage to the company's competitive position.

Lantastic

Lantastic is a small-office, peer-to-peer LAN with advanced security and support for Windows, DOS, and even voice mail. It offers a feature permitting live chat over the LAN cables, and its unique approach allows any station's resources to be either shared or dedicated. So, in some cases, administrators may be able to see everything that a user has saved on his disk and copy it without his knowledge. And of course, with the password of the network administrator, Lantastic will provide complete access to every shared resource, which could be virtually all the PCs in the office.

Windows NT Server

Windows NTS is the high-end product for offices requiring multiple servers and multiprocessing—an easy-to-administer, high-performance server featuring RISC processing and secure network logon; protected by encrypted passwords, secure authentication, and audit features; and meeting level-C2 security (B2 is standard). Often users seem to prefer using the DOS FAT file system mode in NTS servers, which defeats many of the advanced features and benefits. Because of this phenomenon, LAN administrators must make extra efforts to get users adapted to NTS operational mode.

Windows NT

Windows NT is a small high-performance workgroup server for shared applications, offering C2-level security (NCSC per Trusted Computing Base standards). It features secure logon (not displayed).

Carbon Copy and PC Anywhere

These programs allow PC users and Macintosh users to call their PCs from home, performing tasks that might otherwise require them to be at the office. I used to use one of these programs to run a Windows-based application at my office from a laptop at my home. The network design program I ran required lots of memory—which my desktop handled quite nicely. I could never have run this program on my laptop, but my laptop's keyboard controlled my desktop, and my display showed me exactly what was happening on the screen at the office (even if the monitor was off). I could stop the design (or any other) program, start it again, hang up, call back. I could look at files, send output to the printer, and even execute script programs that could auto-dial and make a connection to another computer. I could send and store my new mail, read newsgroup postings, and more.

Needless to say, these programs are very dangerous in the wrong hands. If the right PC were set up with its monitor off, it could serve as a silent burglar in the office. If the hacker obtained administrative passwords, he could inspect, copy, and erase disk files; change user passwords and access attributes—do whatever he wanted to the LAN services and devices. Carbon Copy and PC Anywhere feature password protection, which all office managers should require when this product must be used.

The new version of Carbon Copy (2.0) has many advanced security features that virtually everyone should use—whether doing personal or business computing remotely. The new features include multiple passwords, call-back security, antivirus protection during file transfer, and *GhostScreen* (real screen will be dissapear).

Restricting Access to Cards

Each LAN card, whether Ethernet, token ring, archnet, or another technology, has unique numbers or addresses. Normally, all users on a network can be "filtered" or blocked from attempting to gain access where they aren't permitted. But LAN hackers have ways to get around this.

Sniffing

As the name indicates, LAN hacking is termed "sniffing," where a person attaches a LAN analyzer to loose or exposed LAN cables (using a vampire-type tap or coring a new tap) and looks for valuable data. Sniffing a LAN can take place using hardware or software. Sniffing software can also operate on an attached PC, looking at users, applications, utilization, sometimes without the administrator being able to see it. One underground software package is called "IPX Permissive"; it permits the sniffer to decipher Novell network IP packets without being detected. Here is a list of the places a sniffer could be planted:

1. PC memory
2. PC keyboard memory
3. PC video monitor memory
4. A LAN card or driver software on the PC
5. A LAN cable
6. The network server
7. A peer PC
8. A printer or scanner
9. A host gateway, router, bridge, or anther LAN
10. The WAN
11. The WAN interface connecting the WAN to the LAN
12. The host computer
13. The channel to the host computer (mainframe)
14. The application running on the host[4]

Lockheed installed heavy shielding around its token ring cables at a high security site; both the connector's shielding was equipped with sensors so that disconnection or tampering set off an alarm. The system is not available to the general LAN market.

Protecting the physical premises and properly protecting cables, connectors, taps, jacks, ports, and slots is the best way to minimize the threat of sniffer attacks. Also, encryption of data can prevent sniffers from benefiting from violating a LAN, since busting encrypted data is far out of the budgets of most small-time hackers. Many servers permit encryption of data between nodes, but off-the-shelf Ethernet and token-ring cards are not available with packet encryption at this time (so that packets on the LAN are encrypted transparently and automatically on the LAN cable).

Third-Party Software: LAN Utilities

COTS utility software manages and secures LAN resources, offering utilities and security features including:

1. Access control software
2. Menu systems
3. Data protection and recovery
4. Fault-tolerant processing and networking
5. LAN monitoring, management, and analysis tools

LANs can often provide local and network access to thousands of workers in one campus environment, so it's essential that networks be sufficiently managed and guarded with the proper software and hardware tools.

Maximum LAN Security Procedures

The best way to ensure security is to design a LAN so that it's as far away from trouble sources as possible. If the network has applications, users, and data that are too valuable to risk being compromised, extreme measures may be in order:

- Total disconnection from the Internet
- Complete disconnection from other LANs
- Disabling all access to anonymous ftp, the source of most Internet viruses (or just bar uploads and downloads)
- Tempest cabinets, shielding, and a secured building (anti-Van Eck tapping)
- Comprehensive network management
- Comprehensive physical security procedures
- Firewalls set up between all LAN-attached networks—including other LANs or WANs (including the Internet)
- Use of low-emission media, such as fiber

As a way to maintain as much security as possible on normal LANs, the following test equipment is recommended for all major LAN installations:

- An inductive amp test set to test the amp levels for problems
- A digital voltmeter to detect voltage variations or violations
- An oscilloscope to provide a graphic look at shorts, open circuits, crimps/kinks, and other impedance problems, as well as mismatched cable segments, voltage-level data used to determine attenuation, and signal voltages

- A time-domain reflectometer (TDR) to determine shorts, breaks, taps, and lengths of LAN cable
- An optical TDR, which performs the same function of a TDR, but with fiber cable
- A hand-held cable analyzer and testing device to spot-check for breaks
- A TDR, an oscilloscope, and a printer used together to display waveform reflections from the TDR
- A Mod-TAP Network Analyser NA to detect reverse polarity
- A LAN analyzer, which is a device or PC-based software allowing one to view the LAN traffic online, logged-on users, collisions, line hits, and cable utilization levels.

ENCRYPTION

Who Is
Big Brother?

When we talk about security for telephones, computers, private networks, and the Internet, we're talking about protecting data from interception, alternation, compromise, and destruction. The equipment, time, and personnel required to engage in serious long-term eavesdropping can be quite expensive. The most dangerous spies don't hack unknown dial-up lines found by their *demon dialers*; they target specific organizations, information, and people. You won't typically find a Kevin Mitnik type involved in this class of information warfare; it's reserved for the most powerful threat to security and privacy—*Big Brother*—institutional violations to privacy. When a Big Brother—class eavesdropper decides to violate the privacy of an individual or organization, it's done secretly, comprehensively, and for an extended period of time.

When these spies conduct surveillance, they target a specific subject and are usually looking for specific information. Big Brother—class surveillance operations involve serious money, time, equipment, and personnel. The motives are economic, political, sometimes personal; so it's not in the realm of small-time *phone phreaks, cyber-rebels,* or two-bit *computer nerds.* The Big Brother eavesdropper must be able to separate the targeted communication from the hundreds or thousands of other data messages being tracked, saved, and scanned on the phone, by fax, or on the Internet. Big Brother isn't always the government, and even when it is, his actions aren't necessarily legal. So, who could mount the most serious efforts against your privacy and security? Here are a few examples (not intended in any way to suggest that the parties actually are Big Brother or are involved in anything illegal, just that they have the capabilities and some the historical propensities, for this type of conduct):

1. The federal government
2. Foreign governments
3. State governments
4. Big-city law enforcement (case in point, the LAPD OCID)
5. Organized crime (for instance, Cosa Nostra)
6. Large communications companies
7. Your company's competitor, or hackers working for it
8. Freelance spies, counter spies, double agents; spying independently
9. Colombian drug cartels
10. Terrorist organizations (state sponsored, with political or religious funding, such as the IRA, the PLO, the SLA, violent militias, the KKK, and the Aryan Nations)
11. Individuals with extreme wealth and resources—enough to hire surveillance personnel and put equipment and intelligence apparatus in place

Chapter 07: Encryption: Who Is Big Brother?

Many governments, corporations, even nonprofit organizations possess enormous operating budgets, massive inventories of computer hardware and software, and huge multimillion-dollar espionage budgets. Not only do many large companies have the financial wherewithal and motivation to spy—many (the phone company, computer companies, and so on) also have the surveillance facilities in place—KGB agents had allegedly riddled the American Embassy in Moscow with thousands of bugs while it was still under construction.

AT&T was said to spend over one billion dollars per year to *spy* on its competitors in the late 1980s—and of course that cost was passed on to the American consumer (not all types of corporate "spying" are illegal—when my company offered competitive bids against AT&T, we would often find that my designs and pricing were already matched by AT&T; this was often permitted by law. But sometimes leaks of confidential information caused my employer to lose competitive advantage, and many times, professionals competing against AT&T would feel uncomfortable discussing critical numbers and strategies on the phone).

Industrial spying is illegal, but when nations sponsor spying to steal the trade secrets of other nations, it can affect thousands of jobs and a country's gross national product. American industry has been under constant attack. Large developed countries and developing nations see espionage as a way of helping their economies. It's getting so serious, many are calling for the CIA to increase its efforts to protect U.S. trade secrets, and some are even suggesting that they steal secrets for American industry.

During the 80s, IBM was spied upon by Hitachi, Toshiba, and others; IBM was never caught spying on the Japanese, but like many large companies, it spends big money spying on its own employees, firing or transferring those who date or socialize with competitors or the wrong coworker. Some companies establish unwritten policies about their employees' private activities, hobbies, friends; then they enforce these policies by firing those who don't fit their lifestyle dictums. Employees may be fired for ostensibly unrelated reasons; they often never find out that they have been snooped on. (Many point to conduct like this in explaining why IBM is no longer the "unquestioned" leader in data processing products.)

Unfortunately, while working for companies who want to get into your business, you don't have much defense at work—they can listen to your phone calls, look at your e-mail, and watch everything you do on video cameras. When you leave work, you're supposed to be left alone—but it's not easy to know when you're being snooped on. So the only defense employees have is to work for ethical employers who respect their rights and privacy.

Online Service Scares

In the early 90s, Prodigy was hot because it set trends for slick-looking, easy-to-use graphic user-interfaces. But Prodigy (owned by IBM and Sears) was severely criticized for its poor performance and speed. Prodigy has never been profitable, but its user-friendly approach has attracted a large number of new subscribers. But serious rumors circulated around the Internet about Prodigy uploading private disk information. In 1991, controversy was still brewing over Prodigy's questionable advertising practices and censorship of all postings even mentioning the word "Prodigy." (The service was unwilling to allow users to discuss the e-mail issue after signing a consent decree in Texas, agreeing to stop advertising "fixed rate" service and then charging a surcharge for e-mail.)

Chapter 07: Encryption: Who Is Big Brother?

But after Prodigy's operators thought they had everything under control (people began using code names for Prodigy, such as "*Prodigy" and "P*" and "$P"), in 1991, Prodigy was hit with major subscriber cancellations after being accused of uploading its subscribers' private disk files as they were logged on to Prodigy. The Prodigy user interface for Windows and the Mac (which is still poorly written and slow) uses a file called STAGE.DAT to pre-store screen information. These files increased in size as users continued to use Prodigy, and when old deleted data were found inside of them, rumors spread that Prodigy was using STAGE.DAT to collect private information about its users.

After this controversy had caused much distress and many cancellations, Prodigy hired the national auditing firm of Coopers and Lybrand, who concluded that there was no risk to Prodigy members' data privacy.

Prodigy finally felt compelled to announce that all future releases of user software would include the ability to completely erase all data from the STAGE.DAT and CACHE.DAT area of the hard drive. But they (at this date) have apparently not yet made good on this promise—"STAGE.DAT" is still present on current Prodigy user software.[1]

Mike Goddin, General Council for the Electronic Frontier Foundation, has indicated that in his opinion, there was no widespread practice of snooping by any of the online services, because the cost of implementing and maintaining mass storage facilities and computer-based scanning of user disk data would be preventive. He didn't rule out major problems with individual employees. Throughout the entire scandal and investigations, there were no reports of Prodigy violating private e-mail messages.[2]

But after my own personal experience with e-mail on America Online, I realized that there was strong evidence that e-mail violation was a widespread practice. I knew first hand about the impact of compromised confidential information. But I never fully appreciated how e-mail tampering and viral contamination could create distrust in business. My editor was effectively shut down until she booted up with a CD version of the Macintosh operating system.

The experience left me convinced that security and privacy were sadly lacking in cyberspace; I realized that encryption could help toward that cause. How could anybody be sure about who was doing what online, and could there be accountability? But before we talk about solutions, let's talk more about specific threats from the most dangerous Big Brother—surveillance from government.

Government as Big Brother

Nobody doubts what type of surveillance that governments can impose on their people. But few people realize how widespread surveillance has been, and how little regard government leaders, officials, or agents have had for American rights and the Constitution. Overreaching by government seem to be getting worse since Watergate, not better. Here is a summary of the dark chapters in the last 70 years of federal law enforcement:

- From 1917 to 1975, widespread spying on hundreds of thousands of U.S. citizens: the FBI, the CIA, and military intelligence kept thousands of dossiers, paid thousands of informants.
- In the 1960s, Army Intelligence used thousands of troops and U-2 and SR-71 spy planes to spy on Martin Luther King Jr. and other civilians (not legal for armed forces intelligence).[3]
- It's now known that the investigations of the JFK, RFK, and MLK assassinations were less than thorough, and that the FBI destroyed or lost critical evidence in these cases.

Chapter 07: Encryption: Who Is Big Brother?

- Let's not forget that former FBI Director, J. Edgar Hoover was allegedly blackmailed by the Mob as a child molester and homosexual and so ignored them and vented his wrath on Black people, Jews, those suspected of being gay; it was said that he contrived the Red scare with Joe McCarthy as a power-mad scheme to eavesdrop and censor free speech. Hoover's name is still on the FBI Building in Washington, but he actually crushed the Constitution.

- Consider the three decade—long failure in the interdiction of drug trafficking: rumors of certain high-level officials and agencies benefiting and even aiding cocaine trafficking; most people ignored Michael Levine (the former DEA official and author of *The Great White Lie*), who claims that higher-ups in the federal government were behind the failure of the war on drugs, a charge lent credence by the June 1995 indictment of four top U.S. Justice Department officials accused of working with the drug cartel, some of whom have worked directly for attorney generals in the past. What are citizens to make of this behavior?

- The Inslaw software theft was said to involve the U.S. Justice Department and may have led to the death of the reporter who had apparently just cracked the case. A congressional committee concluded that Justice Department officials were responsible, but nobody has been prosecuted, and former Attorneys General Barr, Smith, and Edwin Meece (the only attorney general to be indicted three times) were said to have benefited.[4]

- Recently, former top Justice Department official Webster Hubble (under Clinton) is awaiting sentencing, and there's still no answer to the question, "Has the Inslaw Promise software been modified to track law-abiding dissenters? Is Big Brother online?"

- At this time of record distrust—the FBI wants access to everybody's e-mail.

Privacy and security are very much related, and recent government and corporate breaches have caused many people to question whether there is privacy on the Internet. There is, however, a technology that—although simple to use—is extremely effective in providing privacy in voice, data, and image communications. The science is called *cryptography*, and the process, *encryption.*

Encryption: the Most Complex Combination Lock in the Universe

Encryption is the calculated rearrangement of data communications messages to render the real message unintelligible or un-meaningful until it's been decoded. The best encryption is implemented with complex algorithmic formulas that use a key to decode the cyphertext.

There are two basic types of encryption technology recognized in computers and telecommunications: *private-key* and *public-key* encryption.

Private-Key Encryption

The first form of encryption is private-key cryptography, used by the federal government and the NSA in the establishment of the DES standard, Triple-DES, RC2, RC4, IDEA, and the Skipjack algorithms. Private-key encryption encodes and decodes data with the same secret key. Some techniques are designed for civilian data, and others, for military communications. For private-key encryption to be efficient, it requires a single key to be present at both sender and receiver sides, where algorithmically encrypted programs use the secret key to both encrypt and decrypt the messages. The secret key can be changed with mutual cooperation between encryption devices; some of which can change keys frequently and randomly, making the decoding of data much more difficult.

Problems with Private-Key Encryption

Private-key cryptography has been

An Example of Private-Key Encryption

Plaintext:
The rain in Spain falls mainly on the plain.
If were you use printable characters, the same message concerted to ciphertext might look like this:
Ciphertext:
dk13k2+3k2j_)%yj;12l3k4j1;23 j31i);a—00#s%5%43-@k

heavily used in military, aerospace, intelligence, and finance because of the need for tight security. Private-key systems have several serious problems, however.

First, there is a major problem with key management and distribution. You can't use e-mail because you can't encrypt until the key is distributed. Next, there is the fact that more than one person must have the key. Finally, if several people each have different private-key pairs for the same recipient, that recipient must use separate keys for each different person. So sending e-mail to just one department, a person might be forced to distribute and maintain twenty secret keys, certainly not simple.

But perhaps the most serious problem with private-key encryption is how relatively easy it is to break the cypher when one discovers the key. Because the same secret key is used to both code and decode—private-key encryption algorithms possess intrinsic weaknesses that yield to faster and more efficient brute-force attacks. This is how they differ from public-key encryption (explained later in this chapter).

DES

The most widely used private-key algorithm is DES (data encryption standard, for commercial use). The DES encryption algorithm is adequate, but because it relies heavily on the secrecy of the key, not the strength of the algorithm, there have been concerns about its toughness. Scientists calculated the time required to bust a DES message, and they concluded that a 10 million-dollar computer could bust any DES message in 21 minutes. With a lot more time and a regular-speed computer, you can still bust a DES message.

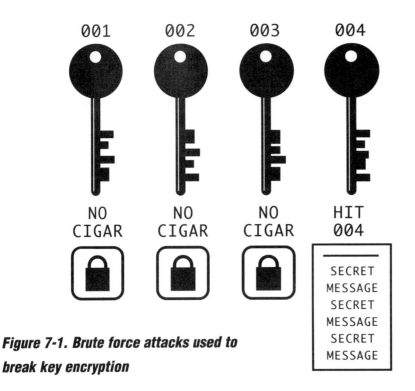

Figure 7-1. Brute force attacks used to break key encryption

Busting DES Keys

Computer	Encryptions/Sec	Years to Crack
Macintosh Quadra	23,200	98,488
1000 Macintosh Quadras	23,200,000	98.5
Power Macintosh 8100	100,000	22,652
1000 Power Macs	1,000,000,000	22.7
PC in Year 2000	1,600,000	1,415
Network of Computers	3,200,000,000	Less than 1[5]

PUBLIC-KEY ENCRYPTION

The second type of encryption is called public-key encryption. Public-key encryption has revolutionized the field of cryptography, because it generates two keys—a private key and a public key. The public has full access to the public key and can *only* send messages to the key's owner. The private key is then used by the owner to decrypt the messages being sent to him using the public key. In order for the owner of a public-key encryption program to send encrypted messages back to the senders, they must provide him with their individual public keys so that he can properly encrypt them. Many people specify on their business cards where their public keys are stored, just as folks are now putting their e-mail addresses there.

Because public-key encryption algorithms encrypt with one key (public) and decrypt with another, they are more secure than private-key encryption algorithms. Because of a mathematical function termed "hashing", neither knowledge of the public key nor access to a decrypted message helps the hacker bust the algorithm used to encrypt—at least not by using brute force key attacks to bust encryption keys. Public-key encryption, as a result, offers significant protection against brute-force attacks.

Phil Zimmermann and PGP

Phil Zimmermann was a civil libertarian and programmer who was inspired by the challenge presented free speech given the government's proposals for eavesdropping in the S.266 Anti-Crime Bill (called the "wiretap ready" bill). Zimmermann realized that private-key encryption wasn't feasible for regular people, so he decided to use a little programming talent to solve a big problem.

In 1991, Zimmermann decided to create a program that would make extremely good encryption available "to the masses." He took existing, working, and test algorithms and integrated them into a PC program, and PGP version 1.0 was born. In the fall of 1992, other programmers took the source code (which, like the program, was available free on many boards) and added nice features for ease of use and authentication features. The resulting program was Pretty Good Privacy versions 2.0 and 3.0.[6]

How to Use PGP

PGP is extremely strong encryption, strong enough to protect data against most "brute force attacks" (normally only achievable by state-sponsored hackers). PGP uses the IDEA, RSA, and MD5 algorithms and features the ability to assure—through software—confidentiality (anonymity), data origin authentication (via digital signature), message integrity, and nonrepudiation of origin. PGP permits the user to determine what level of security he wants (by letting the user determine how long the encryption key will be—384 bits, 512 bits, or 1024 bits. These are casual, commercial, and military grades of security.

Figure 7-2 sketches the stages in PGP encryption. As the figure shows, PGP will also compress data before it encrypts (it can't effectively compress encrypted data since it removes repetitive characters).

PGP allows users to both encrypt and sign(with a digital signature), all of their computer's data and program files. If a file isn't text, PGP will automatically treat it as a binary file. It also has the capability of segmenting messages for e-mail and reassembling them automatically upon receipt (where message sizes are limited).

PGP actually combines private-key and public-key cryptography by first creating a random session key for virtually each message and then using a private-key IDEA algorithm to encrypt that message with the session-level key. PGP then uses the RSA algorithm to encrypt the session key with the receiver's public key. Finally PGP bundles the encrypted message and the session key in the same file for mailing.

To send an encrypted message using PGP is easy; all you have to do is find the program (which is widely available on online services, newsgroups, and ftp sites) and install it. Once it's installed, you create your digital signature

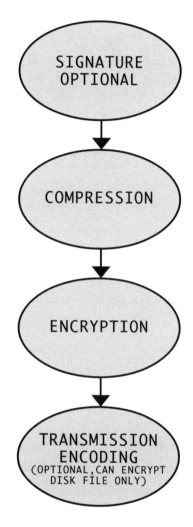

Figure 7-2. Steps in PGP encryption

and your public key. Then you can test the program by sending mail to yourself immediately using your own public key (just as another user would do when sending messages to you). Finally, you can decrypt the same mail using your private key.

Encrypting Disk Files

No matter who may steal your PC or your disk drive, you can provide strong protection for your data by encrypting all files you save. Of course, for maximum protection of your data, you should refrain from putting any data file on your hard drive, but save floppies only! (Then lock up those floppy disks in a secure storage vault in a secure area.)

But if you do put data on hard drives, encryption protects them just as it would protect transmitted data captured en route. If you create a batch file that automatically encrypts new files saved to a specific directory (or Windows 95 folder) , you can set PGP to delete the source files after creating encrypted copies. On your Macintosh, you can do the same thing. It's important to remember to use a "wipe" program (as in Norton Utilities for the PC or the Macintosh) to remove all the bits remaining from deleted files (or use the ERASE command if no disk "wipe" program is available).

Creating a Digital Signature With PGP
Pick your RSA key size:
1) 512 bits- Low commercial grade, fast but less secure
2) 768 bits- High commercial grade, medium speed, good security
3) 1024 bits- "Military" grade, slow, highest security

Choose 1, 2, or 3, or enter desired number of bits: **3**

Generating an RSA key with a 1024-bit modulus.

You need a user ID for your public-key. The desired form for this user ID is your name, followed by your E-mail address enclosed in <angle brackets>, if you have an E-mail address.

For example: John Q. Smith <12345.6789@compuserve.com>

Enter a user ID for your public-key:

<apexapex@aol.com>

You need a pass phrase to protect your RSA secret key.

Your pass phrase can be any sentence or phrase and may have many words, spaces, punctuation, or any other printable characters.

Enter pass phrase: **kodakbrownie**

Note that key generation is a lengthy process.

We need to generate 919 random bits. This is done by measuring the time intervals between your keystrokes. Please enter some random text on your keyboard until you hear the beep:

 0 * -Enough, thank you.

..............++++ ....++++

Key generation completed.

Public-Key Distribution and Key Certification

Once you've created a digital signature and certified yourself, you must perform PGP key certification for your public key ring. Distribution of public keys is unlike distribution of private keys, in that public keys can be openly posted on a BBS or freely e-mailed to the recipient, making distribution less of an extreme burden on the system or key administrator. Seeing the public key will not help the hacker get your data; he must have the private key—but unless you provide it, others don't have access to it.

As previously stated, it's a good idea to indicate how to obtain your public key on your business card, right underneath your e-mail address. You can tell contacts to request your public key via e-mail, or list the BBS or ftp location where they can obtain it. Here's an example of a cyberspace business card:

> HOWARD GROUP CONSULTING
> Network Design, Implementation,
> Business Automation, and Security
> 8306 Wilshire Blvd Suite #6033
> Beverly Hills CA 90211
> HTTP://www.wavenet.com/~HowardGRP
> Request public key at above address.

The distribution of keys is not a security challenge like private-key distribution, because public-key encryption doesn't allow anyone except the owner of the key (who is always the recipient of data encrypted using his or her public key). To give a public key to a user who wants to send mail to you, you must assign it to his specific Internet address (or other e-mail address) and then assign a level of trust to that person. The person must then have a digital signature, which is required for him to use your key and send encrypted mail to you. Verification of another's PGP key, to ensure that messages actually come from the person himself and not an impostor, is accomplished through a concept termed a *web of trust* (not to be confused with the World Wide Web).

You know a person's public key is actually valid either by personal acquaintance or via someone you already trust. When you introduce someone you trust to your friend Sally, she then can trust that your friend's public key is valid. Level of trust is calculated by PGP based on a very sophisticated system that uses user-configurable parameters. Figure 7-3 shows an example of how this web of trust works:

An Example of a Digital Signature

PGP produces a digital signature by asking the user to enter keystrokes and then using the time interval between the keystrokes to generate random numbers, which are in turn used to calculate a unique digital signature. This signature is then applied to a file (not simply appended), and value of the file is then used to produce a unique digital signature.

TO: GARRY HOWARD
FROM: NOEL HARRISON
SUBJECT: RAIN
MESSAGE: The rain in Spain falls mainly on the plain.
-GARRY
u xP
P"H–úß_2:ß_`_–ü_°PWÉÿø((___„_ÿÿÿØ'Nu zy !D_.YO!O_ !!____$ _f_Lp_(-!D_$Nu%_%Mêÿú"ü__BVBnÿö-k_Jÿü-k_Jÿø0_°k__IJ nÿü"nÿø±Ég

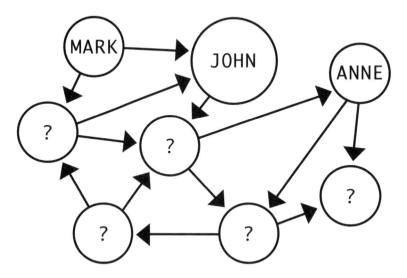

Figure 7-3. PGP web of trust

You can assign users complete trust or partial trust. You also can assign keys to unknown parties, but these keys must be certified by either yourself or two partially trusted key holders.

So, in the above example, key holders A and B could certify unknown signatory I together, but not individually. In the case of unknown signatories K and L, your trusted key-holder D would be able to certify by himself without the knowledge of the owner of the public key (you).

Preventing Forgeries through Validity and Trust

In cyberspace, you don't see who is really on the other end—just texts, images, sounds, and sometimes video. PGP uses key-owner and key-holder assigned "validity" to assure a person's identity. Trust is assigned a person whose honesty and judgment can be relied upon to assign keys. Both these characteristics are used in assessing the holder of your public key. If somebody wanted to forge President Bill Clinton's e-mail by creating a public key with his name, it would be easy using PGP. But this person would have to be certified—he can either validate or assign trust or do both— by the owner (or trusted key holders) in order for his e-mail to be recognized as really belonging to President Bill Clinton. In the above diagram, the person named Bill

An Example of a Fingerprint

Key for user ID: Barry's Books
<bbook@Barry.com>
512-bit key, key ID 43744F09, created
1994/07/07
Key fingerprint =24 38 1A 58 46 AD CC 2D
AB C9 E0 F1 C7 3C 76 EC
This key/userID association is not certified.
Do you want to certify this key yourself?
(y/N)?

Clinton wishing to send mail to the owner of the public key would have a key (let's say key "I") be certified by that owner, another, by a trusted owner or by two partially trusted owners. Then his key would be placed on the owner's key ring. When PGP certifies a key for another user, it prints a fingerprint (not the key but an MD5 message digest). This fingerprint is a set of digits that can be printed on a business card so that the person needing to verify that your digital signature is from you can compare the number on the card with the fingerprint number displayed by any PGP -signed file from that person.

How Many Years to Bust a Secret Key

To break a 128-bit key, experts say that "there simply is not enough time before the sun explodes to crack an IDEA-encrypted message." With PGP's ability to use 1024-bit keys, an entire organization of people equipped with massive computer systems would be required just to break *one* message. So, the economies of time, people, and effort would make it very unfeasible for a Big Brother agent to even think about cracking such a message. In April 1994, with over 600 volunteers engaged, 1600 computers were used to break a 128-bit key—encrypted message. They were successful; in less than one month they had cracked the key for one message. The good news is, PGP uses 1024-bit keys backed up by a session key, so that every new message is encrypted by a different key.

Public-Key Revocation

When you don't want to receive e-mail or any messages from a person who has one of your public keys, simply revoke his key on your key ring, and he won't be able to send encrypted messages to you any more—the messages will be automatically rejected.

PEM

Privacy Enhanced Mail is a standard developed to send mail and have it encrypted automatically. The standard defines user certification through digital signature and encryption and is offered in several new e-mail packages (including Apple Computer's e-mail package).

PEM is excellent for organizations and allows users to send mail quickly and easily that has the weight of a legal document, permitting users to sign e-mail messages with their digital signatures just like real signatures. Key distribution is slightly different but still public-key; it allows key revocation by owner and different levels of security. But PEM does not permit sending anonymous mail, nor is it good for sending mail to anonymous remailers.

Clipper PR Campaign Runs Aground

The FBI has claimed that they worry about outlaws using cryptography to send and receive unreadable secret communications. The FBI "wiretap ready" law passed in late 1994 (with no public hearings, and with many in Congress out of town, it was passed by unanimous consent and President Clinton quickly signed it into law), despite the fact that big computer and telecommunication hardware manufacturers opposed it. Consumer advocates condemned it and blasted the government's allegedly underestimated figures on what the measure would cost taxpayers.

FBI Director Freeh and his cybercop division launched a nationwide public relations campaign for something equal to complete Orwellian tyranny. They advocated something even more dangerous than their successful "wiretap ready" campaign. Not only did they want the capability to examine, analyze, and store everybody's e-mail, data communications, and faxes, they wanted to prevent citizens from fully securing their communications. In 1993 and 1994, FBI proposed the "Clipper Chip" program, a program in which everybody who was a "good citizen" would voluntarily use their (possibly weak) encryption chip, called "Clipper," to pass sensitive data, rather than use any number of better tested commercial and shareware software programs offering encryption.

Government-proof cryptography is now apparently the unofficial target of the FBI, which has claimed that non-Clipper technology could render some criminal investigations "impossible," according to sources at FLETC (Federal Law Enforcement Training Center).[7] But entrepreneurs and businesses who use the Internet overwhelmingly agree that cryptography is absolutely necessary for privacy in a networked environment, and that its absence will threaten both busi-

Within the U.S., patent rights to public-key encryption are jealously guarded by RSA Data Security, a private firm that licensed the patents from their inventors. Although software employing public-key algorithms has been widely published, most people outside the U.S. government cannot use it without risking an infringement suit.

ness and the growth of cyber-commerce. Business on the Internet could conceivably provide hundreds of billions to the U.S. economy in less than two decades.

Businesses, of course, need cryptography for transmitting sensitive financial and other confidential data, but the other market for cryptography is the millions of regular citizens who use electronic mail. Cryptographer Bruce Schneier has said, "Without encryption, e-mail is no more secure than a postcard." Schneier is the author of *E-mail Security: How to Keep Your Electronic Messages Private*, and *Applied Cryptography.*[8]

The Fight for Control of the Internet

The Internet is like a huge mesh of interconnected servers and computers. Attached users are normally dial-up clients or connected via a LAN (local area network). Every day on the Internet, hundreds of time-sharing services, private corporations, and citizens pass hundreds of millions of e-mail messages from one machine to another on the Internet, and an amazing number of computers and people in the middle can read the data as they pass their location.

Computers and networks are extremely vulnerable to break-ins, and stolen passwords are one of the most common keys for the violator. Some companies declare that they don't need cryptography—the expense or the bother.

But Internet users who want to send messages to business associates, physicians, attorneys, accountants, and lovers are adamant about privacy, and the threat of government intrusion has converted ordinary citizens into privacy advocates.

The FBI began communicating two different messages: On one side—they say they support privacy:

"We are totally, enthusiastically supportive of encryption technology for the public"—Jim Kallstrom, the FBI special agent in charge of the Special Operations Division in the New York office.[9]

But Kallstrom then contradicts himself, using language and emotional appeals not linked to constitutional law enforcement practices or successful practices of the past. Kallstrom is seen by many as using McCarthy-type demagogic tactics:

"We merely think that criminals, terrorists, child abductors, perverts, and bombers should not have an environment free from law enforcement or a search warrant. I think most victims of crime agree."[10]

Kallstrom joined the nationwide campaign to support the passage of the "wiretap ready" law and the Clipper Chip proposal—a proposal that would allow police access to all confidential data, voice, and imaging—while still preserving citizen's privacy. Neither he nor anybody supporting Clipper has explained why surveillance is so important, since the number of FBI wiretaps were way up, but resulting convictions, way down.

I participated in an online conference where FBI Special Agent Kallstrom was repeatedly asked, "What will prevent hackers and criminals from using software encryption, or from encrypting data so that it appears not to be encrypted?" He systematically ignored my questions and told other curious attendees that if the public was concerned about law enforcement abusing the Clipper Chip, they should just trust the FBI. He assured concerned attendees that the honest bureaucrats would turn in dishonest law enforcement abusing Clipper, and that they should just trust the FBI.[11]

The FBI had effortlessly enlisted President Clinton into supporting and signing the "wiretap ready" legislation, and with the heavy lobbying by the FBI Director Freeh, Congress passed the 1994 Digital Telephony Act, which requires future telecommunications systems to be "software compatible" for on-demand, push-button, remotely accessible and controllable wiretaps. But Congress—responding to citizen protest that was all but ignored by the White House—began resisting the Clipper Chip proposal in 1992 and 1993, so Vice President Gore issued some confused statements signaling White House backpedaling on Clipper. FBI Director Luis Freeh seemed now to be on his own; with no more big guns backing the Clipper Chip-ship, he seemed more determined than ever to impose it on America.[12]

The Electronic Privacy Information Center's Marc Rotenberg says that the Clipper program would make the Internet an "Information Snooperhighway."[13]

Besides encryption, another trend that gives folks in the FBI bad dreams is anonymous remailers—services that forward e-mail after converting the return addresses to pseudonyms—making the communication essentially untraceable, and if the sender would, anonymous. Many anonymous mailers are in Finland, well out of the reach of American jurisdiction and FBI cybercops, and because pornography laws differ in some countries (the age of majority is 16 in England, but 21 in America—remember the major legal confusion with American porn star Tracie Lords?)

If Clipper were successfully imposed on America, how would it work?

The Clipper Chip: Encryption or Invasion in Disguise?

By pushing the Clipper proposal so hard, the federal government exposed its deep respect for the power of encryption as a means of providing secure transmissions over the telecommunications facilities of America. It recently proposed a new and exciting way to rape every American online of every bit of privacy they may want to have using e-mail; yes—the government wanted the ability to read, see, and hear everything you might send over the Information Superhighway—even things that had to be absolutely, completely kept private.

The entire computer and telecommunications industry gave the Clipper Chip proposal freeze treatment and provoked the biggest mass protest witnessed in cyberspace. The FBI assured everyone in American private and business life that they could voluntarily adopt an unproved standard (initially) and trust that the FBI would never abuse its ability to "back door" the encryption—essentially permitting them to read any person's e-mail, file transfers, voice conversations, faxes, whatever. But there were justifiable concerns; the FBI had already crossed a long-existing boundary separating the phone company from law enforcement. The Clipper proposals would now give the FBI the ultimate power to simulate omnipotence—enabling it—if in the wrong hands—to illegally eavesdrop on law-abiding Americans. With regular letter-mail, citizens at least had assurance of privacy in the contents—Clipper Chips would remove this forever from cyberspace.

What harm could the Clipper standard have caused? Wasn't it just the government trying to catch terrorists, bombers, and child molesters? Statistics indicated that despite hundreds more wiretaps, surveillance didn't seem to assist in recent arrests. In addition to citing the past failures and improprieties of the federal government, experts were talking about major technological and industry problems with Clipper.

Big Brother Key or Private Escrow Key?

The special type of private-key encryption called an *escrow key,* (outlined in Figure 7-4) is the defining characteristic of Clipper. It makes two parties in the government the second holders of the secret key, so that no matter what access hackers had to one system or the other, they would never have the unencrypted key in their disks or memory. It's anticipated that Microsoft will use this technique to provide encryption security for the Microsoft NT Server.

A secret algorithm developed by the National Security Agency for civilian use, the Skipjack algorithm is at the heart of the NSA's Clipper Chip, the chip-

CLIPPER CHIP USES KEY ESCROW

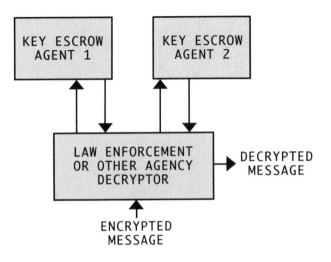

Figure 7-4. The key escrow systemSkipjack

based encryption standard the government insists is "voluntary." Standards for government access would cover voice, data, and image communications. Skipjack utilizes an 80-bit key, so it would take a supercomputer brute-force attack up to ten years to try all the combinations. Skipjack's algorithm is said to be secure, but information encrypted with Clipper Chips would be neither secure nor private; parties using the Clipper Chip would be forced to trust law enforcement officials. Armed "with court-ordered wiretaps" to decrypt messages, they could see any Clipper-transmission they wanted, since a record of every Clipper-user's key would be kept in government databases. And of course, the government insists that because of two separate parties, the law enforcement side and the escrow agent—citizens' rights would be protected. But one of the major fears was, what if other back doors existed and the wrong parties got possession of them? Many such fears arose, but some theorists claimed that Clipper—rather than obstructing the progress of the industry and the free flow of information—would be crushed by economic and technological realities.[14]

A Prediction of Clipper's Failure

Research Associate Michael Schrage of the Massachusetts Institute of Technology published one of the most critical yet relevant articles about Clipper, not just its technological challenges, but what is actually happening in the computer market—a market that has many millions of honest and dishonest users.

Privacy and the Clipper Chip

Michael Schrage, from his article titled, Why the Clipper's Not Likely to ship Away at Privacy, states:

> ....Put the vital issues of privacy and civil liberties aside, however, and, on purely pragmatic terms, the Clipper initiative .... seems destined to produce exactly the opposite effect of what was intended. Instead of creating an encryption standard that gives the government a fighting chance for successful eavesdropping, the feds have encouraged the creation of an encryption market to bypass the threat of government decryption......[15]

The points made are extremely convincing, moreover the FBI never effectively addressed technical questions surrounding conformity and enforcement of the Clipper Standard—they continued to link their demands to preventing acts of terrorism, child molestation, and kidnapping (which weren't statistically relevant to the discussion).

One of the major areas the FBI avoided discussion: there is almost an infinite number of ways to encode and encrypt data—from enveloping very small amounts of data within large data sets filled with garbage to encapsulating data within graphic images to conceal the fact that data was being transmitted. The FBI wouldn't even explain how it would prevent people from using software encryption before subjecting it to Clipper. Nobody from the ranks of the FBI seemed to have a clue of understanding about what implementing the Clipper proposals would involve. Steward A. Baker was the closest the Clipper Chip had to a thinking ally, and Wired Magazine gave him an opportunity to defend Clipper (which had already been broken and found to have an unknown back-door).[16]

Stewart A. Baker, is the chief counsel for the National Security Agency (NSA's top lawyer) and supports the Clipper Initiative. He worked as Deputy General Counsel of the Education Department under President Jimmy Carter. In the Wired Magazine article, he attempted to refute what he terms "seven myths of key escrow encryption." He contended that key escrow encryption would not create a "brave new world of government intrusion into the privacy of Americans", that "Unreadable encryption" (unreadibly only by law enforcement) wasn't "the key to our future liberty", that encryption was not "the key to preserving privacy in a digital world", that key escrow would work—that there was not a secret plan to make key escrow encryption mandatory, that the federal government was not interfering with the free market by forcing key escrow on the private sector, that the National Security Agency was NOT a spy agency, and that the Clipper initiative was NOT "studied in secret and implemented without any opportunity for industry or the public to be heard"......[17]

Unsurprisingly, Backer's attempt to reassure America raised even more criticism by the above response, but it was one of the few intellectual responses by anybody in the federal government. Much of the online world considered Baker's assurances tantamount to a Fox giving assurances to chickens. But when Baker began to suggest that foreign governments also adopt "clipper-like" proposals, he triggered even more ire from cyber-civil libertarians and the multi-billion dollar telecommunications equipment industry. They claimed that wiretap ready Central Office and long distance switches, transmission systems, cellular, pager, cable systems and even operator headsets would be impossible to sell to foreign countries, particularly Europe, where they had already put legal protection on electronic privacy rights. This was not only one of America's largest industries, it was one where we had key advantages—advantages which might be completely undermined if foreign governments barred U.S. wiretappable equipment from their countries.

In a critical analysis of NSA's proposals, Marc Rotenberg, Director Electronic Privacy Information Center states:

"Stewart Baker...backed the biggest obstacle to free-flow on the Internet to date, the agency's own clipper chip. That proposal, if left unopposed, could have shut down private communications on the Internet....

Now the Europeans are trying to put some force into their privacy laws—a step our country should have taken a long time ago — and Baker cries foul....

If the "free flow of information" is now code for helping the National Security Agency monitor private communications, it is time to reconsider our national priorities."

Is the Government the Biggest Threat?

The FBI assumed everybody would discontinue the already widespread use of non-Clipper encryption (which many companies, like RSA Security and Lotus have integrated into their products), and even though the Clipper Chip program had initial flaws that would allow both government and nongovernment (such as foreign spies) agents to tap phones without authorization, they wouldn't explain to the public how security and privacy could be assured. If the Clipper program were adopted, encryption companies could no longer truly certify their products, (since the government wouldn't expose the algorithms for scientific scrutiny, leaving open the possibility, which proved true, that hackers could break the code and steal information from anybody who relied upon the government's ridiculous promise).

The potential result of Clipper standard, according to just about all the computer and telecommunication industry specialists, would be a possibly major widespread loss security for all business and personal voice, data, and fax communication. This is the great fear of industry if the Clipper Chip algorithm turns out to be weaker than the NSA says it is. It has been speculated that former CIA-spy Aldridge Aims has already sold the secrets of Clipper Chip to foreign powers. Spy Johnathan Walker is known to have sold many cyphers to the Soviets. At the very least, critics say, a lost in public confidence would slow or even shut down the growth of the Information Superhighway. If this actually were the case, it would threaten both national security and our economy and affect us emotionally, since confidential information can be used to hurt people deeply. I have consulted in the computer/telecommunications field for about 20 years, and not only have I found the whole Clipper Chip proposal preposterous, but I was outraged to find out that all the money from drug seizures was spent on the stalled proposal. But backers would spend even more before they were done—not promoting the Clipper—but punishing its foes.

Even after one man broke the Clipper Skipjack algorithm (working with NSA), the NSA would not give the scientific community a look at the algorithm. Clinton initially got behind Freeh and the Clipper bandwagon. But a program had already been made available that provided "public-key" based encryption, based on technology that was extremely well tested. One program, called PGP, was written by Phil Zimmermann and distributed by another privacy advocate on hundreds of BBSes across the nation. The existence and availability of PGP alone completely eliminated the government's ability to put forth the argument that they could impose a standard of insecure encryption on a concerned business, technical, and financial community. The FBI was (obviously) outraged, and decided to persecute the developer, Phil Zimmermann, who wasn't accused of violating the law, only of developing software the FBI loathed.[18]

Two days after *MicroTimes* writer Jim Warren editorialized about the Zimmermann case (in the February 1995 San Jose Mercury News), two FBI agents paid him a visit. The agents "asked" for an interview, and refused to let writer Warren tape-record it. Now, Jim Warren is expecting a San Jose grand jury to slap a gag order on him, preventing any further articles on this topic. In 1994, the president of RSA Security, a private firm providing encryption (non-Clipper) for products like Lotus Notes, received death threats (allegedly from the FBI) when he publicly blasted the government's attempt to force citizens to tolerate major compromises to their personal and business security.

Conclusion: the Future of Security in Cyberspace

With so many recent revelations about past FBI, CIA, DEA, and ATF misdeeds, and so many officials being indicted and imprisoned, America has an opportunity to assess the trustworthiness of those who want to stand as sentries on the Information Superhighway.

If the criminal conduct is determined to be widespread, then even President Clinton's sympathetic claims that federal officers were not ". . . some sort of armed bureaucracy acting on private grudges and hidden agendas . . ." won't give much reassurance to citizens concerned about privacy and security. With the recent "wiretap ready," and antiterrorist laws giving federal law enforcement unprecedented powers, how ironic that they would almost simultaneously be subjected to unprecedented negative publicity, allegations of widespread misconduct, and public outrage.

Just to make matters more interesting—out of the blue—House Speaker Newt Gingrich came out opposing the Exon amendment, indicating that it not only threatened the current free state of the Internet but also the First Amendment. There's more debate on the media than ever before, and because many media folk are online; it seems they are sensing the importance of what is facing the nation. Web sites never before displaying photographic material are posting nude pictures in protest. Electronic petitions are being bounced all over cyberspace, collecting the names of Americans preparing for the battle—the battle for freedom, privacy, and security in cyberspace. Meanwhile hundreds of thousands of people are signing onto the Internet, foolishly thinking that their e-mail and data files are secure, and that their freedom will be protected in cyberspace.

Who will win the battle for control of cyberspace? Will it be the Washington bureaucrats, law enforcement, and the President—or the free citizens of America? Will the Constitution be abandoned in cyberspace? It looks like quite a battle is about to begin, perhaps even a second American Revolution in cyberspace. However the battle turns out, I hope that this book will help Internet, phone, and computer users communicate with more privacy and security.

I ponder the big question—will the American consumer; notorious for demanding *faster and better*—demand encryption? If so, the irresistible law of supply and demand will determine the victor in the *War of Cyber-Security*, and it will also encourage software companies to integrate strong encryption (transparently) within every operating system, application program, and communications package of the future. There are strong indications that this process has already begun.

NOTES

Chapter 1

1   Nicholas Baran, *Inside the Information Superhighway*, Coriolis Group Books, Scottsdale, 1995 pp. 1-3

2   Adam Engst, Internet Starter Kit for Macintosh, Hayden Books, Indianapolis, 1995, pp. 16-17

3   ABC News, April 9, 1995

4   ABC News, September 28, 1995

5   Winn Schwartau, *Information Warfare*, Thunder's Mouth Press, N.Y. 1994, p.15

6   Bruce Sterling, *The Hacker Crackdown*, Bantom Books, , N.Y. 1992, pp. 147-178

7   Glamour, Nov. 91, Abstacts; "Is your computer spying on you?", Mark Fiefer.

8   ABC News, March 16, 1995

9   Daryl F. Gates and Diane K. Shah, Chief, Bantam Books, N.Y., 1993, pp. 266, 327

10 L.A. Times, Nov. 16, 1994, March 19, 1995.

11 Simson Garfinkel, *PGP Pretty Good Privacy*, O'Reilly & Associates, Inc. Sebastopol, 1995, pp. 123-127

12 Winn Schwartau, *Information Warfare*, Thunder's Mouth Press, N.Y. 1994, p.15

13 Richard H. Baker, *Network Security*, McGraw-Hill, Inc. N.Y.,1995, pp. 17, 156

14 L.A. Times November 6, 1994

15 Wired, *The Inslaw Octopus Part I and II*, May, 3, 1994, Richard Fricker, downloaded from Wired Online.

16 Ibid

Chapter 2

1   LA Times Feb 26, 1995

2   U.S. Constitution, Excerpt from First Amendment.

3   Michael Levine, Book of Names, Introduction

4   Jwarren@well.com

5   Richard H. Baker, *Network Security*, McGraw-Hill, Inc. N.Y.,1995, p. 304

6   L.A. Times, March 7, 1995

7   Taken from American Online Guidelines

8   Personal Unscientific Survey of Compuserve, AOL and Prodigy (from 1/95 to 5/94)

9   US v LaMaccia, No. 94-10092 -RGS (D.Mass 1994)

10 Ibid

11 U.S. News and World Report, Jan 23, 1995, *Policing Cyberspace*, pp. 58-59

12 Richard H. Baker, *Network Security*, McGraw-Hill, Inc. N.Y.,1995, pp. 282-284

13 Lance Rose; *Netlaw*, Osborne, McGraw-Hill, Berkeley, 1995, pp. 99

14 Ibid, pp. 99-102

15 Ibid, pp. 99-102

16 Ibid, pp. 100-101

17 Ibid, pp. 102-106

18 Ibid, pp. 106-109

19 Ibid, pp. 114-118

20 Ibid, pp. 114-118

21 Ibid, pp. 119-128

22 Ibid, pp. 128-130

23 Ibid, pp. 131-133

24 Ibid, pp. 133-134, Richard H. Baker, *Network Security*, McGraw-Hill, Inc. N.Y.,1995, p. 301

25 Simson Garfinkel, *PGP Pretty Good Privacy*, O'Reilly & Associates, Inc. Sebastopol, 1995, p. 119

26 Ibid p. 119
27 Ibid p. 119
28 Ibid p. 119
29 Ibid p. 119
30 Lance Rose; *Netlaw*, Osborne, McGraw-Hill, Berkeley, 1995, pp. 283-312
31 Ibid, p. 313
32 Ibid, p. 319
33 Ibid, p. 323
34 Ibid, p. 333-348
35 Ibid, p. 349
36 Simson Garfinkel, *PGP Pretty Good Privacy*, O'Reilly & Associates, Inc. Sebastopol, 1995, p. 121-127, Microtimes, Nov 14, 1995
37 ABC NEWS WORLD NEWS TONIGHT 7/15/95
38 Ibid June 28, 1995
39 Ibid June 28, 1995
40 Lance Rose; *Netlaw*, Osborne, McGraw-Hill, Berkeley, 1995, p. 199
41 Ibid, p. 199
42 Ibid, p. 199
43 Ibid, p. 199
44 Ibid, p. 199
45 Ibid, p. 199
46 Ibid, p. 199
47 Ibid 234-235

Chapter 3

1 Bruce Sterling, *The Hacker Crackdown*, Bantom Books, , N.Y. 1992, pp. 147-178
2 Ibid, pp. 147-178

Chapter 4

1 Stanley Foster Reed, The Toxic Executive, pp. 1-210
2 Richard H. Baker, *Network Security*, McGraw-Hill, Inc. N.Y.,199 p. 45
3 Ibid, p. 243

4 Ibid, p. 243
5 Ibid, p. 245
6 S&S Computing, Virus Referecne. S&S Computing, downloaded 8/95 AOL Virus Forum.
7 Richard H. Baker, *Network Security*, McGraw-Hill, Inc. N.Y.,1995,p. 258
8 Virus Ref. S&S Computing, downloaded from AOL Virus ForumMessage Board
9 L.A. Times 2/26/95
10 Scientific American, March 1994, Vol. 270, No. 3, Pages 72-80, Vol. 271, pp. 72-76
11 Don Crabb, Guide to Macintosh *System 7.5*, Hayden Books,Indianapolis, p. 46

Chapter 5

1 Internet Starter Kit, Adam Engst, Hayden Books, Indianapolis, 1995, pp. 16-17
2 U.S. News and World Report, Jan 23, 1995, *Policing Cyberspace*, pp. 58-59
3 TidBITS#268/20, March 1995,*Could It Be... SATAN?*, by Geoff Duncan <geoff@tidbits.com>
4 U.S. News and World Report, Jan 23, 1995, *Policing Cyberspace*, pp. 58-59
5 U.S. News and World Report, Jan 23, 1995, *Policing Cyberspace*, pp. 58-59
6 U.S. News and World Report, Jan 23, 1995, *Policing Cyberspace*, pp. 58-59
7 U.S. News and World Report, Jan 23, 1995, *Policing Cyberspace*, pp. 58-59
8 U.S. News and World Report, Jan 23, 1995, *Policing Cyberspace*, pp. 58-59
9 Simson Garfinkel, *PGP Pretty Good Privacy*. OReilley & Associates, Inc., Sebastopol, 1995, p. 17
10 Bruce Schneier, E-mail Security, John Wiley & Sons, Inc., N.Y. , 1995, pp. 84-86

11 Bruce Schneier, E-mail Security, John Wiley & Sons, Inc., N.Y. , 1995, pp. 84-86

12 Home Office Computing, April 1994, pp. 80-81

13 Scientific American, March 1994, Vol. 270, No. 3, Pages 72-80, Vol. 271, pp. 72-76

14 Siyan Karanjit, *Internet Firewalls and Network Security*, New Riders Publishing, Indianapolis, 1995, p. 275

15 Scientific American, March 1994, Vol. 270, No. 3, Pages 72-80, Vol. 271, pp. 72-76

16 ABC World News Tonight, June 1995.

17 U.S. News and World Report, Jan 23, 1995, p. 58 'Policing Cyberspace'

18 I AOL Rules of the Road

19 Scientific American, March 1994, Vol. 270, No. 3, Pages 72-80, Vol. 271, pp. 72-76

Chapter 6

1 Ellen Dutton, *LAN Security Handbook*, M&T Books, N.Y., 1994 pp. 106

2 Ellen Dutton, *LAN Security Handbook*, M&T Books, N.Y., 1994 pp. 200

3 Schwartau, Winn; *Information Warfare*, Thunder's Mouth Press, N.Y. 1994, pp. 114-136

4 NBC August 20, 1995 Wallstrert Journal Report

Chapter 7

1 Interview with Mike Godwin, chief council for E.F.F., July 20, 1995

2 Phone Interview with Mike Godwin, 7/27/95

3 Memphis Commercial Appeal, March 21, 1993, Stephen G. Tompkins

4 Wired, May, 3, 1994, The Inslaw Octopus Part I&2, Richard Fricker

5 Bruce Schneier,*E-Mail Security*, John Wiley & Sons, Inc., N.Y., 1994 pp. 89-100, 105-120

6 Microtimes, January 2, 1995, p. 90

7 Ibid, p. 90

8 U.S. News and World Report, Jan 23, 1995, *Policing Cyberspace*, pp. 58-59

9 U.S. News and World Report, Jan 23, 1995, *Policing Cyberspace*, pp. 58-59

10 U.S. News and World Report, Jan 23, 1995, *Policing Cyberspace*, pp. 58-59

11 America Online Forum, Janary 19, 1995; 9PM EDT; live chat with Special FBI Agent Jim Kallstrom

12 Microtimes, January 2, 1995, p. 90

13 U.S. News and World Report, Jan 23, 1995, *Policing Cyberspace*, pp. 58-59

14 Simson Garfinkel, *PGP Pretty Good Privacy.* OReilley & Associates, Inc., Sebastopol, 1995, pp. 1-300

15 L.A. Times April 14, 1994, Thursday: PAGE: D-1;MICHAEL SCHRAGE / *Why the Clipper's Not Likely to Chip Away at Privacy*

16 WIRED, Online, vol. 2.03, April 18, 1994, *Electric Word, Security Through Obscurity,*

17 WIRED Online vol. 2.06 (Online Archives), Excepts, May 8 1994, *Don't Worry Be Happy*, (by Stewart A. Baker, Chief Counsel for the NSA)

18 The L.A. Times March 26, 1995, Letter to Editor from Marc Rotenberg, Director Electronic Privacy Information Center Washington

Computer Glossary

application software the term for programs that perform specific tasks such as accounting, word processing, and database management.

AUTOEXEC.BAT A special batch file that DOS searches for when booting up the computer. If DOS finds the AUTOEXEC.BAT file, it automatically carries out the commands contained in the file.

batch file a file to execute often-used DOS commands automatically. You just type in the batch file's name, and the PC carries out the commands contained in that batch file as if you had typed them from the keyboard.

boot a series of events that take place when you turn on the computer. In the boot process, the operating system, DOS for example, is loaded into the computer's internal memory (RAM).

CD-ROM or compact disc, read-only memory. Multimedia mass storage. A form of data storage that uses laser optics rather than magnetic means for reading data. CD-ROMs read compact discs similar to the audio CDs available in music stores.

command a word or string of text that gives the computer instructions on how to manipulate data.

CONFIG.SYS a text file DOS consults at system startup. This file contains commands that tell DOS how to communicate with new hardware, to customize communication with existing hardware, or to adjust your computer's memory usage.

conventional memory RAM (random-access memory) that DOS uses to run programs. Conventional memory is limited to 640 kilobytes.

CPU or Central Processing Unit. Refers to the computer's main processing chip, the "brain" of the machine. The i486SX, the i486DX, the i486DX4, and the Pentium are all processor chips, or CPUs.

current drive the drive your computer is using right now, displayed at the DOS prompt as C> or A>, for instance. "C" stands for the hard drive, and "A" stands for the floppy drive. (If your computer has two floppy drives, "A" represents the first drive, and "B" represents the second.)

cursor a short blinking line that appears underneath the space where the next character is to be typed or deleted. The cursor indicates that the computer is waiting for the user to input a command or information.

data information coded for exchange or transmission inside of, or between computers; typically binary.

database a collection of information organized for easy retrieval. Databases are organized into a hierarchy of *files*, *records*, and *fields*. A file is a group of related information. Information about a particular employee (name, social security number, address) is stored in a record. A record is a collection of related data items called fields. For example, a company's employee file stores information about each employee in a single record consisting of fields for the employee's name, social security number, and address.

desktop publishing one of the fastest-growing applications in personal computing, desktop publishing software offers a relatively inexpensive way for a PC to generate typeset-quality text and graphics.

device driver a program loaded by CONFIG.SYS that controls devices such as a mouse.

digital a signal which has either an "on" or "off" state represented by "1" and "0," respectively.

directory an area of a disk that stores the titles of files and subdirectories. A directory is similar to a table of contents.

DOS extender a superset, or addition to DOS, added to software programs that allows the programs to run in extended memory.

DOS prompt the signal that DOS is awaiting your command. The prompt is usually displayed as the current drive letter and the greater-than symbol (>). Thus C> is a DOS prompt with "C" representing the hard drive.

DOS short for Disk Operating System, software that translates the user's commands and allows application programs to interact with the computer's hardware. Supplies a file management system for efficient disk input and output.

dot-matrix printer a type of printer that employs a moveable print head with pins, or wires, that shoot out and strike a ribbon. Each strike of a single pin creates a dot on the paper. Letters are formed as a pattern, or matrix, of dots.

driver a program that allows the operating system (like DOS or OS/2) to work with a specific hardware device such as a printer, a mouse, or a trackball.

expanded memory memory outside the DOS one-megabyte (MB) limit that is accessed in revolving blocks.

expansion cards electronic circuit cards that fit into slots on the main circuit board inside the case of the computer. Expansion cards are used to add such items as faxes, modems, sound capability, and ports, to a PC.

expansion slot a socket inside the computer case that is designed to hold expansion cards.

extended memory linear memory extending beyond DOS's one-megabyte limit. Extended memory is only available on 286 and-above machines; it is off-limits to XTs.

fax/modem a device that allows a PC to fax documents to another fax/modem or fax machine, as well as to send data to another modem.

file a collection of data. Also the body of a database. A file contains a mass of interconnected parts known as records and fields.

floppy disk a flat piece of flexible plastic covered with a magnetic coating that is used to store data (also called a diskette). The existing standard for floppy disk size is 3.5 inches. Older drives also come in 5.25-inch sizes.

floppy disk drive a drive for flexible, as opposed to "hard," disks. Floppy drives write data to, and read data from, floppy disks that can be removed at will. The two existing standards for floppy diskette sizes are 5.25-inch and 3.5-inch (the latter still called 'floppy" even though they come in rigid plastic cases).

format to prepare a disk so it can store information. Formatting organizes the tracks and sectors that store information. When you format a disk, you erase any information already stored on it.

function keys keys that act as shortcuts for performing certain functions, such as saving or printing data. These keys are labeled Fl through F10 or F12 and they run across the top or down the side of the keyboard.

GUI short for "Graphical User Interface".("gooey"). A user shell in which pictures represent programs or file. GUIs are user-friendly alternatives to character-based interfaces such as DOS's. GUIs allow the user to point at a list of command options instead of typing a character-based command.

hard disk also called hard drives, data storage device for mainframe, mini, and personal computers. Hard drives come in many sizes and with a wide range of capacities. They consists of magnetically coated rigid platters that are fixed inside a sealed casing. A hard disk can store more information and retrieve data faster than can a floppy disk.

hardware any part of a computer system that can be physically touched. Printers, keyboards, monitors (screens), and the computer itself are all hardware.

icon a visual symbol used in a GUI to represent a program or a document. For example, in a DOS interface you'd see "LETTER.DOS" listed in the directory. In a GUI, you'd see a little picture representing the same document.

input device a piece of computer hardware (the keyboard and the mouse being the most popular examples) that is used to enter and manipulate information on a computer.

integrated circuits an arrangement of miniature transistors (silicon chips) used for electronic data transmission.

integrated software integrated software programs pack several applications into one package. These packages usually contain scaled-down versions of spreadsheets, word processors, and database programs.

KB or kilobyte. A unit of measurement of computer memory equivalent to approximately one thousand (1,024) bytes.

laser printer a computer printer that uses the electrophotographic method of printing (like a photocopier) with a laser beam as the light source. Laser printers produce high-resolution copy and are especially popular with business users.

MB or megabyte. A unit of measurement of computer memory equivalent to approximately one million (1,048,576) bytes.

memory management the process of controlling the assignment, use, and access of data storage facilities.

memory manager a program that increases the amount of RAM by making extended or expanded memory available to application programs.

memory an area where your computer stores data. Data can be permanently stored in ROM (read-only memory) or stored temporarily in the computer's RAM (random-access memory). A computer's RAM is emptied when the power is turned off.

menu a list of choices that appears in an application. Menus use graphics but are not GUI, in that commands are invoked by selection of a keyboard character, not double-clicking on a graphic object.

microprocessor an IC containing all the central processing functions of a computer; also called a CPU.

modem modems modulate signals by producing variant levels of frequencies to translate data from digital to analog form and back. They are a form of computer hardware that allows a computer to communicate with other computers (if they also have modems attached) through telephone lines.

multimedia the presentation of information on a computer using a combination of sound, graphics, animation, and video.

online service a dial-up service that provides news, information, and discussion "forums" for users with modem-equipped computers.

operating system the master control program that translates the user's commands and allows application programs to interact with the computer's hardware.

path the route that tells DOS where to search for a program or batch file if it is not found in the current directory.

prompt the DOS prompt usually takes the form of either "C>" or "A>." The "C" refers to the hard drive located inside your computer, and the "A" refers to the floppy disk drive. Most computers sold today come with two floppy disk drives; in this case, one is called the A: drive, and the other is called the B: drive.

software a general term for all types of programs used to manage a computer's operations. Software is essentially a set of instructions the computer uses to perform a task.

spreadsheet a program that simulates an accountant's worksheet, which is made up of rows and columns. It's used to quickly calculate budgets and perform financial analysis.

subdirectory a directory located within another directory (called the parent directory). The root directory is the only directory that is not also a subdirectory.

system files files required to run the computer's operating system.

upgrade any improvement made to your computer system, such as the installation of a new release or version of a software program, the addition of a peripheral such as a printer or modem, or the addition of RAM, a faster microprocessor, or storage space.

Data and Telecommunications Glossary

ADSL (Asymmetrical Digital Subscriber Line) a technology based on existing twisted-pair copper telephone cable that allows transmission speeds of 1.5 megabits per second for video and other broadband services.

algorithm a set of instructions that forms the basis of a computer program, similar to the idea of a recipe.

alternative access carrier a local telephone service provider competing with the regional Bell operating company (RBOC) that services the same area.

analog of a transmission in the form of a continuous wave, analogous to the sound waves produced by the human voice or music. Most audio and video signals are still analog, although equivalent digital signals are the "wave of the future."

analog/digital converter (ADC) an electronic device that converts analog signals to their digital equivalents.

ASCII (American Standard Code for Information Interchange) this code has become the standard code for representing text in binary form (see also *byte*).

ATM (Asynchronous Transfer Mode) a transmission technology that combines features of both circuit-switched and packet-switched networks to enable transmissions speeds ranging from 155 megabits per second up to 2.4 gigabits per second, making it a major contender for use in high-speed, broadband networks. However, ATM is still new.

backbone a term for the primary transmission lines of a telephone or digital network.

backchannel a generally low-bandwidth portion of the network reserved for responses from the subscriber back to the central information provider (for example, a subscriber's menu choices would be transmitted on the backchannel back to the service provider).

bandwidth a measurement of transmission capacity in either Hertz (cycles per second) or bits per second.

baud a somewhat outdated term for modem speeds; equivalent to bits per second. The "baud rate" of a modem is its transmission speed in bits per second (e.g., a 2400 baud modem transmits 2400 bits per second)

BBS an electronic bulletin board system.

bit one unit of digital information (a 0 or a 1); the term comes from "binary digit." bps

bits per second a measure of bandwidth or transmission speed.

branch lines as the name suggests, branch lines are telephone lines that "branch off" the main "trunk lines." Lines going into a local neighborhood are branch lines.

Broadband short for "broad bandwidth," meaning "high transmission capacity." Broadband networks enable transmission of the large volumes of data required for video and audio, as well as text.

byte eight bits is a byte, which is one character in the American Standard Code for Information Interchange (ASCII). ASCII includes all the letters of the alphabet, the numbers, and a variety of special characters.

CD-ROM (Compact Disc-Read Only Memory) currently the primary storage and distribution medium for multimedia applications on computers. CDs can hold about 600 MB of data, making them suitable for storing audio and video data as well as text and graphics.

CDMA (Code Division Multiple Access) an emerging digital transmission technology for cellular communications, which is supposedly 10 to 20 times faster than current analog cellular transmission techniques.

CDPD (Cellular Digital Packet Data) a digital transmission technique that uses existing analog cellular circuits to transmit packets of data, enabling data transmission speeds of up to 19.2 Kbps. CDPD uses a technique called "channel hopping" to take advantage of unused bandwidth on analog channels. CDPD is just being introduced for commercial use as this book goes to press.

cell (cellular) the geographic area serviced by a single radio transmitter/receiver in a "cellular network." In other words, a cellular network is a network of cells, with each cell "handing off" the signal to the next cell to connect the parties of a cellular phone call.

circuit switching the primary analog transmission technique used in today's telephone systems. The basic characteristic of circuit switching is that it requires an "end to end" connection between the calling and receiving parties and is therefore very inefficient for data communications.

Clipper Chip a government-developed encryption technology supported by the NSA and the FBI but not too many other parties (even some in government admit privately that it is doomed).

coaxial cable (Coax) the single copper cable wrapped in insulation that, for instance, enters most homes to connect to cable TV networks. Coaxial cable is also used for many other types of communications applications, from satellite and VCR video cable to ethernet-based local area networks.

codec short for coder/decoder, primarily referring to devices and software used for compressing and decompressing data, although it can also refer to the coding and decoding of encrypted data.

common carriage this is regulatory jargon for the provision of basic telephone service on a universal basis.

compression See *data compression.*

compression algorithm a particular set of instructions for compressing and decompressing data.

conduit a term for the means of data transmission. For example, copper telephone cable and fiber-optic cable are both types of "conduit."

content the data that travel along the conduit. For example, electronic mail or digitized movies are "content."

cyberspace the medium of electronic communications. When you're in cyberspace, you communicate "online" over the phone lines or over wireless radio waves.

dark fiber fiber-optic cable that has been installed but is not in use. Many telephone companies have installed "dark fiber" alongside fiber cable that is already in operation as a means of planning ahead for the expansion of fiber-optic networks. Dark fiber also refers to unused capacity of operational fiber-optic cable.

e-mail electronic mail, an electronic message containing text, graphics, even audio and video, which can be sent from one computer user to another over a computer network. Users of computer networks generally have an "e-mail address," to which you can send an e-mail message.

encryption disguising information so it cannot be understood without a means of undisguising or decrypting the information.

ethernet the most popular network protocol, based on 802.3 and other standards, used widely on PC file servers and UNIX systems. Patented by Xerox, Ethernet was one of the first packet network protocols. Each Ethernet station has a unique address shared by no other Ethernet card or NIU.

FCC (Federal Communications Commission) the agency charged with establishing regulatory policy for all forms of telecommunication in the United States and therefore instrumental in determining the future of the Information Highway.

FDDI (Fiber-Distributed Data Interface) a high-speed fiber-optic-based network that can be interfaced with local area networks.

fiber-optic cable glass fiber cable that sends signals by means of light pulses, allowing much faster transmission speeds than have been possible using copper cable.

firewalls data networks that can connect with the Internet but are tightly monitored, filtered, or controlled to prevent hacker access.

flame an abusive or angry message on an online network.

freenet a community-sponsored network on the Internet, allowing citizens free access to the Internet.

full-motion video a minimum of 30 frames per second is considered full-motion video. The digital storage and transmission of full-motion video requires enormous storage capacity and high bandwidth, thus representing one of the major technical challenges of the Information Highway.

Gbps billions of bits per second.

Ghz billions of cycles per second (gigahertz).

Gigabyte one billion bytes.

Hertz (Hz) cycles per second, which is the unit of measurement of frequency.

hybrid fiber/coax telecommunications jargon for a network consisting of a combination of fiber and coaxial cable. Fiber-to-the-curb systems are hybrid fiber/coax networks.

interactive live, two-way communications the ability to immediately send and receive responses on a computer or on a network.

interexchange carriers another term for long distance telephone companies (IXC or LDC).

ISDN (Integrated Services Digital Network) a digital transmission technology that operates on standard copper telephone cable, providing a standard bandwidth of 64 Kbps and with options for bandwidth up to 1.5 Mbits per second. Available through most major telephone companies, ISDN is more popular in Europe and Japan.

LAN a local area network, usually Ethernet, token ring. The most popular implementation of Ethernet utilizes twisted pair (10 base T).

local exchange carriers a fancy term for local phone companies.

Mbps millions of bits per second.

Megabits millions of bits.

MHz millions of cycles per second (megahertz).

MPEG compression Motion Pictures Experts' Group compression algorithm for motion-picture images (video), which is likely to become the standard compression scheme used on the Information Highway.

multimedia integration of audio, video, text, and graphics in computer applications; available on CD-ROM or on the WWW.

node a term used for a computer or other device (e.g., a laser printer) that is part of a network. Information on the WAN or a LAN travels from one node to another.

online service large computer system that provides commercial electronic messaging and conferencing services to a network of subscribers (e.g., CompuServe, America Online).

operating system the base level software that controls the input, output, and processing for a computer system (e.g., MS-DOS, Macintosh Finder).

packet-switching networks networks where data is assembled into small packets, transmitted to a specific destination node, and then put back into its original form. Data can be retransmitted or rerouted, if necessary.

personal communicator small palm-sized computing and communications device such as Apple's Newton.

pipes telecommunications jargon for the means of transmitting data, such as fiber-optic cable, coaxial cable, radio waves (see also *conduit*).

platform a specific computer system and/or its operating system environment. For example, the Macintosh is a platform, as is MS-DOS. Unfortunately, there may be different and incompatible platforms on the Information Highway.

POTS (Plain Old Telephone System) jargon for the current analog, copper-based telephone system.

protocol an agreed-upon set of instructions or commands that form a basis for communications.

RBOC one of the Regional Bell Operating Companies or "baby Bells," resulting from the court-mandated breakup of AT&T in 1984.

real-time real-time is live.

SONET (Synchronous Optical Network) a standard fiber-optic transmission technology.

TCP/IP (Transport Control Protocol/Internetworking Protocol) the networking protocol that has become standard on the Internet, which primarily uses UNIX-based computers (see also *UNIX*).

TDMA (Time Division Multiple Access) like its cousin CDMA, TDMA is an emerging form of digital wireless communications, which may be 10 to 20 faster than current analog transmission techniques.

telco jargon for "telephone company."

token ring a packet network protocol that is second only to Ethernet in popularity. This product was developed by IBM and uses a logical "token" to allow a station to send or receive messages on a LAN cable.

topology the layout of telephone cable. The "trunk and branch topology" of modern telephone systems means that long distances are connected by "trunks" (as in tree trunks), with local access provided by branches that connect to the trunks.

trunk lines long-distance telephone lines (see also Topology).

twisted-pair current copper phone wire into most residences is so-called "twisted pair" wiring (two copper wires twisted together), in contrast to coaxial cable, which is a single copper cable.

UNIX an operating system developed in the early 1970s that is still the most popular operating system in universities and the federal government and thus is the basic operating system used in the Internet networks.

upstream of the channel from the network subscriber back to the central server.

user interface the software interface that allows users to gain access to operating system commands. Microsoft Windows and Macintosh icons are graphical user interfaces (GUIs). They are considered the most user-friendly and advanced human-computer interfaces.

WAN wide area network; a network that operates over long distances as opposed to within a building or campus.

Cryptography Glossary

Encryption
- Privacy of messages
- Using ciphers and codes to protect the secrecy of messages
- DES is the most common symmetric cipher (same key for encryption and decryption)
- **RSA is the most common asymmetric cipher (different keys for encryption and decryption)**

Signatures and authentication
- Proving who you are
- Proving you (and not someone else) signed a document

Untraceable mail
- Untraceable sending and receiving of mail and messages
- Focus: defeating eavesdroppers and traffic analysis
- DC protocol (dining cryptographers)

Cryptographic voting
- Focus: ballot box anonymity
- **Credentials for voting**
- Issues of double voting, security, robustness, efficiency

Digital cash
- Focus: privacy in transactions, purchases
- Unlinkable credentials
- Blinded notes
- "Digital coins" may not be possible

Crypto-anarchy

- Using the preceding techniques to evade government, to bypass tax collection, etc.
- A technological solution to the problem of too much government

Terms

agoric systems open, free market systems in which voluntary transactions are central.

Alice and Bob cryptographic protocols are often made clearer by considering parties A and B, or Alice and Bob, performing some protocol. Eve the eavesdropper, Paul the prover, and Vic the verifier are other common stand-in names.

ANDOS all-or-nothing disclosure of secrets.

anonymous credential a credential that asserts some right or privilege or fact without revealing the identity of the holder. This is unlike CA driver's licenses.

asymmetric cipher same as public-key cryptosystem.

authentication the process of verifying an identity or credential, to ensure you are who you said you were.

biometric security a type of authentication using fingerprints, retinal scans, palm prints, or other physical/biological signatures of an individual.

bit commitment e.g., tossing a coin and then committing to the value without being able to change the outcome. The blob is a cryptographic primitive for this.

blinding *or* blinded signature a signature that the signer does not remember having made. A blind signature is always a cooperative protocol, and the receiver of the signature provides the signer with the blinding information.

blob the crypto equivalent of a locked box. A cryptographic primitive for bit commitment, with the properties that a blob can represent a 0 or a 1, that others cannot tell be looking whether it's a 0 or a 1, that the creator of the blob can "open" the blob to reveal the contents, and that no blob can be both a 1 and a 0. An example of this is a flipped coin covered by a hand.

channel the path over which messages are transmitted. Channels may be secure or insecure and may have eavesdroppers (or enemies, or disrupters, etc.) who alter messages, insert and delete messages, and so on. Cryptography is the means by which communications over insecure channels are protected.

chosen-plaintext attack an attack where the cryptanalyst gets to choose the plaintext to be enciphered, e.g., when an enciphering machine or algorithm is in the possession of the cryptanalyst.

cipher a secret form of writing, using substitution or transposition of characters or symbols.

ciphertext the plaintext after it has been encrypted.

code a restricted cryptosystem where words or letters of a message are replaced by other words chosen from a code book. Not part of modern cryptology, but still useful.

coin flipping an important crypto primitive, or protocol, in which the equivalent of flipping a fair coin is possible. Implemented with *blobs.*

collusion wherein several participants cooperate to deduce the identity of a sender or receiver, or to break a cipher. Most cryptosystems are sensitive to some forms of collusion. Much of the work on implementing DC Nets, for example, involves ensuring that colluders cannot isolate message senders and thereby trace origins and destinations of mail.

computationally secure where a cipher cannot be broken with available computer resources but in theory could be broken with enough computer resources. Contrast with *unconditionally secure.*

countermeasure something you do to thwart an attacker.

credential clearinghouse a bank, credit agency, insurance company, police department, etc., that correlates records and decides the status of records.

credentials facts or assertions about some entity, for example, credit ratings, passports, reputations, tax status, insurance records, etc. Under the current system, these credentials are increasingly being cross-linked. Blind signatures may be used to create anonymous credentials.

cryptanalysis methods for attacking and breaking ciphers and related cryptographic systems. Ciphers may be broken, traffic may be analyzed, and passwords may be cracked. Computers are of course essential.

crypto-anarchy the economic and political system after the deployment of encryption, untraceable e-mail, digital pseudonyms, cryptographic voting, and digital cash. A pun on "crypto," meaning "hidden," and as when Gore Vidal called William F. Buckley a "crypto-fascist."

cryptography another name for cryptology.

cryptology the science and study of writing, sending, receiving, and deciphering secret messages. Includes authentication, digital signatures, the hiding of messages (steganography), cryptanalysis, and several other fields.

DC protocol, or DC-Net the dining cryptographers' protocol. DC-Nets use multiple participants communicating with the DC protocol.

DES, Security of many have speculated that the NSA placed a trapdoor (or back door) in DES to allow it to read DES-encrypted messages. This has not been proved. It is known that the original Lucifer algorithm used a 128-bit key and that this key length was shortened to 64 bits (56 bits plus 8 parity bits), thus making exhaustive search much easier (so far as is known, brute-force search has not been done, though it should be feasible today). Shamir and Bihan have used a technique called "differential cryptanalysis" to reduce the exhaustive search needed for chosen plaintext attacks (but with no import for ordinary DES).

DES the Data Encryption Standard, proposed in 1977 by the National Bureau of Standards (now NIST), with assistance from the National Security Agency. Based on the "Lucifer" cipher developed by Horst Feistel at IBM, DES is a secret-key cryptosystem that cycles 64-bit blocks of data through multiple permutations with a 56-bit key controlling the routing. "Diffusion" and "confusion" are combined to form a cipher that has not yet been cryptanalyzed (see *DES, Security of*). DES is in use for interbank transfers and as a cipher inside of several RSA-based systems; it is also available for PCs.

description Let p and q be large primes, typically with more than 100 digits. Let $n = pq$ and find some e such that e is relatively prime to $(p - 1)(q - 1)$. The set of numbers p, q, and e is the private key for RSA. The set of numbers n and e forms the public key (recall that knowing n is not sufficient to easily find p and q . . . the factoring problem). A message M is encrypted by computing M^e mod n. The owner of the private key can decrypt the encrypted message by exploiting number theory results, as follows. An integer d is computed such that $ed = 1$ (mod $(p - 1)(q - 1)$). Euler proved a theorem that $M^{(ed)} = M$ mod n, and so $M^{(ed)}$ mod $n =$

M. This means that in some sense the integers *e* and *d* are "inverses" of each other. [If this is unclear, please see one of the many texts and articles on public key encryption.]

differential cryptanalysis the Shamir-Bihan technique for cryptanalyzing DES. With a chosen plaintext attack, they've reduced the number of DES keys that must be tried from about 2^{56} to about 2^{47} or less. Note, however, that rarely can an attacker mount a chosen plaintext attack on DES systems.

digital cash, digital money protocols for transferring value, monetary or otherwise, electronically. Digital cash usually refers to systems that are anonymous. Digital money systems can be used to implement any quantity that is conserved, such as points, mass, or dollars. There are many variations on digital money systems, ranging from VISA numbers to blinded signed digital coins. A topic too large for a single glossary entry.

digital pseudonym basically, a "crypto identity." A way for individuals to set up accounts with various organizations without revealing more information than they wish. Users may have several digital pseudonyms, some used only once, some used over the course of many years. Ideally, the pseudonyms can be linked only at the will of the holder. In the simplest form, a public key can serve as a digital pseudonym and need not be linked to a physical identity.

digital signature Analogous to a written signature on a document. A modification to a message that only the signer can make but that everyone can recognize. Can be used legally to contract at a distance.

digital timestamping one function of a digital notary public, in which some message (a song, a screenplay, a lab notebook, a contract, etc.) is stamped with a time that cannot (easily) be forged.

dining cryptographers' protocol (a.k.a. DC protocol, DC nets) the untraceable message-sending system invented by David Chaum. Named after the "dining philosophers" problem in computer science, a protocol in which participants form circuits and pass messages in such a way that the origin cannot be deduced, barring collusion. At the simplest level, two participants share a key between them. One of them sends some actual message by bitwise exclusive-ORing the message with the key, while the other one just sends the key itself. The actual message from this pair of participants is obtained by XORing the two outputs. However, since nobody but the pair knows the original key, the actual message cannot be traced to either one of the participants.

discrete logarithm problem given integers a, n, and x, find some integer m such that $a^\wedge m$ mod $n = x$, if m exists. Modular exponentiation, the $a^\wedge m$ mod n part, is straightforward (and special-purpose chips are available), but the inverse problem is believed to be very hard, in general. Thus it is conjectured that modular exponentiation is a one-way function.

DSS, Digital Signature Standard the latest NIST (National Institute of Standards and Technology, successor to NBS) standard for digital signatures. Based on the El Gamal cipher, some consider it a weak and poor substitute for RSA-based signature schemes.

eavesdropping, or passive wiretapping intercepting messages without detection. Radio waves may be intercepted, phone lines may be tapped, and computers may have RF emissions detected. Even fiber-optic lines can be tapped.

factoring some large numbers are difficult to factor. It is conjectured that there are no feasible—i.e., "easy," less than exponential in size of number—factoring methods. It is also an open problem whether RSA may be broken more easily than by factoring the modulus (e.g., the public key might reveal information that simplifies the problem). Interestingly, though factoring is believed to be "hard," it is not known to be in the class of NP-hard problems. Professor Janek invented a factoring device, but he is believed to be fictional.

information-theoretic security "unbreakable" security, in which no amount of cryptanalysis can break a cipher or system. One-time pads are an example (providing the pads are not lost nor stolen nor used more than once, of course). Same as *unconditionally secure.*

key exchange, or key distribution the process of sharing a key with some other party, in the case of symmetric ciphers, or of distributing a public key in an asymmetric cipher. A major issue is that the keys be exchanged reliably and without compromise. Diffie and Hellman devised one such scheme, based on the discrete logarithm problem.

key a piece of information needed to encipher or decipher a message. Keys may be stolen, bought, lost, etc., just as with physical keys.

known-plaintext attack a cryptanalysis of a cipher where plaintext-ciphertext pairs are known. This attack searches for an unknown key. Contrast with the *chosen-plaintext attack,* where the cryptanalyst can also choose the plaintext to be enciphered.

mail, untraceable a system for sending and receiving mail without traceability or observability. Receiving mail anonymously can be done with broadcast of the mail in encrypted form. Only the intended recipient (whose identity, or true name, may be unknown to the sender) may be able to decipher the message. Sending mail anonymously apparently requires mixes or use of the *dining cryptographers' (DC) protocol.*

mechanical principles eavesdroppers alter the quantum state of the system and so are detected. Developed by Brassard and Bennett, only small laboratory demonstrations have been made.

minimum-disclosure proofs another name for zero knowledge proofs, favored by Chaum.

mixes David Chaum's term for a box that performs the function of mixing, or decorrelating, incoming and outgoing electronic mail messages. The box also strips off the outer envelope (i.e., decrypts with its private key) and remails the message to the address on the inner envelope. Tamper-resistant modules may be used to prevent cheating and forced disclosure of the mapping between incoming and outgoing mail. A sequence of many remailings effectively makes tracing sending and receiving impossible. Contrast this with the software version, the DC protocol.

modular exponentiation raising an integer to the power of another integer, modulo some integer. For integers a, n, and m, a^m mod n. For example, 5^3 mod $100 = 25$. Modular exponentiation can be done fairly quickly with a sequence of bit shifts and adds, and special-purpose chips have been designed. See also *discrete logarithm problem*.

National Security Agency (NSA) the largest intelligence agency, responsible for making and breaking ciphers, for intercepting communications, and for ensuring the security of U.S. computers. Headquartered in Fort Meade, Maryland, with many listening posts around the world, the NSA funds cryptographic research and advises other agencies about cryptographic matters. The NSA once obviously had the world's leading cryptologists, but this may no longer be the case.

negative credential a credential that you possess that you don't want any one else to know, for example, a bankruptcy filing. A formal version of a negative reputation.

NP-complete a large class of difficult problems. "NP" stands for nondeterministic polynomial time, a class of problems thought in general not to have feasible algorithms for their solution. A problem is "complete" if any other NP problem may be reduced to that problem. Many important combinatorial and algebraic problems are NP-complete: the traveling salesman problem, the Hamiltonian cycle problem, the word problem, and on and on.

oblivious transfer a cryptographic primitive that involves the probabilistic transmission of bits. The sender does not know if the bits were received.

one-time pad a string of randomly-selected bits or symbols that is combined with a plaintext message to produce the ciphertext. This combination may be shifting letters some amount, bitwise exclusive-ORed, etc. The recipient, who also has a copy of the one-time pad, can easily recover the plaintext. Provided the pad is only used once and then destroyed, and is not available to an eavesdropper, the system is perfectly secure, i.e., it provides *information-theoretic security.*

one-way function a function that is easy to compute in one direction but hard to find any inverse for, e.g., modular exponentiation, where the inverse problem is known as the discrete logarithm problem. Compare the special case of trapdoor one-way functions. An example of a one-way operation is multiplication: It is easy to multiply two prime numbers of 100 digits to produce a 200-digit number, but hard to factor that 200-digit number.

P ?=? NP Certainly the most important unsolved problem in complexity theory. If P = NP, then cryptography as we know it today does not exist. If P = NP, all NP problems are "easy."

padding sending extra messages to confuse eavesdroppers and to defeat traffic analysis. Also, adding random bits to a message to be enciphered.

plaintext also called "cleartext," the text that is to be enciphered.

Pretty Good Privacy (PGP) Philip Zimmermann's implementation of RSA, recently upgraded to version 2.0, with more robust components and several new features. RSA Data Security has threatened Zimmermann so that he no longer works on it. Version 2.0 was written by a consortium of non-U.S. hackers.

prime numbers integers with no factors other than themselves and 1. The number of primes is unbounded. About 1 percent of the 100-decimal-digit numbers are prime. Since there are about 10^{70} particles in the universe, there are about 10^{23} 100-digit primes for each and every particle in the universe!

probabilistic encryption a scheme by Goldwasser, Micali, and Blum that allows multiple ciphertexts for the same plaintext, i.e., any given plaintext may have many ciphertexts if the ciphering is repeated. This protects against certain types of known ciphertext attacks on RSA.

proofs of identity proving who you are, either your true name or your digital identity. Generally, possession of the right key is sufficient proof (guard your key!). Some work has been done on "is-a-person" credentialling agencies, using the so-called Fiat-Shamir protocol. Think of this as a way to issue unforgeable digital passports. Physical proof of identity may be done with biometric security methods. Zero-knowledge proofs of identity reveal nothing beyond the fact that the identity is as claimed. This has obvious uses for computer access, passwords, etc.

protocol a formal procedure for solving some problem. Modern cryptology is mostly about the study of protocols for many problems, such as coin-flipping, bit commitment (blobs), zero-knowledge proofs, dining cryptographers, and so on.

public-key cryptosystem the modern breakthrough in cryptology, designed by Diffie and Hellman, with contributions from several others. Uses trapdoor one-way functions so that encryption may be done by anyone with access to the "public key" but decryption may be done only by the holder of the "private key." Encompasses public-key encryption, digital signatures, digital cash, and many other protocols and applications.

public-key encryption the use of modern cryptologic methods to provided message security and authentication. The RSA algorithm is the most widely used form of public-key encryption, although other systems exist. A public key may be freely published, e.g., in phonebook-like directories, while the corresponding private key is closely guarded.

public-key patents MIT and Stanford, due to the work of Rivest, Shamir, Adleman, Diffie, Hellman, and Merkle, formed Public Key Partners to license the various public-key, digital signature, and RSA patents. These patents, granted in the early 1980s, expire in between 1998 and 2002. PKP has licensed RSA Data Security Inc., of Redwood City, CA, which handles the sales, etc.

public key the key distributed publicly to potential message senders. It may be published in a phonebook-like directory or otherwise sent. A major concern is the validity of this public key to guard against spoofing or impersonation.

reputations the trail of positive and negative associations and judgments that some entity accrues. Credit ratings, academic credentials, and trustworthiness are all examples. A digital pseudonym will accrue these reputation credentials based on actions, opinions of others, etc. In crypto-anarchy, reputations and agoric systems will be of paramount importance. There are many fascinating issues of how reputation-based systems work, how credentials can be bought and sold, and so forth.

RSA the main public-key encryption algorithm, developed by Ron Rivest, Adi Shamir, and Kenneth Adleman. It exploits the difficulty of factoring large numbers to create a private key and public key. First invented in 1978, it remains the core of modern public-key systems. It is usually much slower than DES, but special-purpose modular exponentiation chips will likely speed it up. A popular scheme for speed is to use RSA to transmit session keys and then a high-speed cipher like DES for the actual message text.

secret-key cryptosystem a system that uses the same key to encrypt and decrypt traffic at each end of a communication link. Also called a symmetric or one-key system. Contrast with *public-key cryptosystem*.

smart card a computer chip embedded in a credit card. They can hold cash, credentials, cryptographic keys, etc. Usually these are built with some degree of tamper-resistance. Smart cards may perform part of a crypto transaction, or all of it. Performing part of it may mean checking the computations of a more powerful computer, e.g., one in an ATM.

spoofing, or masquerading posing as another user. Used for stealing passwords, modifying files, and stealing cash. Digital signatures and other authentication methods are useful to prevent this. Public keys must be validated and protected to ensure that others don't substitute their own public keys that users may then unwittingly use.

steganography a part of cryptology dealing with hiding messages and obscuring who is sending and receiving messages. Message traffic is often padded to reduce the signals that would otherwise come from a sudden beginning of messages.

symmetric cipher same as *private-key cryptosystem*.

tamper-responding modules, tamper-resistant modules (TRMs) sealed boxes or modules that are hard to open, requiring extensive probing

and usually leaving ample evidence that the tampering has occurred.
Various protective techniques are used, such as special metal or oxide layers
on chips, armored coatings, embedded optical fibers, and other measures to
thwart analysis. Popularly called "tamper-proof boxes." Uses include: smart
cards, nuclear weapon initiators, cryptographic key holders, ATMs, etc.

tampering, or active wiretapping interfering with messages and
possibly modifying them. This may compromise data security, help to
break ciphers, etc. See also *spoofing*.

token some representation, such as ID cards, subway tokens, money, etc.,
that indicates possession of some property or value.

traffic analysis determining who is sending or receiving messages by
analyzing packets, frequency of packets, etc. A part of *steganography*.
Usually handled with traffic padding.

transmission rules the protocols for determining who can send messages
in a DC protocol, and when. These rules are needed to prevent collision
and deliberate jamming of the channels.

trap messages dummy messages in DC Nets that are used to catch
jammers and disrupters. The messages contain no private information and
are published in a *blob* beforehand so that the trap message can later be
opened to reveal the disrupter. (There are many strategies to explore here.)

trap-door one-way functions functions that are easy to compute in
both the forward and reverse direction but for which the disclosure of an
algorithm to compute the function in the forward direction does not
provide information on how to compute the function in the reverse
direction. More simply put, trap-door one-way functions are one way for
all but the holder of the secret information. The RSA algorithm is the best-
known example of such a function.

trapdoor In cryptography, a piece of secret information that allows the holder of a private key to invert a normally hard-to-invert function.

unconditionally secure where no amount of intercepted ciphertext is enough to allow the cipher to be broken, as with the use of a one-time pad cipher. Contrast with *computationally secure.*

voting, cryptographic various schemes have been devised for anonymous, untraceable voting. Voting schemes should have several properties: privacy of the vote, security of the vote (no multiple votes), robustness against disruption by jammers or disrupters, verifiability (voter has confidence in the results), and efficiency.

zero-knowledge proofs proofs in which no knowledge of the actual proof is conveyed. Peggy the Prover demonstrates to Sid the Skeptic that she is indeed in possession of some piece of knowledge without actually revealing any of that knowledge. This is useful for access to computers, because eavesdroppers or dishonest sysops cannot steal the knowledge given. Also called minimum disclosure proofs. Useful for proving possession of some property, or credential, such as age or voting status, without revealing personal information.

Glossary Resources:

Timothy C. May | Crypto Anarchy: encryption, digital money, tcmay@netcom.com | anonymous networks, digital pseudonyms, zero
408-688-5409 | knowledge, reputations, information markets, W.A.S.T.E.: Aptos, CA | black markets, collapse of governments.
Higher Power: 2^756839 | PGP Public Key: by arrangement.
Crypto Glossary
Compiled by Tim May (tcmay@netcom.com) and Eric Hughes
(hughes@soda.berkeley.edu), circa September 1992.*American Eagle Publications*
602-888-4957

Security and Privacy Publications

Computers and Security	011-44-865-512242
The Computer Law and Security Report	212-989-5800
Computer Security Digest	313-459-8787
Consumertronics	505-434-0234
Data Pro Research	800-328-2772
EMC Technology	703-347-0030
Full Disclosure	708-395-6200
Gyptologia	516-378-0263
Hactic	011-31-20-6001480
Info Security News	508-879-7999
Intelligence Solutions Newsletter	800-877-9138
International Journal of Intelligence	212-737-7923
International Privacy Bulletin	202-544-9240
Internet World	203-226-6967
Low Profile Newsletter	800-528-o559
Monitoring Times	704-837-9200
PIN Magazine	301-652-9050
Privacy Journal	401-274-7861
Ross Engineering Newsletter	703-318-8600
Security Book Catalog	800-366-2655
Security Insider Report	813-393-6600
Security Magazine	708-635-8800
Security Management	703-522-5800
Security Technology News	301-340-7788
Telecom and Network Security Review	800-435-7878
Virus Bulletin	011-44-235-555139
Wired	415-904-0660
2600: The Hacker Quarterly	516-751-2600

Magazines Worth Checking

Gray Areas
P.O. Box 808
Bromall, Pennsylvania 19008-0808

Mondo 2000
P.O. Box 10171
Berkeley, California 94709

Axcess
4640 Cass St. #9309
San Diego, California 92169

Black Ice (Mondo-Wired style, with
a British accent.)
P.O. Box 1069
Brighton BN2 4YT
United Kingdom

Boing Boing
11288 Ventura Blvd. #818
Studio City, California 91604

FringeWare Review
P.O. Box 49921
Austin, Texas 78765

Nuts & Volts
430 Princeland Court
Corona, California 91719

Intertek
13 Daffodil Lane
San Carlos, California 94070

Phrack Magazine
603 W. l3th #lA-278
Austin, Texas 78701

Boardwatch
8500 Lo. Bowles Ave. Suite 210
Littleton, CO 80123
800-933-6038

U.S. Government Resources

National Institute of Standards and Technology
Computer Security Labs
Gaithersburg, Maryland 20899
301-975-2000

National Computer Security Center
9800 Savage Road
Fort Meade, Maryland 20755
301-859-4371

Government Services Canada (GSC)
Industrial and Corporate Security Branch
Hull, Quebec
Canada

Computer Bulletin Boards

National Institute of Standards and Technology Bulletin Board
301-948-5717 (300, 1200, 2400 baud)
301-948-5140 (9600 baud)
Use N, 8, 1 or E, 7, 1

Computer Security BBS
303-962-9536

Computer Security Connection
703-756-8333
CompuServe: Type: GO NCSA
Comsec BBS 415-495-4642

The WELL
415-332-4335

Phantom Access Technologies, Inc.
212-989-2418

Security Newsgroups

On Usenet, subscribe to:

alt.2600

alt.cellular

alt.cyberpunk

alt.dcom.telecom

alt.hackers

alt.hackers.cough.cough.cough

alt.hackers.malicious

alt.os.multics

alt.privacy

alt.privacy.anon-server

alt.privacy.clipper

alt.security

alt.security.index

alt.security.keydist

alt.security.pgp

alt.security.ripem

alt.society.cu-digest

bit.listserv.security

bit.listserv.virus-l

comp.dcom.telecom

comp.privacy

comp.risks

comp.security.announce

comp.security.misc

comp.security.unix

comp.society.privacy

comp.virus

de.comp.security

misc.security

sb.security

sub.security

sura.security

uwo.comp.security

LOD Communications

E-mail lodcom@mindvox.phantom.com for info.

603 W. l3th #lA-278

Austin, Texas 78701

Lots of security-related BBS messages from the great hacker BBSs of the past.

Security FTP Sites

ftp.netsys.com

The official *Phrack* ftp site. /pub/phrack

ftp.eff.org

The CuD ftp site with hundreds of underground publications online. /pub/cud *The Hacker Chronicles*. PC-compatible CD-ROM with thousands of underground files.

Security Information Publishers

P-80 Systems

304-744-2253 (data)

Forbidden Subjects. A PC-compatible CD-ROM with thousands of underground files.

Profit Press

824 E. Ft. Lowell Rd.
Tucson, Arizona 85719

Security-Related Electronic Mailing Lists

Firewalls

The best mailing list going for issues dealing with securing systems through the implementation of system firewalls. E-mail majordomo@greatcircle.com and in the body of the message write "SUBSCRIBE FIREWALLS."

The BugTraq

Serious security-related discussions pinpointing actual bugs, their invocations, and workarounds. E-mail bugtraq@crimelab.com and ask to be put on the list.

BBS-Related Publications

Modem USA, Second Edition

Allium Press
P.O. Box 5752-55
Takoma Park, MD 20912

Provides listings of BBSs. Their BBS is also a gateway to more than 100 other government-agency bulletin boards.

Other Bulletin Board Systems

Audiophile Network
Modem: 818-988-0452

About audio equipment and state-of-the-art music systems.

Aviation TotalInformation Systems
Voice: 703-242-0161; Modem: 703-242-3520 or 703-242-3534

CompuFarm BBS
Modem: 403-556-4243

Farm and livestock, agricultural information.

Exec-PC
Voice: 414-789-4200; Modem: 414-789-4210

The largest BBS in the country, with a focus on business-oriented discussions and software.

Federal Communications Commission (FCC) PublicAccess Link

Voice: 301-725-1585 Modem: 301-725-1072

FedWorld

Modem: 703-321-8020

If you're interested in getting the latest information that the U.S. federal government puts out, you'll need to access this BBS.

Association of Online Professionals (AOP)

1818 Wyoming Avenue NW, Washington, DC 20009

Voice: (202)265-1266

E-mail: 70631.266~compuserve.com, CompuServe: GO IBMBBS, AOL Section.

Advocacy and resource organization for smaller online and bulletin board systems, Newly formed as this book goes to press. Intends to act as voice for smaller online systems in national policy and affairs, coordinate responses to local regulation of online activities, and maintain resources of use to those who operate online systems.

Computer Underground Digest (CuD)

Usenet: alt.society.cu-digest

A weekly electronic newsletter covering legal and cultural issues, with contributions from hackers, activists, and other non-mainstream sources. On various online systems, and in its own Usenet newsgroup at alt.society.cu-digest.

U.S. Government

Government Printing Office BBS (GPO Access)

Voice: 202-512-1530; Modem: 202-512-1387

Online access to federal documents such as the Congressional Record *and the* Federal Register, *supports Wide Area Information Server (WAIS) search and retrieval software for Internet users.*

Other Useful Sources of Information on Government, Security, Privacy, the Internet, the Media

HerpNet
Voice: 215-464-3561; Modem Number: 215-464-3562
BBS on reptiles and herpetology.

HouseNet
Modem: 410-745-2037
This BBS provides useful information on every household-related topic you can think of from repairing your roof to adding a security door.

Legal Ease BBS
Modem: 509-326-3238

Movies-by-Modem
Voice: 216-861-0467; Modem: 216-694-5736

NASA Space Link
Voice: 205-544-6360 Modem: 205-895-0028

National Genealogical Society

Voice: 703-525-0050; Modem: 703-528-2612

The place to go for information on genealogy, tracking your ancestry.

On-line Bookstore

Voice: 800-233-0233; Modem: 215-657-6130

People's Electronic Exchange

Modem: 908-685-0948

This is the BBS to check when you are looking for a new job.

Small Business Administration BBS

Voice: 800-827-5722; Modem: 800-859-INFO (2400 bps), 800-692-INFO (9600)

Software Creations

Modem: 508-368-7036

Software Creations was voted the best BBS in the country by readers of the leading online magazine, Boardwatch. This BBS is the clearinghouse for great game software, shareware, freeware, graphics files, and much more.

Superdemocracy Foundation BBS

Voice: 305-370-7850; Modem: 305-370-9376

Discuss electronic democracy and other issues related to democracy.

Trader's Connection (computerized classified ads)

Voice: 800-753-4223 (call for local access modem numbers); Modem (central modem number, where you can find local access numbers and also get a "guided tour" of the system): 317-359-5199

U.S. Census Bureau
Voice: 301-763-7662; Modem: 301-763-4574

Windows Online
Modem: 510-736-8343

This BBS offers more than 12,000 files of Windows software for downloading.

Index